SCOTLAND

Susanne Arbuckle, Colin Baird, Kay Gillespie, Laurie Goodlad, Mike MacEacheran, Joseph Reaney, Neil Robertson, Neil Wilson

Contents

Best Experiences 04
Calendar 16
Trip Builder 24
7 Things to Know About Scotland 32
Read, Listen, Watch & Follow 34

Edinburgh 36

Edinburgh Festival Fringe 42
History & a Royal Mile 44
The Water of Leith........... 46
Writers, Witches & Wizards 48
Seven Hills 50
Foodie Leith 52
Listings 54

Glasgow 56

A Night on the Town........ 62
A Splash of Colour 64
Glasgow's Story 66
Footsteps of Legends 70
Listings 72

Southern Scotland 74

Immersion in the Lowlands 78
Majestic, Stately Homes 80
Lands of Sieges & Raids 82
Ride to the Sea 84
Listings 86

Stirling, Fife & Perthshire 88

Sea Food & Sea Views 94
The Road to Rannoch 96
Kings, Queens & Castles 100
Listings 106

The Northeast 108

A Coastal Trail................. 114
Whisky Tour of Speyside..................... 118
Dundee Design Trail 120
Listings 122

Southern Highlands & Islands 124

Inner Hebrides Hopscotch 130
Whisky Island Discovery 132
From Sea to Plate.......... 136
Secret Coast Road-Trip 138
Enter the Ancient Kingdom 140
Listings 144

Central Highlands 146

Monster Hunting........... 152
Up Ben Nevis................. 156
Royal Road Trip.............. 158
Listings 160

Northern Highlands 162

Rails to the North.......... 166
Cape Wrath.................... 170
On the Clearances Trail.............. 172
Remote Caithness 174
Listings 178

Skye & the Outer Hebrides 180

Hiking Trotternish 186
Driving Skye's West Coast 190

JANE BARLOW/GETTY IMAGES ©

Above *St Mungo* mural by artist Smug (p65), Glasgow

Skye's Secret Sister........192
St Kilda: Edge of the World 194
Cycling South Harris.......196
History on Lewis..............198
Listings 200

Orkney **202**

Hop to Papa Westray 206
Neolithic Orkney 208
Creative Orkney Trail.......210
St Magnus Way Walk 214
Listings 216

Shetland **218**

Exploring Fair Isle........... 222
Unforgettable Unst 226
Mousa Broch's Petrels... 230
Exploring Geology.......... 232
Listings 234

Practicalities **236**

Arriving 238
Getting Around............... 240
Safe Travel 242
Money 243
Responsible Travel 244
Accommodation 246
Essentials 248

ESSAYS

What Makes Glasgow So?..................... 68
The River Tay.................... 98
Meet the Master Distiller............................134
5000 Years of Orkney Creativity 212
Land of the Vikings 224

VISUAL GUIDES

A Castle Glossary............104
Treasures of Kilmartin Glen 142
On Screen: The Highlands on Film 154
Highland Games 176
Flora & Fauna 228

WHISKY STATS

- There are more than 130 malt and grain distilleries – making Scotland home to the world's greatest concentration of whisky production.
- Opened in 1786, Strathisla is the oldest continuously operating distillery in the Highlands.
- Whisky exports totalled £4.9bn in 2019.

WHISKY **COUNTRY**

Nowhere else in the world is as indebted to a drink as Scotland is to whisky. The country's bounty of ingredients, from soft spring water gushing from the mountains to fields of barley flourishing in the peaty highlands, helps create a landscape that's ripe for exploration. Then there are the scenic distilleries and joyous whisky festivals – they burst with history, flavour and the potential for a long, if life-affirming, night out.

Left Strathisla Distillery.
Right Copper stills at Glenfiddich Distillery (p119)
Below A whisky tasting

→ THE MALT WHISKY TRAIL

If the number of distilleries to choose from leaves you feeling dizzy, the world's only Malt Whisky Trail offers the perfect introduction. The route introduces you to the guardians of Glenlivet, Glenfiddich, Glen Moray and Glen Grant, among others, as well as Cardhu – the only distillery pioneered by a woman.

▶ Learn more about the Malt Whisky Trail on p118

ISLAY WHISKY

With nine distilleries – soon to be 10 with the reopening of Port Ellen – on an island only 25 miles wide, Islay could be described as the 'whiskiest' place in the world. Most distilleries offer tours and tastings, exclusive drams and food pairings.

▶ See our guide to Islay whisky on p132

↑ HOW TO DRINK A SINGLE MALT

Whiskies vary as much as wine: so treat both a single origin malt and blended whisky (a mix of different cask spirits) with respect. Drink it straight at room temperature, or mix it with a little still water to bring out its flavours and aromas. Before drinking, inhale deeply and raise your dram with the traditional toast: slainte mhath!

Best Whisky Experiences

▶ **Savour a beach tasting on the sand at Machir Bay to learn all about Islay's only farm distillery.** (p133)

▶ **Discover the highest distillery in Scotland with an original smoke stack that can be seen for miles.** (p160)

▶ **Explore the Speyside Cooperage to watch Britain's only barrel makers mastering their craft.** (p119)

LAND OF ISLANDS

With 900 islands to choose from, and with most offering silvery sands, craggy mountains, charming croft villages and bucket-list wildlife, it's not hard to find an offshore paradise. Reassuringly, despite the timely ferry connections to the mainland, many remain secluded spots where you can get away from it all. Almost castaway bliss.

Harris

Photo-worthy beaches

North of the Sea of the Hebrides, this stunning island does vast beaches, sweeping mountains and trendsetting knitwear in spades. For the picture-postcard Scottish beach, beeline to the powdery sands and primrose-dotted machair of Seilebost (pictured below right).

1hr 40min ferry to Tarbert from Uig on Skye

▶ p196

Skye

Scotland in miniature

Simply put, the Isle of Skye has it all. Two clan-rich castles, Michelin-star restaurants with rooms, Jurassic-era dinosaur fossils, dazzling coral beaches, the lunar landscapes of the Trotternish peninsula, the seismogram-ragged Cuillin mountains and the smoky whisky at Talisker Distillery.

Drive across the Skye Bridge from Kyle of Lochalsh

▶ p180

Mull

Wildlife and island-hopping

Gateway to the Inner Hebrides, Mull offers the best of the islands in microcosm – it's a marriage of beaches, mountains and coastal villages inhabited by friendly locals and Scotland's big five (golden eagles, red deer, otters, common seal and harbour porpoise). The adventure continues with island-hopping to Iona and Ulva, or day-tripping to Staffa and the Treshnish Isles.

50min ferry from Oban

▶ p131

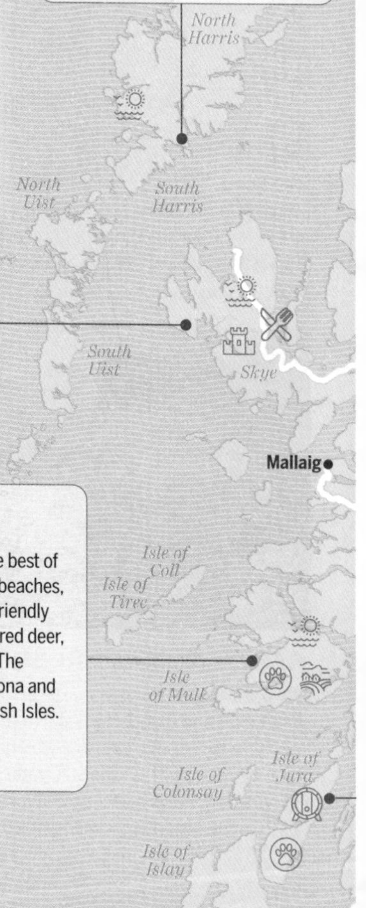

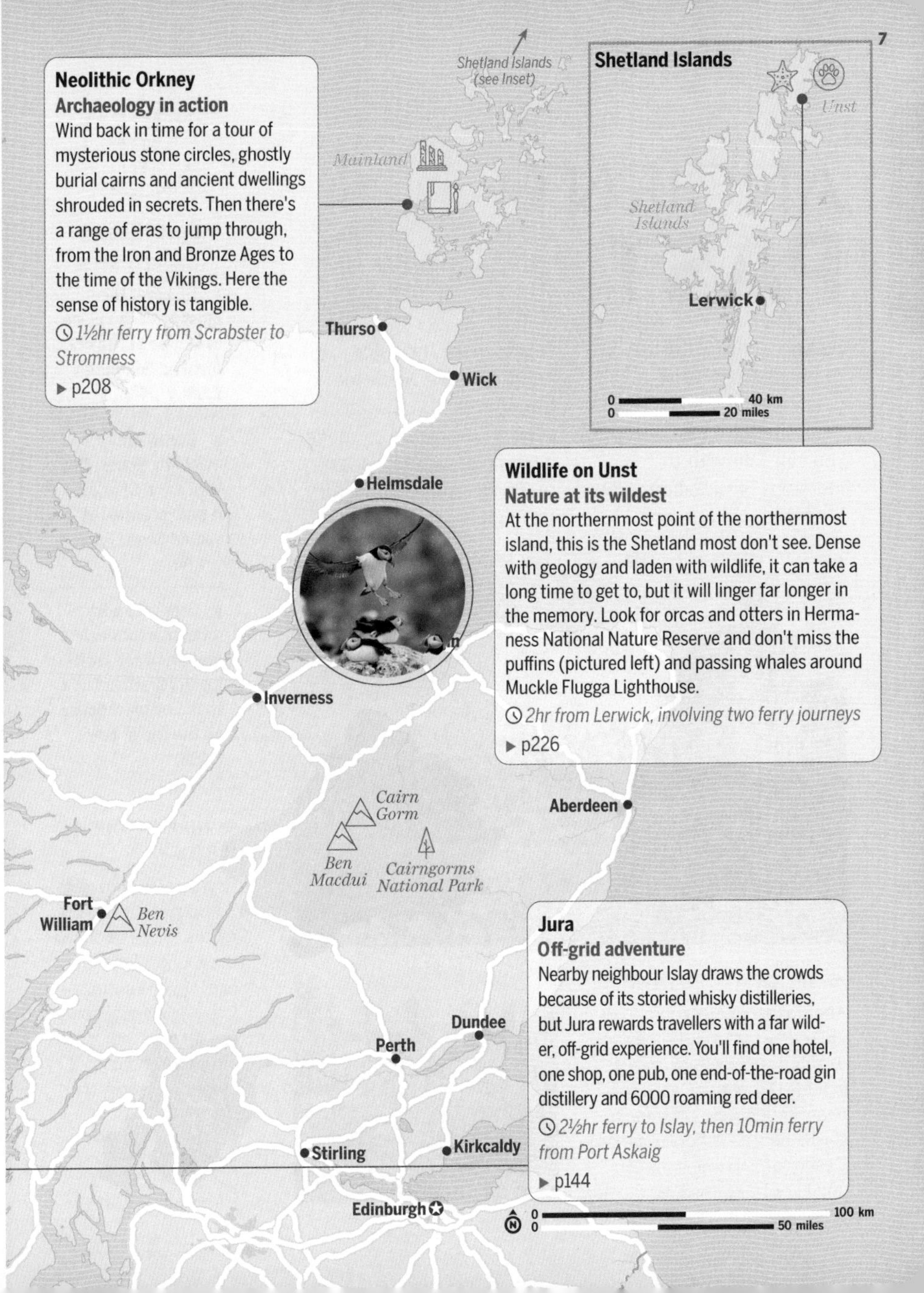

Neolithic Orkney

Archaeology in action

Wind back in time for a tour of mysterious stone circles, ghostly burial cairns and ancient dwellings shrouded in secrets. Then there's a range of eras to jump through, from the Iron and Bronze Ages to the time of the Vikings. Here the sense of history is tangible.

1½hr ferry from Scrabster to Stromness

▶ p208

Wildlife on Unst

Nature at its wildest

At the northernmost point of the northernmost island, this is the Shetland most don't see. Dense with geology and laden with wildlife, it can take a long time to get to, but it will linger far longer in the memory. Look for orcas and otters in Hermaness National Nature Reserve and don't miss the puffins (pictured left) and passing whales around Muckle Flugga Lighthouse.

2hr from Lerwick, involving two ferry journeys

▶ p226

Jura

Off-grid adventure

Nearby neighbour Islay draws the crowds because of its storied whisky distilleries, but Jura rewards travellers with a far wilder, off-grid experience. You'll find one hotel, one shop, one pub, one end-of-the-road gin distillery and 6000 roaming red deer.

2½hr ferry to Islay, then 10min ferry from Port Askaig

▶ p144

ANCIENT
PAST

▬▬ Exploring history is so much more satisfying when you have so many strata to delve into. Here you can follow in the footsteps of time-honoured kings and queens, or tread where Jurassic-era dinosaurs, Neolithic humans or Vikings once roamed, rewarding you with a whole new perspective of a place rich with history through the ages.

Best History Experiences

▶ Discover the most besieged place in Europe at heavily fortified Edinburgh Castle. (p45)

▶ See where Macbeth, Robert the Bruce and Charles II were crowned at sacred Scone Palace. (p106)

▶ Step into a traditional Hebridean home and see crofting life firsthand at a thatched blackhouse on the Isle of Lewis. (p198)

LEFT: JULIETPHOTOGRAPHY/SHUTTERSTOCK ©BOTTOM: TOMASZ WOZNIAK/SHUTTERSTOCK ©

← HIKE THROUGH HISTORY

Dozens of pilgrim trails and long-distance routes thread through the country. From the Fife Pilgrim Way to the Rob Roy Way, the routes are studded with standing stones, abbeys, stories and secrets.

→ SEE CASTLE COUNTRY

Aberdeenshire has more than 260 castles, stately homes and turreted chateaux. Must-sees include Dunnottar Castle (p116) near Stonehaven; Crathes Castle near Banchory; Balmoral Castle (p159) near Braemar; and fairy-tale Craigievar Castle in Ballater.

Above left St Andrews Castle (p106)
Left Dunnottar Castle (p116)

TANTZI13/SHUTTERSTOCK ©

↘ CELTIC DELICACIES

Don't miss these only-in-Scotland treats:

Tablet A sweeter-than-fudge sugary confection (pictured).

Cranachan Raspberries, oats, cream and whisky in a dessert glass.

Cullen Skink Thick, smoked fish and potato soup.

LOCAL **FLAVOURS**

Forget the deep-fried Mars bar. This is a country with a larder jam-packed with just-landed langoustine, mussel and lobster, estate-reared venison, hand-dived scallops, wood-smoked salmon, Aberdeen Angus beef, Stornoway black pudding, Ayrshire cheddar, sea-salt fudge (pictured), crumbly oatcakes, vegan haggis and stovies, Arbroath smokies, Dundee cake, bubblegum-like Irn Bru, and the world's best single malt whisky. Put simply, Scotland is the kind of place where indulging is practically a human right.

Best Food Experiences

- **For crab feasts, curries and whisky, head to Glasgow's trendiest neighbourhood for a big night out.** (p62)
- **Fish and chips, farmers markets, Michelin stars and local lobster – loosen your belt for the foodie hot spot of Fife.** (p94)
- **All gannets flock to Oban, the 'Seafood Capital of Scotland', for sustainable shellfish platters.** (p136)

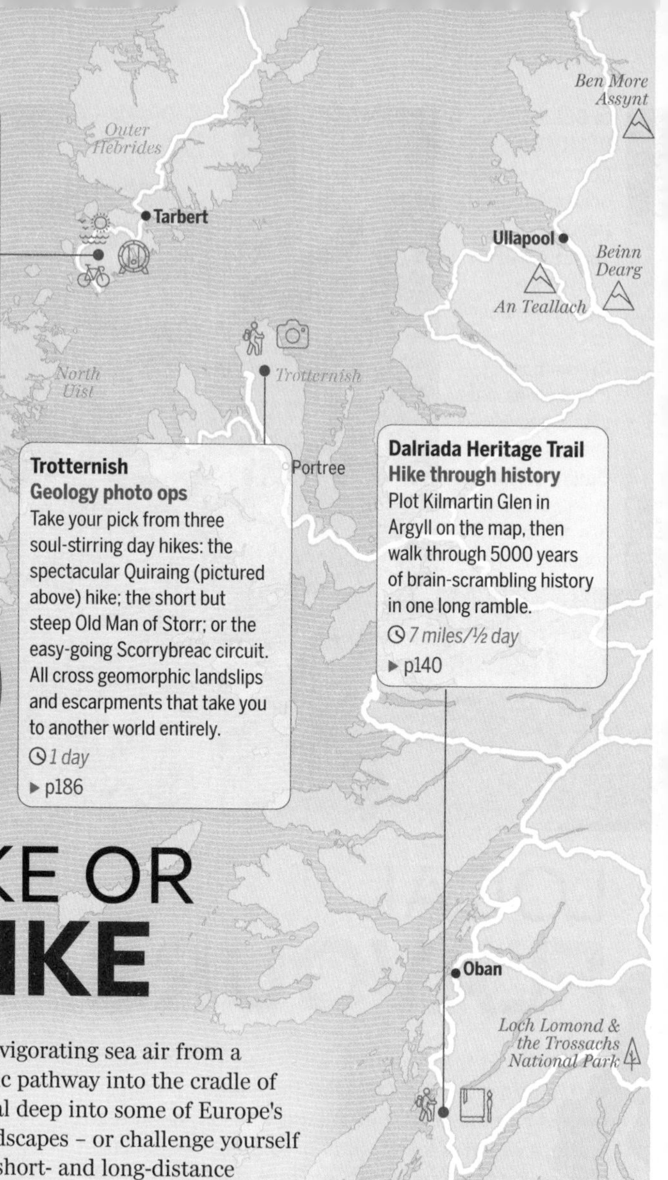

South Harris
Coastline circuit
It's a challenging cycle, with your journey beginning and ending in Tarbert. But navigate the climbs and twisting east coast and you'll be rewarded with glorious beaches, the loch-strewn east coast and a gin distillery at the finish line.
52 miles/2 days
▶ p196

Trotternish
Geology photo ops
Take your pick from three soul-stirring day hikes: the spectacular Quiraing (pictured above) hike; the short but steep Old Man of Storr; or the easy-going Scorrybreac circuit. All cross geomorphic landslips and escarpments that take you to another world entirely.
1 day
▶ p186

Dalriada Heritage Trail
Hike through history
Plot Kilmartin Glen in Argyll on the map, then walk through 5000 years of brain-scrambling history in one long ramble.
7 miles/½ day
▶ p140

BY HIKE OR **BY BIKE**

Breathe in the invigorating sea air from a clifftop, follow a historic pathway into the cradle of a silent mountain, pedal deep into some of Europe's most undiscovered landscapes – or challenge yourself to all three. Scotland's short- and long-distance walking trails and bike routes reward you with a wealth of second-to-none history, culture and wildlife experiences.

Rannoch Moor

Scenic bike adventure

Follow the twisty-turn road from Pitlochry to Rannoch Station, past glittering lochs and beautifully contoured mountains, to arrive at the daunting expanse of Rannoch Moor (pictured right).

35 miles/2 days

▶ p96

West Highland Way

Wild walks and wild camping

This rollercoaster route (pictured right) through the Highlands' finest scenery starts north of Glasgow and winds to Fort William. Wild camping is a thrill among the heather, but a permit is needed while in Loch Lomond and The Trossachs National Park.

96 miles/7–10 days

▶ p161

Fife Coastal Path

Seafood-packed shores

The country's most delicious long-distance trail, stringing together portrait-posing fishing villages, is packed with places to enjoy the sea harvest, from humble fish and chip shops to gourmet restaurants.

117 miles/5 days

▶ p94

SPEED LIMITS

MOTORWAYS

70 mph (112 km/h) for cars / 60 mph (96 km/h) for caravans/camper vans

CITIES

30 mph (48 km/h)

OUTSIDE BUILT-UP AREAS

60 mph (96 km/h) for cars / 50 mph (80 km/h) for caravans/camper vans

ON THE ROAD

Driving across Scotland isn't for the faint-hearted. The single-track roads and moving obstacles (sheep, cattle, deer) offer a crash course in the slower pace of life beyond the main cities. But the country's highways and coastal routes open up a world of adventure that lives up to the hype. Seen through the windscreen or during spontaneous pit stops, it will blow you away.

Left Sheep on a Scottish road.
Right Kylesku Bridge, on the North Coast 500 (p179)
Below Motorist approaching Dumfries and Galloway.

→ THE ROAD TRIP BOOM

Following the success of the North Coast 500, there are plenty of sign-posted touring routes to pack your itinerary with. The K66 around the Kintyre Peninsula; the South West Coastal 300 around Dumfries and Galloway; the Deeside Tourist Route from Perth to Aberdeen; or The Coig, around Ayrshire and the Clyde Islands.

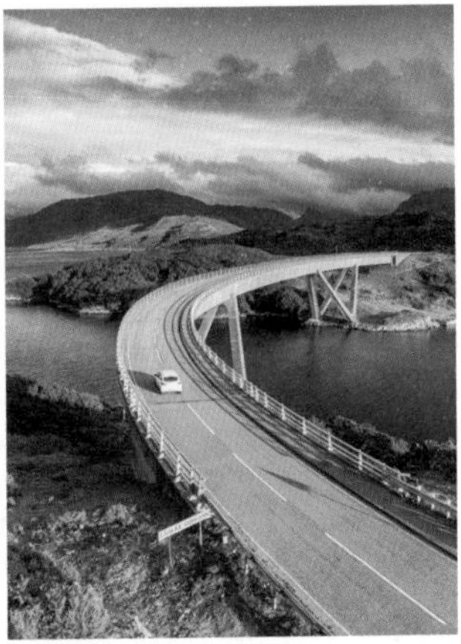

RICHARD P LONG/SHUTTERSTOCK ©

THE ULTIMATE PLAYLIST

When touring, you need a fitting soundtrack. The folky and ambient refrains of Erland Cooper and Kris Drever are ideal for Orkney, while Runrig remains Skye's most popular rock band. The Gaelic lilts of Mànran, Skipinnish and Julie Fowlis help bring the Outer Hebrides to life, while bands such as The Proclaimers, Chvrches and Franz Ferdinand will have you singing down the M8 motorway.

▶ Learn about more Scottish albums on p34

RIGHT: HELEN HOTSON/SHUTTERSTOCK ©
LEFT: OTMARW/SHUTTERSTOCK ©

↑ DON'T DRINK & DRIVE

There is a zero tolerance policy for driving under the influence of alcohol in Scotland. The legal limit is 50mg of alcohol in 100mL of blood – just one drink can put you over the threshold.

Best Road Trips

Stop off at chalky lighthouses, soft-sieved sands and cliff-hugging harbours on the Aberdeenshire Coastal Trail. (p114)

Hit the road to discover forest paths, hidden beaches and gastro highlights on the crowd-free Cowal Peninsula. (p138)

Follow the Snow Roads Scenic Route to see a royal palace, ancestral clan homes and distilleries east of the Cairngorms. (p160)

Take in Skye's dramatic west coast to explore stunning coastal scenery, historic castles and rarely seen wildlife. (p190)

ARTS &
CULTURE

For all the wild landscapes and scenic excursions, this is a country imbued with a deep-rooted love for Scots, Gaelic and Celtic cultures in all their forms. From Hogmanay and the Highland Games to the world's largest arts festival in Edinburgh, there's plenty of art, song, design, poetry, literature, theatre and film to capture your imagination – and your heart.

Best Culture Experiences

▶ **Snap up tickets for a premiere at the genre-defying Edinburgh Festival Fringe.** (p42)

▶ **Gawp at Glasgow's larger-than-life murals on an ever-changing street art tour.** (p64)

▶ **Meet the artisans who carve, spin, engrave, paint and weave on the Creative Orkney Trail.** (p210)

← **MUST VISIT**

Dundee's V&A Museum encapsulates a city that is on the rise. The country's first design museum, its galleries are spectacular: expect identity-unravelling exhibits on fashion, art, furniture and architecture.

▶ Follow the design trail on p121

★ **FAB FESTIVALS**

Not a month goes by without a memory-making festival and there are as many small-scale events as there are zeitgeist-defining epics like the Edinburgh Festival Fringe, Glasgow's Celtic Connections and Belladrum's Tartan Heart Festival. There are more than 200 every year.

▶ Find out more at scotland.org/events

Above left V&A Dundee (p121)
Left Street performers, Edinburgh Festival Fringe (p42)

LEFT: DOUBLECLIX/SHUTTERSTOCK ©. BOTTOM: IAN KRANENDONK/SHUTTERSTOCK ©

↘ GO CROWD FREE

Leave the tourists behind for somewhere new:

Isle of Raasay A wilder alternative to Skye. (p192)

Angus Glens Swap Glencoe for the Grampians.

East Lothian Stay on the coast, rather than in Edinburgh.

LEE WALKER/SHUTTERSTOCK ©

WIDE OPEN SPACES

There is no more rewarding way to experience Scotland than to really get away from it all. Words such as remote and off-grid are buzz-worthy today and Scotland is, in effect, a gigantic outdoor classroom, delivering a lesson on how to lose yourself in a landscape. Whether you hike in to cut-off Knoydart (Europe's so-called last wilderness) or tour Flow Country (Europe's largest expanse of blanket bog), there's a wide open space waiting for you.

Best Wide Open Spaces

- **Wild camp or stargaze amid the epic beauty and rolling silence of Galloway Forest Park.** (pictured above; p79)
- **Explore the wilderness of Cape Wrath with birdwatching and beach camping.** (p170)
- **Discover Loch Ness away from the crowds and be rewarded with rolling moorlands, mountains and clear waters.** (p152)

Demand for accommodation peaks in summer, particularly during the school holidays in July and August. Book tours and overnight adventures in advance. lonelyplanet.com/bookings

↙ The World Pipe Band Championships

Ditch the earplugs: pipers and drummers compete to see who's the best in the world.

Glasgow

▶ theworlds.co.uk

Belladrum Tartan Heart Festival

Inverness-shire does Woodstock at this alternative rock festival held every July.

▶ Beauly

▶ tartanheartfestival.co.uk

It's golf season: the home of golf has a course for every day of the year (550, in fact), but 18 holes are best played under sunny skies.

JUNE

Average daytime max: 17°C
Days of rainfall: 10

JULY

Scotland in SUMMER

↓ Edinburgh Festival Fringe

The world's largest arts festival brings the capital to a standstill in August.

Edinburgh

▶ edfringe.com

↑ Royal Highland Show

Scotland's largest agricultural get-together – a showcase of rural life, farm produce, arts and crafts.

Edinburgh

▶ royalhighlandshow.org

↑ The Hebridean Whale Trail

Cetacean sightings peak from June to September, when long summer nights make it easier than ever to shore watch along Scotland's west coast.

Average daytime max: 19°C
Days of rainfall: 10

AUGUST

Average daytime max: 19°C
Days of rainfall: 10

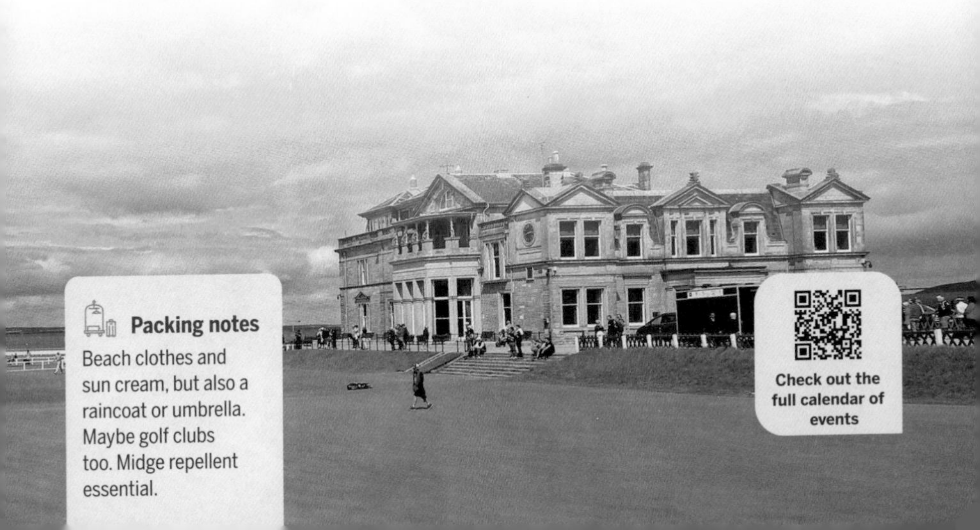

Packing notes

Beach clothes and sun cream, but also a raincoat or umbrella. Maybe golf clubs too. Midge repellent essential.

Check out the full calendar of events

Go stargazing: autumnal skies and shooting stars light up Galloway Forest Park, the UK's first Dark Sky Park.

↘ Braemar Gathering

Skirling, whirling, caber tossing, tug of war and highland dancing – the world-famous Highland Games is a one-day bash (literally) in September. Always a sell-out.

▶ p158

As part of the breeding season, stag ruts are shows of strength from the largest population of red deer in Europe. Best seen before dusk or dawn in the Highlands.

↘ Halloween

The Celtic roots of this scare-fest are celebrated nationwide on 31 October. Take a ghost tour in Edinburgh, or follow Scotland's Ghost Trail.

▶ visitscotland.com/blog/attractions/ghost-trail

SEPTEMBER

Average daytime max: 16°C
Days of rainfall: 10

OCTOBER

Scotland in AUTUMN

SIMON PRICE/ALAMY STOCK PHOTO © LORENZO ... NEWS/ALAMY STOCK PHOTO © CKP1001/SHUTT... SHUTTERSTOCK ©

↘ St Andrews Day

A celebration of Scotland's patron saint and the country's national day. Expect haggis, whisky and tipsy singalongs of 'Auld Lang Synev'.

Seal watching

Witness 10,000 grey seals – the largest number in Europe – coming ashore to have their pups on the Monach Islands off the coast of North Uist.

Royal National Mòd

The biggest celebration of Gaelic literature, song, arts and culture. Held in October in a different city each year.

▶ ancomunn.co.uk

Largs Viking Festival

More than an excuse to dress up in a horned helmet: a commemoration of the last great battle between the Scots and the Vikings.

Largs

▶ largsvikingfestival.org

Average daytime max: 12°C
Days of rainfall: 12

NOVEMBER

Average daytime max: 9°C
Days of rainfall: 11

Packing notes

A backpack and hiking boots for forest rambles, plus a fleece or puffy jacket for cooler nights.

↘ Winter sports

Scotland's six ski resorts are a great way to see the country's most spine-tingling scenery. Choose Glenshee or Cairngorm for beginners, or Glencoe for gnarlier terrain.

Glencoe

▶ p161

Christmas Day, Boxing Day, New Year's Day and 2 January are all public holidays. Restaurants and pubs are busy with revelry and especially welcoming.

↘ Burns Night

A celebration of the life and poetry of the national bard and poet, Robert Burns, on 25 January.

DECEMBER

Average daytime max: 3°C
Days of rainfall: 12

JANUARY

Scotland in WINTER

Celtic Connections

The UK's largest Celtic music festival, with folk, roots and jazz. Late-night sessions and stadium stars.

Glasgow

▸ celticconnections.com

↘ Up Helly Aa

Viking-themed fire festival held at the end of January – a no-holds-barred carnival, culminating in 1000 men setting a replica longboat ablaze.

Shetland

▸ uphellyaa.org

Edinburgh's Hogmanay

A carnival of Hogmanay – the Scottish celebration of New Year – with *ceilidhs*, a torchlit procession and a city-stopping street party.

Edinburgh

▸ edinburghshogmanay.com

Get lucky, and on a clear night Scotland's night sky turns into a disco. Sutherland, Caithness and Shetland are prime areas for the Northern Lights.

Average daytime max: 4°C
Days of rainfall: 12

FEBRUARY

Average daytime max: 5°C
Days of rainfall: 9

Snow Roads Scenic Route

Drive the 90-mile road through the Cairngorms National Park – it's the highest mountain road in the UK.

Packing notes

Warm hat, gloves and a puffy jacket to keep you wrapped up in the cold, often snowy, conditions.

Spirit of Speyside Whisky Festival

Tastings, tours and morning-after sore heads at this single malt extravaganza. In a word: slainte!

Speyside

▶ spiritofspeyside.com

→ Six Nations

Pan-European rugby tussle that brings the UK together every spring. Hard to get a ticket, but the pubs around Murrayfield Stadium are just as packed.

Edinburgh

▶ scottishrugby.org

Beltane Fire Festival

Celtic festival in April which heralds the beginning of summer. Don't miss the Calton Hill bonfire.

Edinburgh

▶ beltane.org

Demand for accommodation on the popular West Highland Way hiking route peaks in summer – tackle it in late April or May.

▶ westhighlandway.org

MARCH

Average daytime max: 9°C
Days of rainfall: 10

APRIL

Scotland in SPRING

↘ Mountain biking

All eyes are on Fort William in May for the annual World Cup event, which attracts thousands from around the globe.

📍 Fort William

▶ fortwilliamworldcup.co.uk

The beginning of the salmon-fishing season starts in February, but the most reliable time for landing a whopper is April and May. The Spey, Tay and Tweed have the best spring runs.

Average daytime max: 12°C
Days of rainfall: 9

MAY

Average daytime max: 15°C
Days of rainfall: 10

The long Easter holiday from school (and work) lasts for two to three weeks every spring.

World Whisky Day

The centrepiece of Scotland's Whisky Month held every May (yet another excuse for a dram).

▶ worldwhiskyday.com

Packing notes

Woolly sweater and waterproof jacket, plus scarf and warm hat. Feeling brave? Pack shorts for Easter.

CITIES & THE SOUTH
Trip Builder

TAKE YOUR PICK OF MUST-SEES AND HIDDEN GEMS

Experience Scotland's two extremes: the here-and-now arts, music, dining and drinking scenes of its two greatest cities, then take the road less travelled to the serene landscapes and scenic coastlines of Arran, Ayrshire, the Borders, and Dumfries and Galloway.

Trip Notes

Hub towns Edinburgh, Glasgow

How long Allow for 10–12 days

Getting around Take the bus or train to see the cities, then pick up a hire car to go at your own pace. Otherwise, public transport will take you to all but the most remote destinations.

Tips Plan for more time than you think you will need: many roads hide a castle, cove or creaky historic attraction that you'll want to stop and linger at. The roads here are designed to be driven slowly.

Islay
Breathe in the peaty aromas, then sample single malt whisky on a trail around the Southern Hebrides.
2 days

Arran
Hike, bike, wildlife watch, distillery tour or beach comb – maybe all five. This west coast isle's 'best-in-Scotland' billing lives up to expectation.
2 days

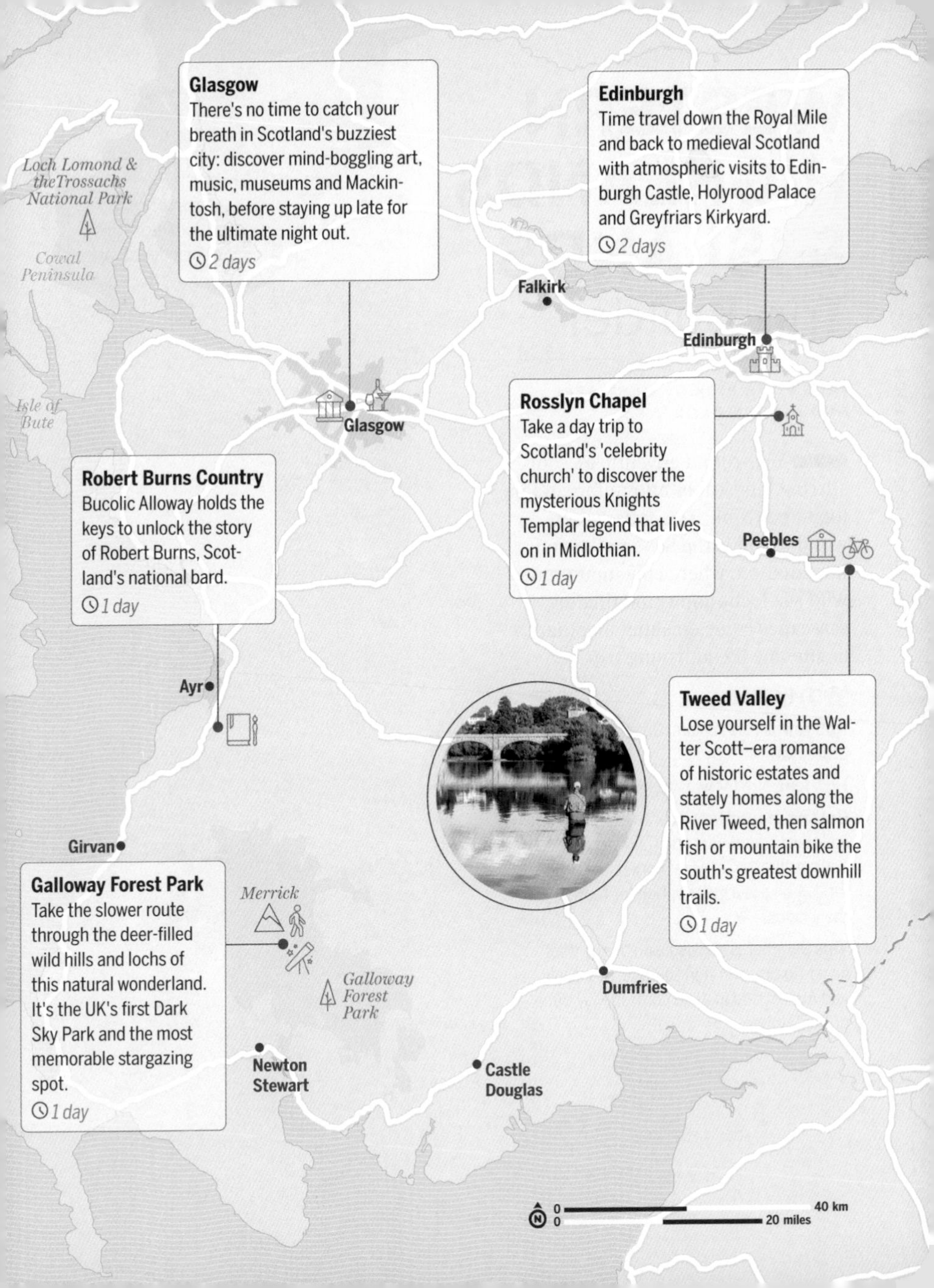

Glasgow
There's no time to catch your breath in Scotland's buzziest city: discover mind-boggling art, music, museums and Mackintosh, before staying up late for the ultimate night out.
2 days

Edinburgh
Time travel down the Royal Mile and back to medieval Scotland with atmospheric visits to Edinburgh Castle, Holyrood Palace and Greyfriars Kirkyard.
2 days

Rosslyn Chapel
Take a day trip to Scotland's 'celebrity church' to discover the mysterious Knights Templar legend that lives on in Midlothian.
1 day

Robert Burns Country
Bucolic Alloway holds the keys to unlock the story of Robert Burns, Scotland's national bard.
1 day

Tweed Valley
Lose yourself in the Walter Scott–era romance of historic estates and stately homes along the River Tweed, then salmon fish or mountain bike the south's greatest downhill trails.
1 day

Galloway Forest Park
Take the slower route through the deer-filled wild hills and lochs of this natural wonderland. It's the UK's first Dark Sky Park and the most memorable stargazing spot.
1 day

WESTERN HIGHLANDS & ISLANDS
Trip Builder

TAKE YOUR PICK OF MUST-SEES AND HIDDEN GEMS

Year-round adventures, soul-stirring landscapes and unforgettable food and drink. This four-season wonderland is the Scotland of your imagination, where epic mountains, wild sea lochs and spine-tingling seascapes come crashing together to create one life-affirming trip.

Trip Notes

Hub towns Fort William, Oban, Portree, Stornoway

How long Aim for two weeks

Getting around Hire a car to explore at your own speed. Bus and train travel are limited, but the ferry network makes up for it. A bike is a great option for touring the islands.

Tips Summer is peak season on the west coast. To discover it in solitude, avoid July and August and instead come in May, June or September.

St Kilda
St Kilda
See soaring sea cliffs and rare birdlife on this remote Atlantic outpost.
1 day
North Uist
South Uist

JAROSLAV MORAVCIK, JAJA, JAROSLAV SEKERES./SHUTTERSTOCK ©.

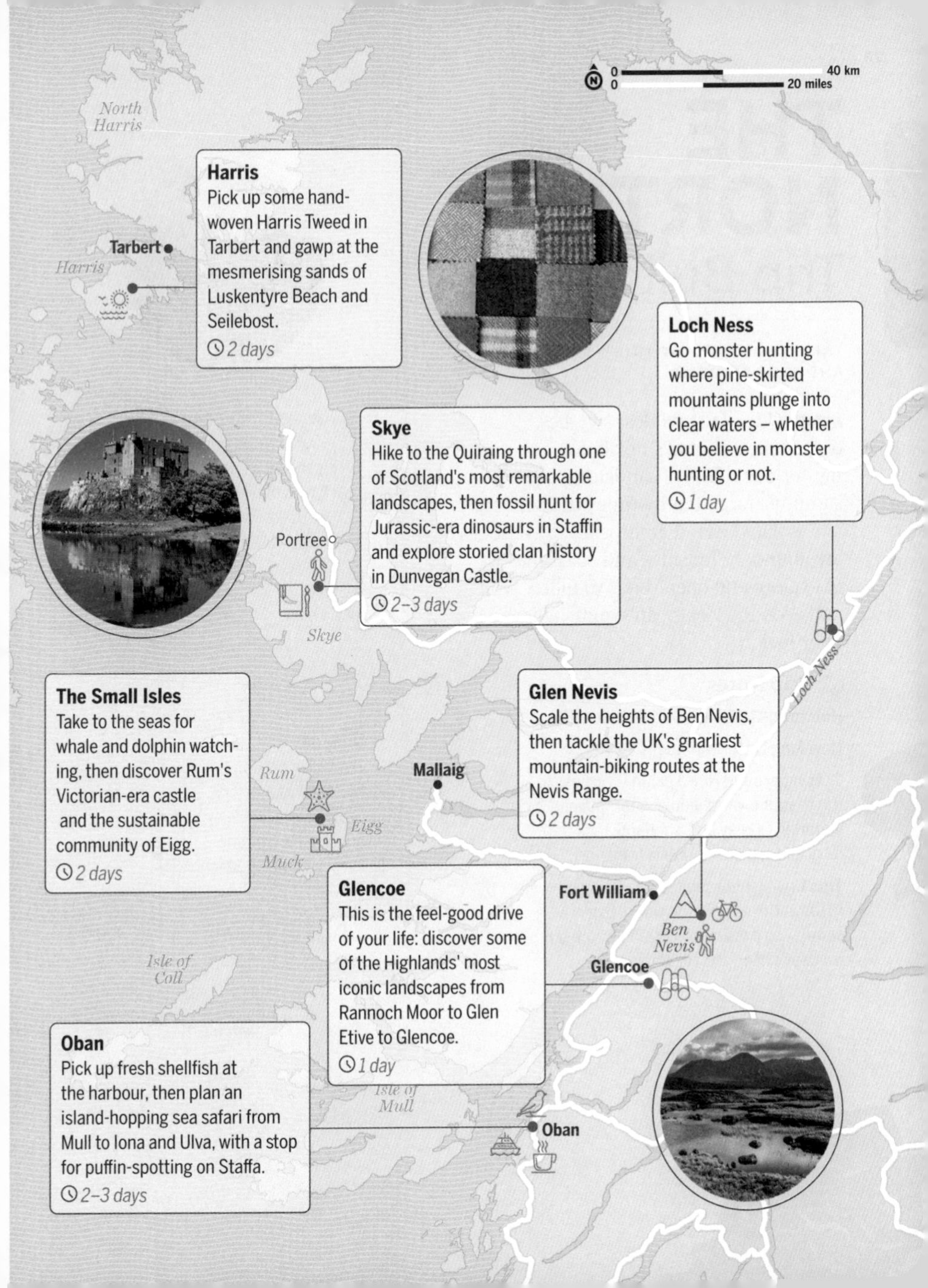

Harris
Pick up some hand-woven Harris Tweed in Tarbert and gawp at the mesmerising sands of Luskentyre Beach and Seilebost.
2 days

Loch Ness
Go monster hunting where pine-skirted mountains plunge into clear waters – whether you believe in monster hunting or not.
1 day

Skye
Hike to the Quiraing through one of Scotland's most remarkable landscapes, then fossil hunt for Jurassic-era dinosaurs in Staffin and explore storied clan history in Dunvegan Castle.
2–3 days

The Small Isles
Take to the seas for whale and dolphin watching, then discover Rum's Victorian-era castle and the sustainable community of Eigg.
2 days

Glen Nevis
Scale the heights of Ben Nevis, then tackle the UK's gnarliest mountain-biking routes at the Nevis Range.
2 days

Glencoe
This is the feel-good drive of your life: discover some of the Highlands' most iconic landscapes from Rannoch Moor to Glen Etive to Glencoe.
1 day

Oban
Pick up fresh shellfish at the harbour, then plan an island-hopping sea safari from Mull to Iona and Ulva, with a stop for puffin-spotting on Staffa.
2–3 days

THE NORTH
Trip Builder

TAKE YOUR PICK OF MUST-SEES AND HIDDEN GEMS

One of the wildest swathes of Europe, Scotland's north is a mysterious riddle of sandstone summits, forgotten-by-time sea lochs and isolated island archipelagos. There are abundant hillsides and coastlines to explore and open roads to follow – and even the locals can't quite believe their luck.

Trip Notes

Hub towns Inverness, Kirkwall, Lerwick

How long Go for two weeks

Getting around Hire a car in Inverness to run to your own schedule. Alternatively, if touring Orkney and Shetland, take the ferry and explore by public transport.

Tips Driving here can feel like being on roads at the edge of the world. Explore slowly, use passing places and watch out for deer, sheep and Highland cows.

CLIFF HANDS/SHUTTERSTOCK ©, COLIN WARD/SHUTTERSTOCK ©, COLOMBO NICOLA/SHUTTERSTOCK ©

Assynt
Experience mind-boggling geology, where three billion years of history collide with dramatic beauty and sigh-triggering outdoor thrills.
1 day

Ullapool
Stop off in this mini Highland capital for seafood, seal-spotting, cruising the Summer Isles or climbing Stac Pollaidh.
1–2 days

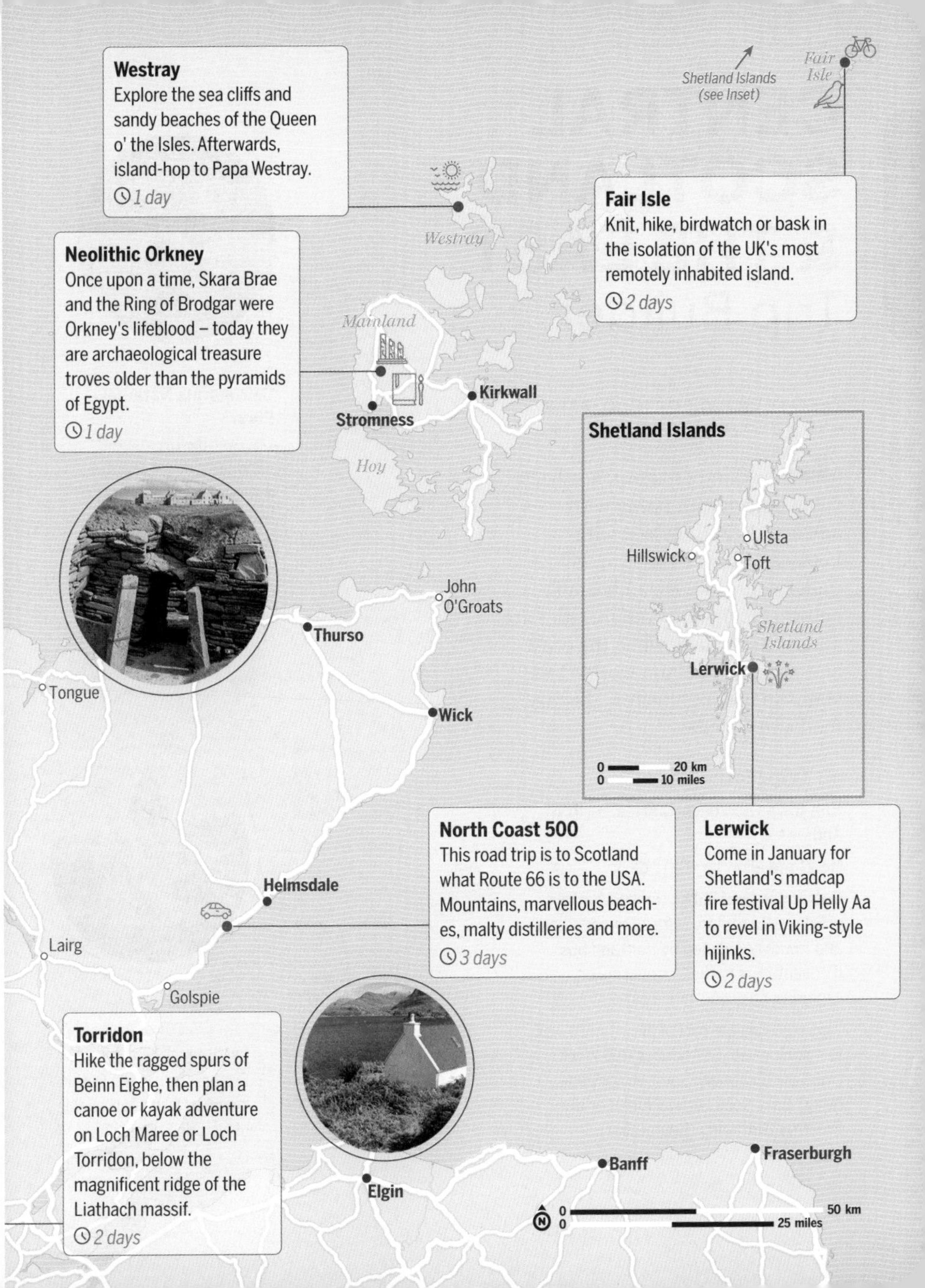

Westray

Explore the sea cliffs and sandy beaches of the Queen o' the Isles. Afterwards, island-hop to Papa Westray.

1 day

Fair Isle

Knit, hike, birdwatch or bask in the isolation of the UK's most remotely inhabited island.

2 days

Neolithic Orkney

Once upon a time, Skara Brae and the Ring of Brodgar were Orkney's lifeblood – today they are archaeological treasure troves older than the pyramids of Egypt.

1 day

North Coast 500

This road trip is to Scotland what Route 66 is to the USA. Mountains, marvellous beaches, malty distilleries and more.

3 days

Lerwick

Come in January for Shetland's madcap fire festival Up Helly Aa to revel in Viking-style hijinks.

2 days

Torridon

Hike the ragged spurs of Beinn Eighe, then plan a canoe or kayak adventure on Loch Maree or Loch Torridon, below the magnificent ridge of the Liathach massif.

2 days

CENTRAL SCOTLAND & THE EAST
Trip Builder

TAKE YOUR PICK OF MUST-SEES AND HIDDEN GEMS

Scotland's historic northeast is big on pride, bursting with adventures and blessed with landscapes and cities that will get under your skin. For unbeatable culture, its up-and-coming cities are almost unrivalled, while the coast and mountains claim world-class status in art, architecture, history, food and beaches.

Trip Notes

Hub towns Aberdeen, Dundee, Perth, St Andrews

How long Allow for 10–12 days

Getting around Public transport is a great way to explore, with all major cities and towns connected by train and bus. If adventuring to the Cairngorms or exploring Speyside, hire a car.

Tips Festivals are part of life – time a visit to coincide with St Andrews Golf Week (April and October), Spirit of Speyside (May), East Neuk Festival (July) or the Braemar Gathering (September).

ESCOCIA/SHUTTERSTOCK ©, FOTO-JAGLA.DE/SHUTTERSTOCK ©, LUCAS FERGUSON/SHUTTERSTOCK ©

Cairngorms National Park
Discover the UK's largest national park – it offers a smorgasbord of hiking, biking, canoeing, wildlife watching and winter sports.
2–3 days

Stirling
Explore the castles, Gothic landmarks and battlefields of historic Stirling.
1 day

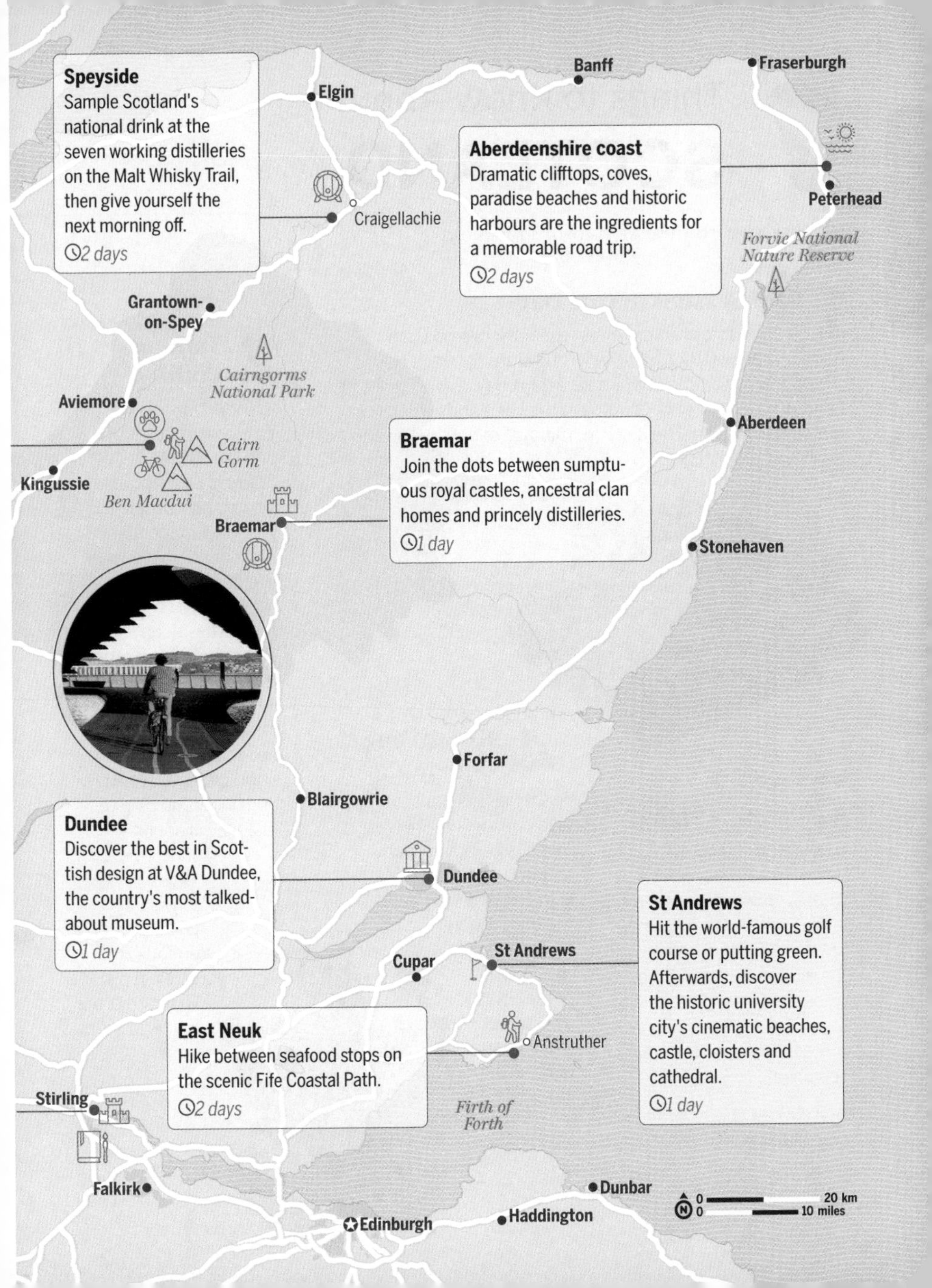
Speyside
Sample Scotland's national drink at the seven working distilleries on the Malt Whisky Trail, then give yourself the next morning off.
2 days
Elgin
Banff
Fraserburgh
Aberdeenshire coast
Dramatic clifftops, coves, paradise beaches and historic harbours are the ingredients for a memorable road trip.
2 days
Craigellachie
Peterhead
Forvie National Nature Reserve
Grantown-on-Spey
Cairngorms National Park
Aviemore
Cairn Gorm
Kingussie
Ben Macdui
Aberdeen
Braemar
Join the dots between sumptuous royal castles, ancestral clan homes and princely distilleries.
1 day
Braemar
Stonehaven
Forfar
Blairgowrie
Dundee
Discover the best in Scottish design at V&A Dundee, the country's most talked-about museum.
1 day
Dundee
St Andrews
Hit the world-famous golf course or putting green. Afterwards, discover the historic university city's cinematic beaches, castle, cloisters and cathedral.
1 day
Cupar
St Andrews
East Neuk
Hike between seafood stops on the scenic Fife Coastal Path.
2 days
Anstruther
Stirling
Firth of Forth
Falkirk
Dunbar
Haddington
Edinburgh
0 20 km
0 10 miles

7 Things to Know About SCOTLAND

INSIDER TIPS TO HIT THE GROUND RUNNING

1 Four Seasons in One Day

Scotland's old adage rings true – there's no such thing as bad weather, just the wrong clothing. Pack a raincoat, even on the sunniest Glasgow day. Expect gales in Edinburgh. And monsoon rains in the Highlands when the forecast is for sun. The key is to manage expectations and dress appropriately.

▶See more about the weather on p16

2 Talking Politics

Scotland is entering an era-defining period and the country's future is up for grabs. On one hand, there is a growing independence movement, fuelled by Brexit, and another referendum on leaving the UK has been promised; on the other, there are those who want to maintain the status quo. The next five years could see unprecedented change and understanding the history will not only deepen the pleasure of travelling, but act as a reminder that you are not just visiting a place but also a time.

3 Wi-fi & Mobile Signal

Broadband and 4G coverage is improving across rural Scotland, particularly in the Highlands and Islands, but don't be surprised if there is none. While this is a blessing for many, it's best to download any essentials or maps before your plans are scotched!

▶See more about getting connected on p238

4 Know Your Geography

Few things get Scots as riled up as visitors not knowing that it is an independent country. It's part of a union with England, Wales and Northern Ireland and referring to Scotland or the UK as England will only result in glowers.

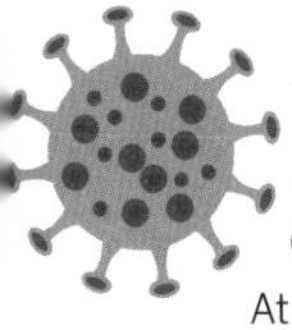

5 Covid-19

At the time of writing, international travellers entering Scotland needed to follow different rules depending on their vacination status. Note that travel from other parts of the UK, Ireland and the Crown Dependencies is not considered international travel. Check your government's advice before travelling and visit gov.scot for the latest information.

▶See more about safe travel on p242

6 Local Lingo

Learning some Scots vernacular will help you get by and make local friends along the way.

Munro bagging – hiking Scotland's highest mountains

gutties – shoes

banter – chat

fizzy juice, ginger – a soft drink or soda

scran – food

dreich – cold, wet and miserable

gie it laldy – give it your best

roaster, rocket, walloper – an idiot

blootered, bladdered, hammered, steamin', smashed, wrecked – drunk

If you're visiting the Highlands and Islands, particularly the Outer Hebrides, a few token words of Gaelic will go a long way with locals. Many road signs are in both English and Gaelic.

madainn mhath – good morning

ciamar a tha sibh? – how are you?

slainte mhath – (pronounced slanj-a-va) cheers

Alba – Scotland

uisge beatha – literally water of life, but also the name of whisky

7 Midges

Scotland's most ferocious foe can single-handedly ruin a summer's evening. From May to September, the hard-to-see biting insects swarm riverbanks, lochsides, campsites and anywhere without a breeze. Pack midge repellent and cover up to avoid itchy red spots. If they're bad, put a stocking over your head and run for cover. Seriously.

▶See more about midges on p242

Read, Listen, Watch & Follow

READ

Trainspotting (Irvine Welsh; 1993) A literary assault on the senses, hinged on the dark exploits of heroin users in 1980s Edinburgh.

Lanark (Alasdair Gray; 1981) A dystopian, surrealist distillation of Glasgow in four colossal parts.

The Prime of Miss Jean Brodie (Muriel Spark; 1961) A love letter to Edinburgh, as well as a story of betrayal at an all-girls school.

Sunset Song (Lewis Grassic Gibbon; 1932) Rural life in the Northeast, as seen through the lens of postwar Scotland.

LISTEN

Bandwagonesque (Teenage Fanclub; 1991) Beloved pop-grunge hooks from Bellshill that led Kurt Cobain to call the 'Fannies' the greatest band in the world.

Screamadelica (Primal Scream; 1991) Rave-meets-rock-meets-gospel-meets-psychedelic-acid-house, spanning 11 tracks that changed British music forever.

Sunshine on Leith (The Proclaimers; 1988) Scotland's favourite sons, thanks to the country's unofficial singalong national anthem, 'I'm Gonna Be (500 Miles)'.

The Boy with the Arab Strap (Belle and Sebastian; 1998) Breakthrough third album from Glasgow's unlikely pop-folk troubadours.

TOM ROSE/SHUTTERSTOCK ©

Divinely Uninspired to a Hellish Extent (Lewis Capaldi; 2019) Broody, blue-eyed soul and torch ballads from busking singer-songwriter turned down-to-earth Billboard superstar.

WATCH

Harry Potter saga (2001–11) Wizards, witches and whomping willows – JK Rowling's epic inspired by and shot in her homeland.

Braveheart (1995) Mel Gibson channels his inner warrior for this Oscar-winning classic about claymore-wielding hero William Wallace.

Gregory's Girl (1981) Ageless high school coming-of-age comedy.

Brave (2012) Disney does Scotland, with kilts, curses and a fiery cartoon princess.

Whisky Galore! (1949) Ealing Studio classic about a shipwrecked cargo and the Hebridean community out to hijack it.

FOLLOW

bbc.com/scotland News, sports and culture from the country's largest broadcaster.

scottishrugby.org Follow the biggest match days #AsOne.

list.co.uk Culture and events listings.

@VisitScotland Visit Scotland's official account.

gigsinscotland.com Gigs, ticket sales and music news.

EDINBURGH

CULTURE | HISTORY | FESTIVALS

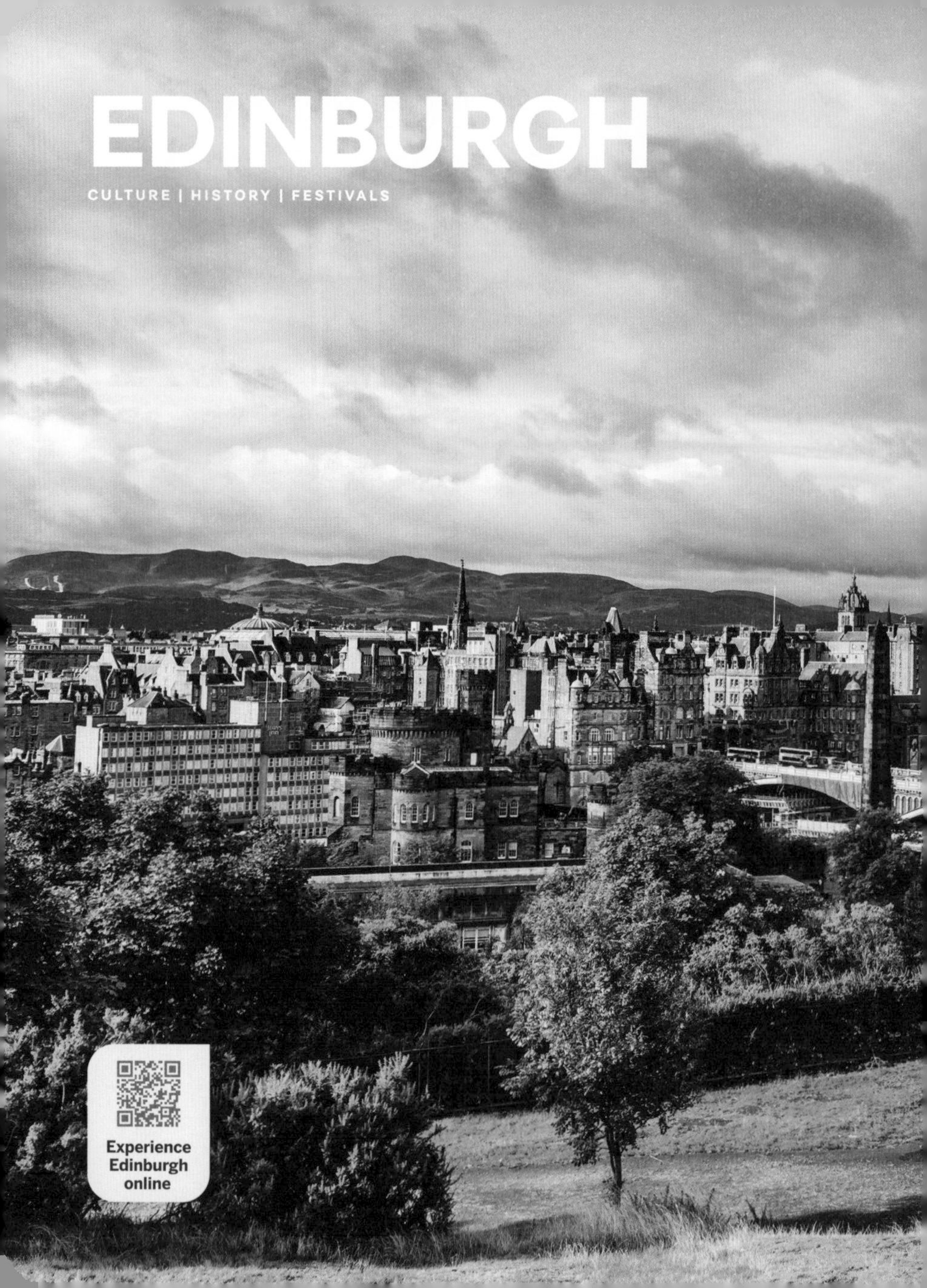

Experience Edinburgh online

- **Edinburgh Festival Fringe** (p42)
- **History & a Royal Mile** (p44)
- **The Water of Leith** (p46)
- **Writers, Witches & Wizards** (p48)
- **Seven Hills** (p50)
- **Foodie Leith** (p52)
- **Listings** (p54)

Bonus Online Experiences

- **Hogmanay Survival Guide**
- **Edinburgh by Design**

EDINBURGH
Trip Builder

Where history, hospitality and higgledy-piggledy hills collide you'll find this soul-soaring city. It's a wellspring of castles and cathedrals, with storybook alleys that inspired the greatest minds in science, philosophy and literature, but it's also where visitors can experience new waves of art, design and culture.

Firth of Forth
TRINITY
WARRISTON
INVERLEITH
Inverleith Park
CANONMILLS
DRYLAW
BLACKHALL
NEW TOWN
DEAN VILLAGE
WEST END
LAURISTON
MARCHMONT

Stroll the **Water of Leith** to **Stockbridge** for a window on local Edinburgh life (p46)
1 day

Get smart and land tickets for the best shows at the world's largest **arts festival** (p42)
2–3 days

Discover life as it was during the Middle Ages at **Edinburgh Castle** (p45)
½ day

Take a scenic trip to **Rosslyn Chapel** for divine masonry and mystery (p45)
½ day

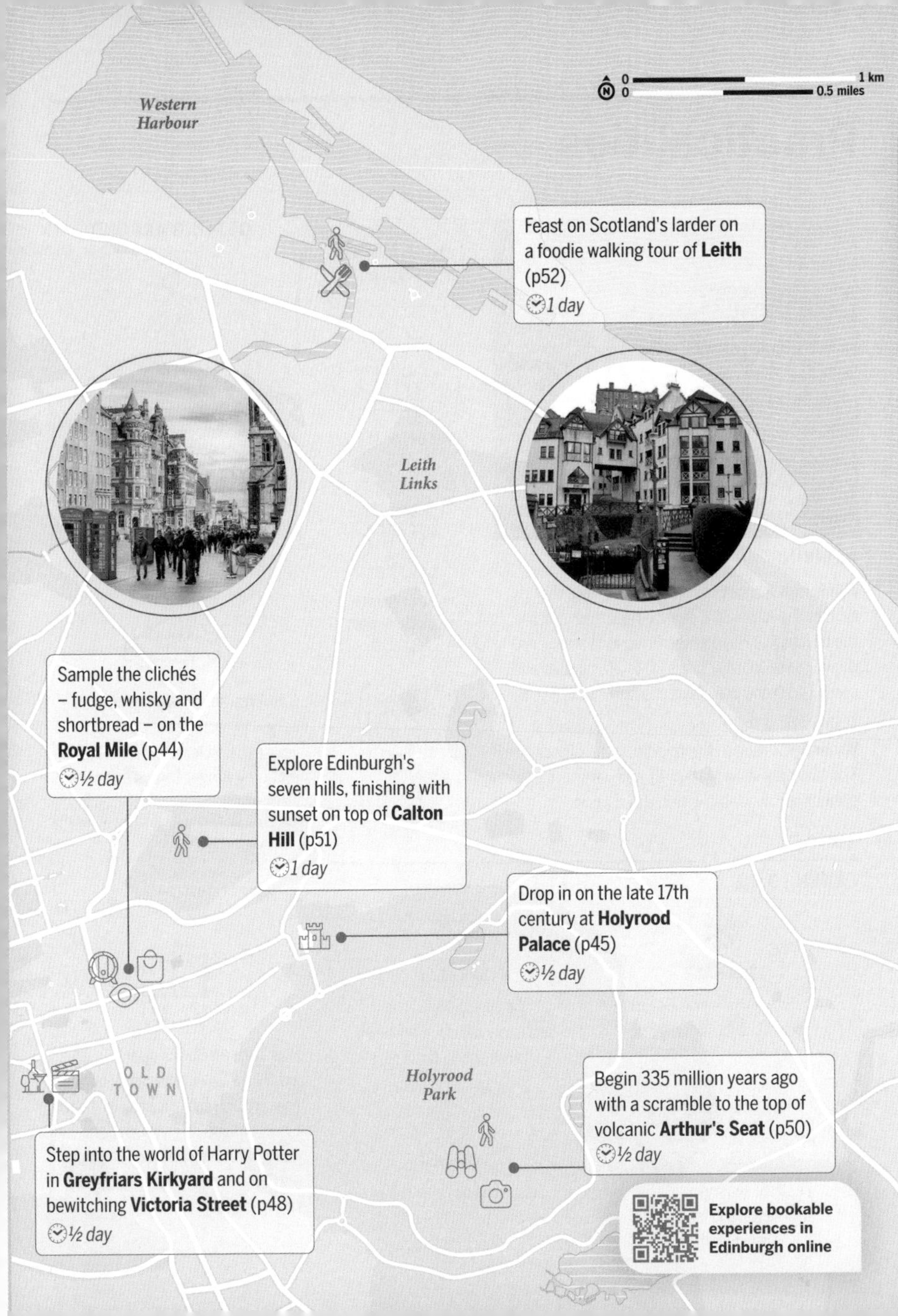
Western Harbour
Leith Links
OLD TOWN
Holyrood Park
Feast on Scotland's larder on a foodie walking tour of **Leith** (p52) 1 day
Sample the clichés – fudge, whisky and shortbread – on the **Royal Mile** (p44) ½ day
Explore Edinburgh's seven hills, finishing with sunset on top of **Calton Hill** (p51) 1 day
Drop in on the late 17th century at **Holyrood Palace** (p45) ½ day
Begin 335 million years ago with a scramble to the top of volcanic **Arthur's Seat** (p50) ½ day
Step into the world of Harry Potter in **Greyfriars Kirkyard** and on bewitching **Victoria Street** (p48) ½ day
Explore bookable experiences in Edinburgh online

Practicalities

NITSAWAN KATERATTANAKUL/SHUTTERSTOCK ©

ARRIVING

Edinburgh Airport Located 8 miles from the city centre. The Airlink 100 service runs from outside the terminal to Haymarket, Princes St and St Andrew Sq. The journey takes 20 to 25 minutes and costs £4.50 one way. Taxis cost around £25 to £30.

Trains Arrive from other parts of Scotland at Waverley Station in the middle of the city centre. The taxi rank is on Market St and various car-hire options are available within the station.

HOW MUCH FOR A

Pint of local beer
£5

Edinburgh Castle ticket
£17.50

Haggis meal
£14

GETTING AROUND

Walking Edinburgh is compact, easily navigable and best explored in a pair of comfy shoes. The city has seven hills – offering a different perspective from almost every angle.

Car A rental car isn't necessary – in fact, street parking is very expensive. Hire one only if planning longer forays out of the city centre.

Bus Lothian Buses operates an extensive 24/7 network around the city and the suburbs. If it can't take you, you might question going in the first place. All maps and timetables can be found on the website.

WHEN TO GO

JAN–MAR
Chilly weather, snow-globe scenery and dark nights.

APR–JUN
Comfortably warm, relatively rain free and with blossoming flowers.

JUL–SEP
Festival season, with the sunniest weather and the most visitors.

OCT–DEC
Thinner crowds, but busy around the city's raucous winter festivals.

EATING & DRINKING

Michelin menus Edinburgh has more Michelin-star restaurants and fine-dining affairs than the rest of Scotland put together. Blow your budget on a tasting menu with paired wines at The Little Chartroom, Fhior or Wedgwood (p55).

Coffee and cake Artisan Roast (p54) is the connoisseur's choice, with three barista hot spots dotted around the city.

Must-visit The Bow Bar (p54)

Best whisky alternative Edinburgh Gin Distillery (p55)

WHERE TO STAY

Area	Pro/Con
Old Town	Buzzing hub of restaurants, shops, pubs and hotels, with excellent transport links and views. Pricey accommodation.
West End	Upmarket streets with terrace houses and hotels, boutiques and cocktail bars. Perfectly quiet in the evening.
Stockbridge	Gentrified suburb wedged between the Royal Botanic Gardens and the Water of Leith. Wonderful restaurants, cafes, pubs and markets with a family-friendly feel.
Leith	Hipster central with hostels and the city's most happening restaurants and nightlife. A little rough around the edges.
Bruntsfield	Colourful southern suburb overlooking the green spaces of The Meadows with a village-like vibe.
Newington	Up-and-coming neighbourhood in the shadow of Arthur's Seat. Popular with students and right in the thick of things come Festival Fringe time in August.

CONNECT & FIND YOUR WAY

Wi-fi All hotels, bars, cafes and restaurants have guest wi-fi, while the city has its own free wi-fi service (edinburghfreewifi.com) with no restrictions on time.

Navigation The city centre is one of the smallest in Europe and a joy to explore on foot. Use Google Maps or grab a free local map from the VisitScotland Edinburgh iCentre on the Royal Mile.

FESTIVALS

The Scottish capital is turned upside down in August, December and at Hogmanay with more than three million visitors. Arrange your trip for midweek, when the crowds are more bearable.

MONEY

Plenty of Edinburgh's most popular attractions are free, including the National Museum of Scotland, the Scottish National Gallery and Scottish National Gallery of Modern Art. All are certainly worthy of a donation.

01 Festival FRINGE

ARTS | CULTURE | LATE NIGHT

From performances in pubs and playhouses to genre-defying shows in caravans and even toilets, the Edinburgh Festival Fringe turns the capital into an intoxicating cultural Xanadu every August. Nothing beats it for drama or spectacle. Weirdness, too. But with so much to make sense of, knowing where to start can leave you spinning.

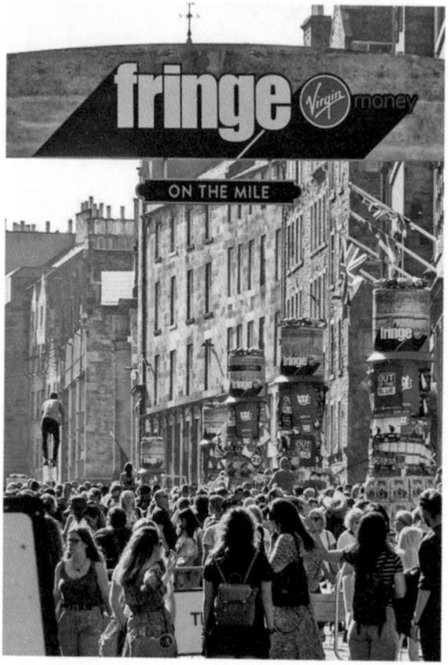

KENNY TELFER/SHUTTERSTOCK ©

How to

When to go August. Stay longer than you think you'll need. Three days is ideal.

How much Ticket prices vary from free to upwards of £40 for a marquee act. 2-for-1 previews over the first weekend are the norm. Consider the Half Price Hut (The Mound) for last-minute bargains.

Don't forget An umbrella or raincoat. August is notoriously fickle weather-wise and queueing outside a venue in torrential rain is no one's idea of a great day out.

Get smart With 3500 shows, 1900-odd premieres and around 55,000 performances spread across 300 city-wide venues, deciding on what to see is a minefield. For the most memorable shows, read up on the critics' picks beforehand in *The Scotsman*, trust word of mouth, and remember that spontaneity is key. For the quintessential day, settle on one of the big four venues, turn up by lunchtime with at least one show pre-booked in advance, then see where the mood takes you.

The venues The four main Fringe hubs all offer something different. Try the

Above left Edinburgh Festival Fringe on the Royal Mile
Above right A Festival Fringe street perfomer
Right A street musician plays for a Festival Fringe crowd

YATZEK PHOTOGRAPHY/SHUTTERSTOCK ©

POWEROFFLOWERS/SHUTTERSTOCK ©

Other Festivals

Edinburgh's Hogmanay The world's biggest Hogmanay bash sees an international tartan army crammed beneath Edinburgh Castle to *ceilidh* and quaff whisky every 31 December.

Edinburgh International Film Festival This carnival in late June sees red carpet galas, world premieres and talks with both local and A-list stars and directors.

Edinburgh International Book Festival Held from mid to late August, with 1000 writers, conversations and Q&As.

Pleasance for celeb-spotting and comedy; take a picnic blanket to Assembly at George Sq for street food and the big top Spiegeltent; consider Underbelly for cabaret; and catch topical comedy and theatre at the Gilded Balloon. Elsewhere, Summerhall is a stellar multi-arts venue, while The Stand is a don't-miss basement comedy club.

Need to know By the second and third weeks, the critics' picks are often sold out. Conversely, newcomers and on-the-up performers hand out free or next-to-nothing tickets outside venues. You might see a flop, but before they were famous the likes of Stephen Fry, Mike Myers and Flight of the Conchords performed for less than £5.

02 History & a ROYAL MILE

HISTORY | CULTURE | WALK

With a storied skyline of Gothic tollbooths, Georgian turrets and gasp-inducing spires, Edinburgh is Britain's most full-blooded city. There are dozens of world-class sights to discover, with each offering time travel of a sort through the centuries, from the medieval to the present day.

ESSEVU/SHUTTERSTOCK ©

How to

Getting around Most sights are easily navigable through Edinburgh's most romantic cobbled passageways. To get to Rosslyn Chapel, take Service 37 with Lothian Buses, or hire a bike for the 10-mile round-trip along Route 61 (The Rosslyn Chapel Way).

When to go Summer sees the city's high-profile attractions at their busiest; spring and September are quieter times to visit.

Best photo op From rugged Salisbury Crags, next to Holyrood Palace at last light.

FOTOKON/SHUTTERSTOCK ©

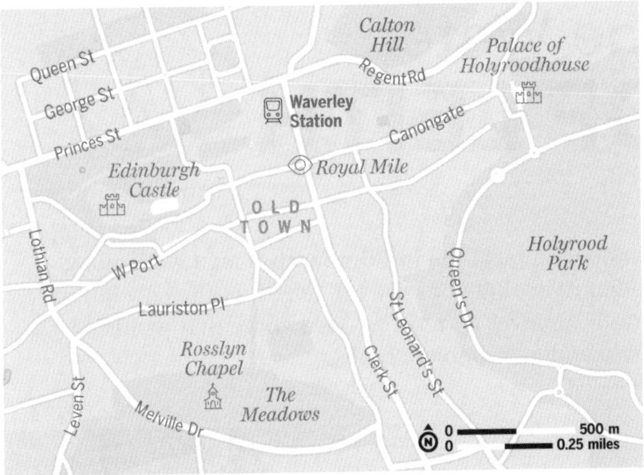

Left Edinburgh's Royal Mile
Below left Canongate Tolbooth

Skyline views Edinburgh Castle is the Scotland of fantasies. Stride past the Braveheart face-painters and bagpipe-players to the top of Castle Rock to discover 10 centuries of nation-defining wars. To bypass the crowds, go straight to the Honours of Scotland, Britain's oldest surviving set of crown jewels, and take a quiet moment in St Margaret's Chapel, Edinburgh's oldest building.

Living history The Royal Mile is the city's larger-than-life high street, where then and now come face to face. Start in front of the Castle Gate House before strolling east, past the Tolbooth Kirk, St Giles' Cathedral and Mercat Cross. Between glimpses of 73 time-stopped closes (medieval alleyways), highlights include the Canongate Tolbooth, John Knox House and the Scottish Parliament.

Of kings and queens The Royal Mile abruptly ends at the gates to Holyrood Palace, the official residence of Her Majesty The Queen in Scotland. Join a morning private tour to learn the secrets of the Throne Room and State Apartments before the palace opens for the day.

All saints A sanctuary for the faithful since 1446, mysterious Rosslyn Chapel took on a second life as a 'celebrity' church following its role in Dan Brown's *The Da Vinci Code*. Try to find connections to the Knights Templar in the crypt, then ogle at 200-plus keystone carvings that cover the nave, apse and altar.

Fortress Edinburgh

With more time to explore further afield, here are three other medieval keeps to help inspire your imagination.

Craigmillar Castle The capital's 'other' imposing castle, located 2.5 miles southeast of the Royal Mile. Once a safe haven for Mary Queen of Scots and brimming with nooks and crannies.

Lauriston Castle A supposedly haunted 16th-century tower house with lovely Japanese garden, museum and family-run bakery.

Blackness Castle A sea-front garrison and prison stronghold with second-to-none Firth of Forth views. Located 15 miles west near Linlinthgow.

03 The Water OF LEITH

WALK | ART | FOOD

There's no better window on local life in Edinburgh than a walk along the Water of Leith, the hidden river that runs the full length of the city. Slip into your comfiest shoes and you'll discover a secret wooded gorge that winds past impeccable gardens, galleries and gastronomic highs.

KORNELIJA CAKARUN/SHUTTERSTOCK ©

Trip Notes

Getting around At 12 miles long, this walk is best broken into chunks. Our featured section can be reached on a bus or tram from Princes St to Murrayfield Stadium. Alternatively, hire a bike from Cycle Scotland (29 Blackfriars St) to tackle it in one go.

When to go Year-round, but especially on Sunday when the Stockbridge Market is in full swing.

Top tip The Scottish National Gallery of Modern Art is split into Modern One and Modern Two: fuel up at Modern One's garden cafe.

Wildlife Watching

The Water of Leith isn't only home to strolling couples, harried dog walkers and weekend joggers. It's an urban sanctuary for a staggering 250 species of wildlife and there's almost as much diversity as at nearby Edinburgh Zoo. Look for heron, kingfisher, mink and otter, as well as swan, fox, squirrel and bat.

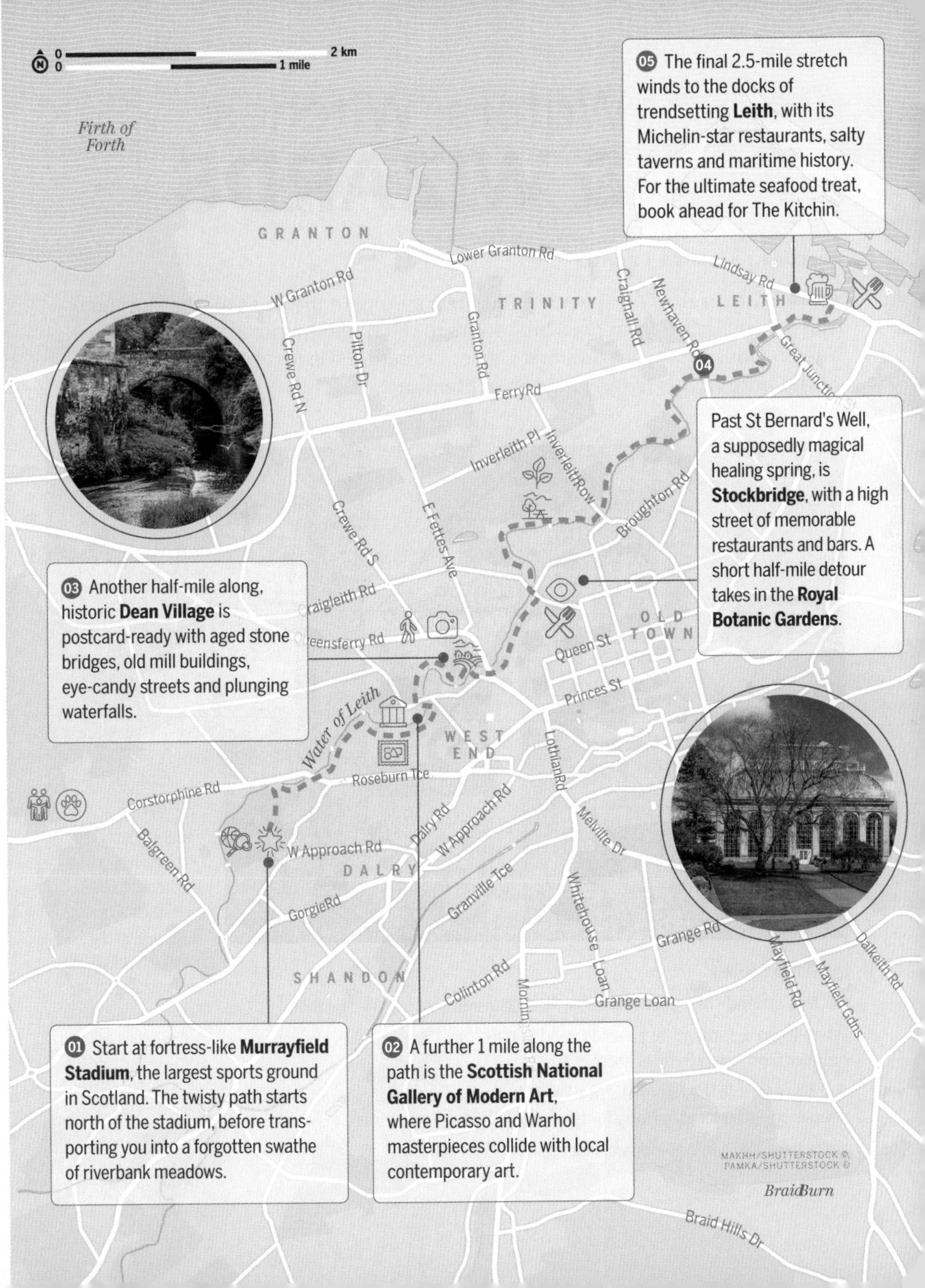

01 Start at fortress-like **Murrayfield Stadium**, the largest sports ground in Scotland. The twisty path starts north of the stadium, before transporting you into a forgotten swathe of riverbank meadows.

02 A further 1 mile along the path is the **Scottish National Gallery of Modern Art**, where Picasso and Warhol masterpieces collide with local contemporary art.

03 Another half-mile along, historic **Dean Village** is postcard-ready with aged stone bridges, old mill buildings, eye-candy streets and plunging waterfalls.

Past St Bernard's Well, a supposedly magical healing spring, is **Stockbridge**, with a high street of memorable restaurants and bars. A short half-mile detour takes in the **Royal Botanic Gardens**.

05 The final 2.5-mile stretch winds to the docks of trendsetting **Leith**, with its Michelin-star restaurants, salty taverns and maritime history. For the ultimate seafood treat, book ahead for The Kitchin.

MAKHH/SHUTTERSTOCK ©, PAMKA/SHUTTERSTOCK ©

04 Writers, Witches & WIZARDS

CULTURE | HISTORY | FAMILY

Edinburgh's Old Town is a fairy tale sprung to life, with all the storybook traits of a classic – from macabre towers to the romantic castle, it's no wonder Unesco named it the world's first City of Literature. Discover the bestselling stories born in this living museum of literature.

FOTOKON/SHUTTERSTOCK ©

Trip Notes

Getting around The Old Town is easily navigable and best explored on foot.

When to go Year-round, but keep in mind that the most popular sites can get crowded with Fringe Festival goers in August.

Top tip Duck into the National Museum of Scotland to see the medieval Lewis chessmen, as featured in Harry Potter and the Philosopher's Stone.

Extra help Join a free guided walking tour with The Potter Trail.

Eat, Drink, Sleep

The Balmoral is the city's grandest hotel and home to the magical JK Rowling Suite, where the novelist penned the final instalment of her wizarding saga. A short walk away, some of the most vivid stories can be heard in The Oxford Bar (Young St), a pub where crime writer Ian Rankin regularly sups a pint.

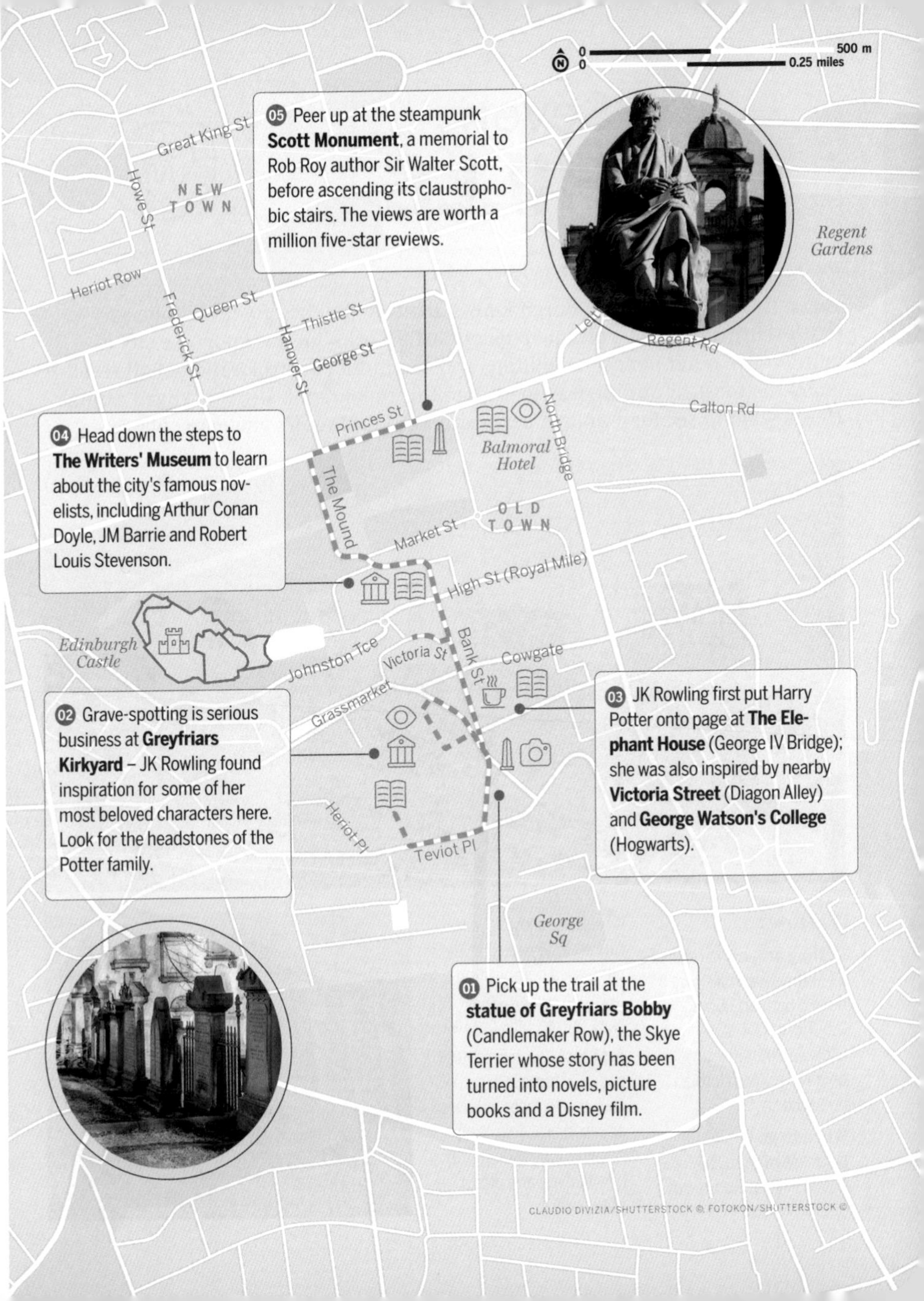

01 Pick up the trail at the **statue of Greyfriars Bobby** (Candlemaker Row), the Skye Terrier whose story has been turned into novels, picture books and a Disney film.

02 Grave-spotting is serious business at **Greyfriars Kirkyard** – JK Rowling found inspiration for some of her most beloved characters here. Look for the headstones of the Potter family.

03 JK Rowling first put Harry Potter onto page at **The Elephant House** (George IV Bridge); she was also inspired by nearby **Victoria Street** (Diagon Alley) and **George Watson's College** (Hogwarts).

04 Head down the steps to **The Writers' Museum** to learn about the city's famous novelists, including Arthur Conan Doyle, JM Barrie and Robert Louis Stevenson.

05 Peer up at the steampunk **Scott Monument**, a memorial to Rob Roy author Sir Walter Scott, before ascending its claustrophobic stairs. The views are worth a million five-star reviews.

05 Seven HILLS

WALK | HISTORY | ADVENTURE

Every visitor to Edinburgh knows about Arthur's Seat and Edinburgh Castle, sitting atop the volcanic plug of Castle Rock. But few know the city is built on five other handsome hilltops and combining an exploration of all seven offers the most rewarding way to explore this topographically challenged capital. Here's what to see for a unique perspective of Edinburgh's cinematic plateau.

MAKHH/SHUTTERSTOCK ©

How to

Getting around To reach all of the seven hills, you'll need a Lothian Buses Day Ticket (£4.50), which allows unlimited journeys on day services (lothianbuses.com).

When to go It might be an allusion to the Seven Hills of Rome, but it remains a joy all year round. June sees a hotly contested competition between runners of all ages (seven-hills.org.uk).

Fast fact It's an Edinburgh badge of honour to run or walk the 14 miles between all seven hills, marrying pavement pounding with hill climbing and urban orienteering.

MIGUEL ALMEIDA/SHUTTERSTOCK ©

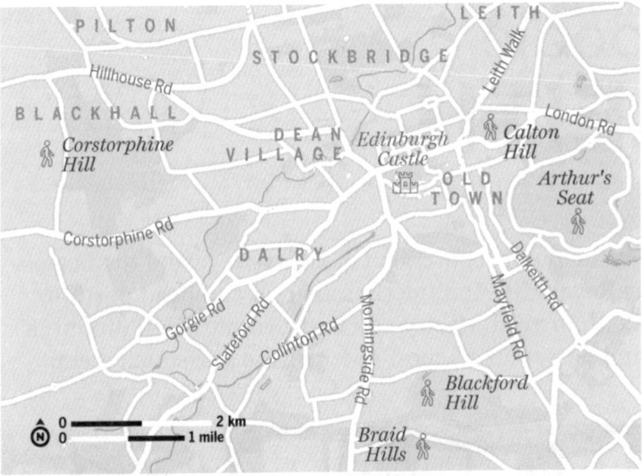

Pick Your Perfect Hill

The panoramic one About 2 miles south of the city centre, **Blackford Hill** is the locals' preferred option on a summer's day. It begins with a ramble through a wooded glen past Hermitage House, a stunning example of 18th-century architecture, before rising steeply through gorse onto a bald summit. From here, you'll discover a tear-inducing view of the trinity of Edinburgh Castle, the Old Town and Arthur's Seat.

The family-friendly one Easy to reach in the city centre, and even easier to climb, Unesco-worthy **Calton Hill** is the gateway to the city's most photographed sunset view, as well as a series of memorials and crenellated buildings that are a delight to explore. A memorable lunch is an option at The Lookout by Gardener's Cottage restaurant, while late spring sees the hill at its busiest. On 30 April, the Beltane Fire Festival takes place on the hilltop – cue bonfires, masked dancers and Gaelic tradition.

The golf escape Knowing Scotland is the home of golf helps explain why **Braid Hills**, the southernmost of the seven hills, is blanketed with fairways, putting greens and bunkers – it's home to two golf courses, 27 holes and a driving range. For something other than golf, there's a circular walk that's open to hikers, bikers and horse riders – take muddy boots.

The wild hill Above Edinburgh Zoo, **Corstorphine Hill** is a forest-topped ridge and nature reserve with a smattering of wooded walks and Corstorphine Hill Tower, a memorial to Sir Walter Scott. As well as a walled garden and gorgeous swathes of oak and birch woods, it's home to a disused stone quarry and a nuclear bunker that's now being converted into a visitor attraction.

Left Royal Observatory (p54), Blackford Hill
Below left National Monument of Scotland, Calton Hill

The Pentlands

To the southwest of Edinburgh is the Pentland Hills, which offer a cornucopia of outdoor thrills.

Threipmuir Reservoir Wild swim, canoe or stand-up paddle on this hill-cradled reservoir.

Allermuir Hill The hike to the summit is a 5-mile round-trip, but the reward is views of the entire city.

Scald Law The highest point of the Pentlands at 579m and a 7.5-mile walk from Flotterstone. Plan a whole day to savour all of Edinburgh's heather-topped Himalaya.

06 Foodie LEITH

WALK | FOOD | DRINK

For food and drink – the purest expression of any city – avoid the haggis-touting tourist traps on the Royal Mile and the Grassmarket and head north by northeast to trendsetting Leith instead. Here you'll find a carousel of Edinburgh's most vibrant restaurants and bars, plus its most enterprising grassroots scene.

LONELY PLANET/GETTYIMAGES ©

By the Sea

Plenty of seafood in Edinburgh is landed at Newhaven Harbour, a 10-minute walk north from Leith. It's home to a boardwalk promenade, a lighthouse and two memorable fish restaurants. Try the sustainably sourced fish and chips from **The Fishmarket**.

Trip notes

Getting around Before Leith gets connected to the rest of the city by tram (expected spring 2023), you'll have to make do with bus, bike or your own two feet. For an organised tour, Eat Walk Edinburgh is highly recommended (eatwalkedinburgh.co.uk).

When to go Year-round, but especially on a Friday or Saturday, when the tasting rooms, bars and ad hoc summer markets are at their liveliest.

Top Tip Take a piece of Leith home with you from Valvona & Crolla, Scotland's oldest delicatessen and wine merchant.

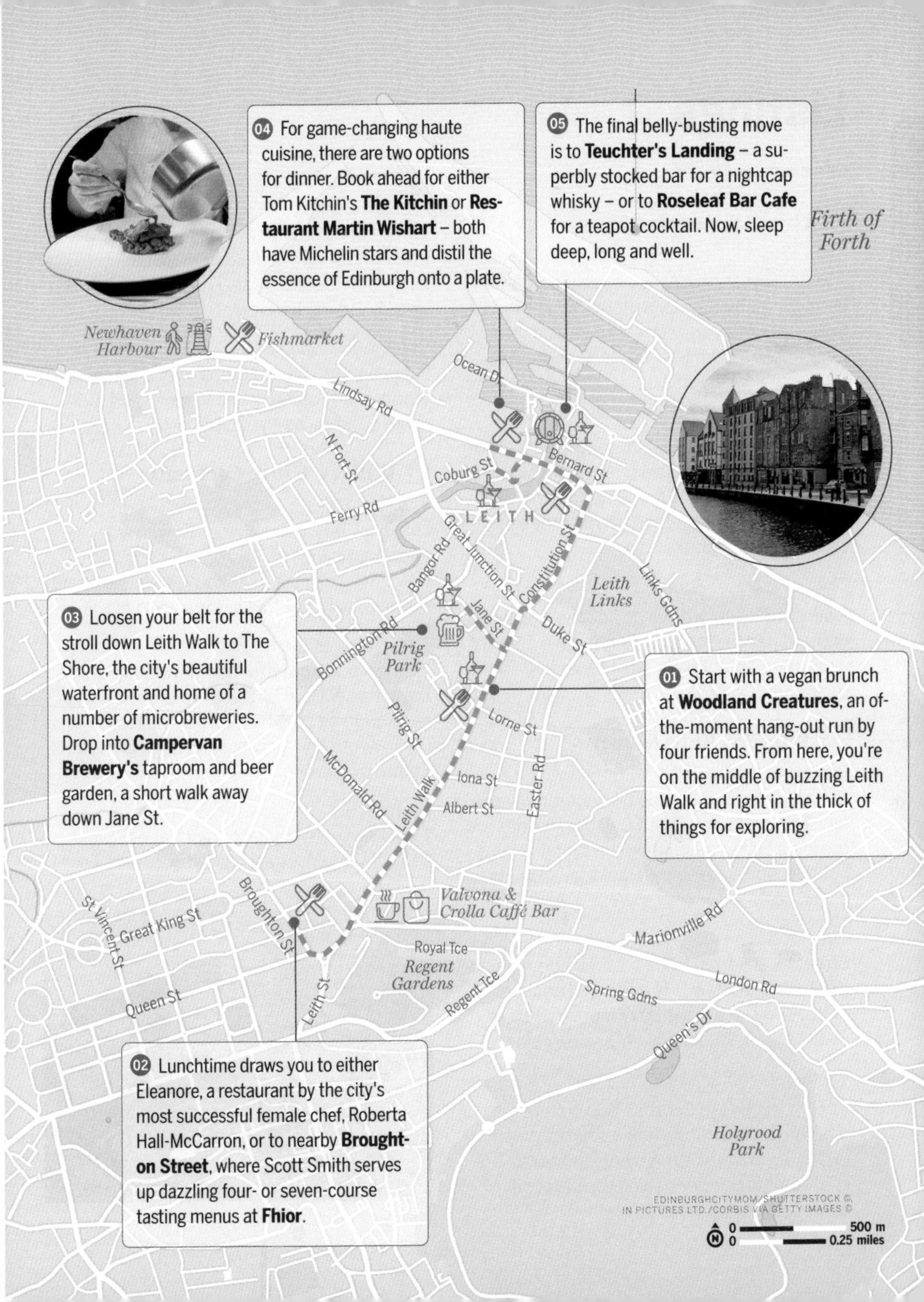

01 Start with a vegan brunch at **Woodland Creatures**, an of-the-moment hang-out run by four friends. From here, you're on the middle of buzzing Leith Walk and right in the thick of things for exploring.

02 Lunchtime draws you to either Eleanore, a restaurant by the city's most successful female chef, Roberta Hall-McCarron, or to nearby **Broughton Street**, where Scott Smith serves up dazzling four- or seven-course tasting menus at **Fhior**.

03 Loosen your belt for the stroll down Leith Walk to The Shore, the city's beautiful waterfront and home of a number of microbreweries. Drop into **Campervan Brewery's** taproom and beer garden, a short walk away down Jane St.

04 For game-changing haute cuisine, there are two options for dinner. Book ahead for either Tom Kitchin's **The Kitchin** or **Restaurant Martin Wishart** – both have Michelin stars and distil the essence of Edinburgh onto a plate.

05 The final belly-busting move is to **Teuchter's Landing** – a superbly stocked bar for a nightcap whisky – or to **Roseleaf Bar Cafe** for a teapot cocktail. Now, sleep deep, long and well.

Listings

BEST OF THE REST

Green Spaces & Views

Calton Hill
A moody skyline, crowned by Edinburgh Castle, is for many the city's ultimate panorama. Spires, steeples and turrets pose as if for a family portrait, while Arthur's Seat provides the geological theatre.

Arthur's Seat
Once an amped-up volcano, now a knuckle of dormant rock, this 251m piton is to Edinburgh what the Sugarloaf is to Rio de Janeiro. Hike through the heather, then gawp at the ludicrous summit panorama.

The Royal Observatory
Sweeping Blackford Hill beside the Hermitage of Braid park is home to Edinburgh's premier stargazing spot. Take a bus to Morningside for the round-trip hike.

Burgers, Buns & Brews

Bread Meats Bread £
Burger dreams are made on once-drab, now-fab Lothian Rd. Smashed Cali beef patties are the local cult classic, while the signature is a Lothian Wolf, with spicy 'Nduja sausage and pulled pork.

The Pitt £
Street food – from buffalo sauce burgers and gelato to craft beer – is all served under blue or bruised skies in a groovy industrial lot in Leith Market. Weekends only.

The Scran and Scallie ££
All the best bits of Scottish pub culture crammed into the one neighbourhood spot in Comely Bank. It's run by tousle-haired chef Tom Kitchin, who raids the seasonal Scots larder with glee.

Artisan Roast £
Three coffee hot spots to pick from: in Stockbridge, Bruntsfield or on Broughton St near Leith. Serves freshly roasted brews from award-winning baristas.

Cairngorm Coffee £
Funky community brew labs, with minimalist outposts on Frederick St and Melville Pl. Grilled cheese and cakes also a speciality.

Whisky, Gin & Cocktails

The Bow Bar £
Laid-back boozer on Victoria St with an encyclopaedia's worth of single malts and ever-changing cask ales. It's no-frills and standing room only, but that's why locals flock in.

The Voyage of Buck ££
Taking a cue from *Around the World in 80 Days,* this William St favourite is a showstopper. Food and cocktails come courtesy of Delhi, Kyoto and Casablanca, but the decor is Scottish chic.

Bramble £
Tiny if hard-to-find basement bar on Queen St, but worth it for acclaimed cocktails, beats

Edinburgh cityscape, seen from Arthur's Seat

and resident DJs. The bartenders are as creative as they come.

Edinburgh Gin Distillery £
A banner couple of years for Scottish gin has seen this subterranean small-batch distillery thrive. Try raspberry-, rhubarb- or bramble-infused recipes on a behind-the-scenes tour off Lothian Rd.

Memorable Meals

Prestonfield House ££
Highland-style lodge south of the centre with its own strutting peacocks and herd of Highland cows. Come for afternoon tea, served amid a riot of stag antler armchairs and gilded mirrors.

The Little Chartroom ££
Chef Roberta Hall-McCarron is at the vanguard of new Scots cuisine. Her poky Leith bistro, packed with an ever-changing menu of risky, remarkable food, shows why.

Fhior ££
Chef Scott Smith's vaunted Broughton St restaurant looks modest from the outside but is rewriting Scotland's cultural cookbook. Seasonal cooking at its best.

Wedgwood ££
On the Royal Mile, chef Paul Wedgwood's farm-to-fork philosophy and fondness for herb foraging means every dish has a local story behind it. Wild foraging courses on offer, too.

The Witchery by the Castle £££
Take a jaunt back to the 18th century at this decadent restaurant beside the Edinburgh Castle gates. Enough romantic baroque flourishes to put Casanova in the mood.

Arts & Culture

National Museum of Scotland
The only place to time travel through Scotland's history and modern culture. Standout exhibits include Bonnie Prince Charlie's picnic set and Dolly, the first cloned mammal and the most famous sheep in the world.

Inchcolm Abbey

Edinburgh Music Tours
Like The Bay City Rollers, The Proclaimers and David Bowie? Every city corner has an echo and it comes to life on a trivia-loaded tour of the city's pop, punk and folk temples.

Day Trips

Inchcolm Abbey
Set sail from the city's Forth Bridges to eerily empty Inchcolm island to see the best-preserved group of monastic buildings in Scotland.

Blackness Castle
The Firth of Forth estuary has its own toothy ruin, complete with three towers, great hall and dazzling shoreline views. *Mary Queen of Scots,* with Saoirse Ronan and Margot Robbie, was filmed here.

Jupiter Artland
Thirty minutes west of the city, they say the Guggenheim has competition. This sprawling sculpture park and art gallery in the grounds of Bonnington House is ideal for eye-rubbing art encounters. Open May to September.

Scan to find more things to do in Edinburgh online

GLASGOW

FRIENDLY | GRITTY | DYNAMIC

Experience Glasgow online

▸ **A Night on the Town** (p62)

▸ **A Splash of Colour** (p64)

▸ **Glasgow's Story** (p66)

▸ **What Makes Glasgow So?** (p68)

▸ **Footsteps of Legends** (p70)

▸ **Listings** (p72)

GLASGOW
Trip Builder

Glasgow is a place of excitement and round-the-clock energy, offering one of the best nightlife and dining scenes in Europe, backed by superb cultural attractions and eye-catching architecture. Prepare for new friendships and plenty of surprises.

Explore the vast treasure trove of **Kelvingrove Art Gallery & Museum** (p67)
½ day
Kelvingrove Park
KELVINGROVE
Taste a dram straight from the source at **The Clydeside Distillery** (p73)
½ day
GOVAN
River Clyde
IBROX
Applaud Charles Rennie Mackintosh's **House for an Art Lover** (p72)
1–2 hours
Bellahouston Park
Gorge on seafood, curries, whisky and more in the food and drink hub of **Finnieston** (p73)
½ day
SOUTH CARDONALD
Admire one of the world's finest personal art collections at **The Burrell Collection** (p72)
½ day
Pollok Country Park

Explore bookable experiences in Glasgow online

0 2 km
0 1 mile
Whisk yourself around town on the wonderfully retro **Glasgow Subway** (p60) 1 hour
Marvel at marble in the Victorian masterpiece that is **The City Chambers** (p72) 1–2 hours
COWCADDENS
GARNETHILL
TOWNHEAD
RIDDRIE
Step back in time at medieval **Glasgow Cathedral** (p67) 1–2 hours
DENNISTOUN
CARNTYNE
Dance the night away at locally iconic music venue **The Barrowland Ballroom** (p72) ½ day
Glasgow Green
BRIDGETON
HUTCHESONTOWN
Lose yourself in shopping along the city centre's **Style Mile** (p61) ½ day
RUTHERGLEN
HAMPDEN PARK
BANKHEAD

Practicalities

EQROY/SHUTTERSTOCK ©

ARRIVING

Glasgow Airport A round-the-clock shuttle bus service operates from Glasgow Airport's main terminal exit, going to Buchannan St Station in the city centre. Single/return tickets cost £9/15. Taxis are also available outside the terminal. The journey time for both to the city is 20 to 30 minutes.

Train In the city centre, trains coming from the south (including direct from London) arrive at Glasgow Central Station while arrivals from the north and Edinburgh pull in at Queen St Station.

HOW MUCH FOR A

Dram of whisky
£3

Haggis pakora
£6

Gig ticket
£7–9

WHEN TO GO

DEC–MAR
Cold and rainy in the quiet season, with short days that call for cosy drams.

APR–JUN
Very mixed weather but a good number of beautiful days.

JUL–AUG
Peak season with stretching days, mild temperatures and moderate rainfall.

SEP–NOV
Autumn weather with crisp days and photogenic light.

GETTING AROUND

Subway The delightfully retro Subway has only 15 stops and travels in a constant loop, making it the most convenient means of getting between the centre and West End.

Bike Hiring bikes is increasingly popular in the city and there are 800 bikes in circulation across 79 locations – cyclists can pick up and drop off at any of them. Look for the pink People Make Glasgow branding on the bikes or download the Nextbike app.

Bus There are City Sightseeing hop-on, hop-off buses with stops at all the major attractions in the city centre and West End, including audio guides in multiple languages.

EATING & DRINKING

Where to go The West End – and Finnieston in particular – offers the best concentration and range of dining options. Late-night bars and clubs are more prevalent in the city centre.

Regional produce The west coast Highlands and Islands have played a big role in the evolution of the city's social culture, and sampling produce (seafood, venison, lamb, whisky, gin) from these parts is well advised.

Must-try local beer

WEST Brewery's St Mungo lager

Best for seafood

Crabshakk (p63)

CONNECT & FIND YOUR WAY

Wi-fi Available throughout the city in restaurants, bars, cafes and attractions. Glasgow City Free Wi-fi is also available in central locations.

Navigation The city centre is built up with a grid system that can be hard to navigate for first-time visitors. Use navigation apps on your phone (or ask the friendly locals) to keep you right.

WHERE TO STAY

Scotland is rarely cheap but highly competitive Glasgow offers some of the best value. Book ahead wherever possible, certainly in summer peak season and at weekends.

Area	Pro/Con
Merchant City	Trendy, boisterous and best for nightlife seekers, within walking distance of the central bars and clubs.
City centre	On and around Sauchiehall St you'll find loads of choice from the familiar chain hotels.
Kelvinbridge and Kelvingrove	A relatively quiet happy medium with close proximity to the West End's attractions and restaurants.
Hillhead	Pricey but with immediate access to the West End's main thoroughfare of Byres Rd and its energetic, youthful buzz.
South Side	Less choice but best for mingling with the locals in the calmer residential neighbourhoods south of the Clyde.

SHOPPING

Most city centre shops and centres are open 9am to 7pm daily. Late night shopping is on Thursday, when this extends to 8pm for many shops.

MONEY

Most of Glasgow's museums and galleries are free to enter. There are shopping bargains to be had both on the competitive Style Mile and in the West End's vintage shops. All-day tickets on the Subway give unlimited travel.

07 A Night on THE TOWN

NIGHTLIFE | DINING | LIVE MUSIC

From time immemorial, Glaswegians have loved to be entertained. They love having a good laugh at themselves, and each other. They love a good feast, a suitable bevvy, a night of dancing and a singalong. You'd be well advised to join in.

MARION CARNIEL/SHUTTERSTOCK ©

Trip Notes

Getting around While the weather may have other plans, the West End of the city is very navigable by foot. By evening, getting back into the city centre is best done by hailing a taxi.

When to go Friday and Saturday nights are relentlessly boisterous and energetic.

Top tip Keep moving. There are dozens of terrific nightspots in the city so don't settle down too comfortably and keep seeking out the next best thing.

Memories Are There for the Making

Perhaps it was Will Fyffe who captured it best in the 1920s with his timeless song 'I Belong to Glasgow'. Engrossed in conversation with a merry local, Fyffe enquired knowingly if the man belonged to Glasgow. He was slyly reassured that, after a drink or two, on the contrary, it was Glasgow that belonged to him.

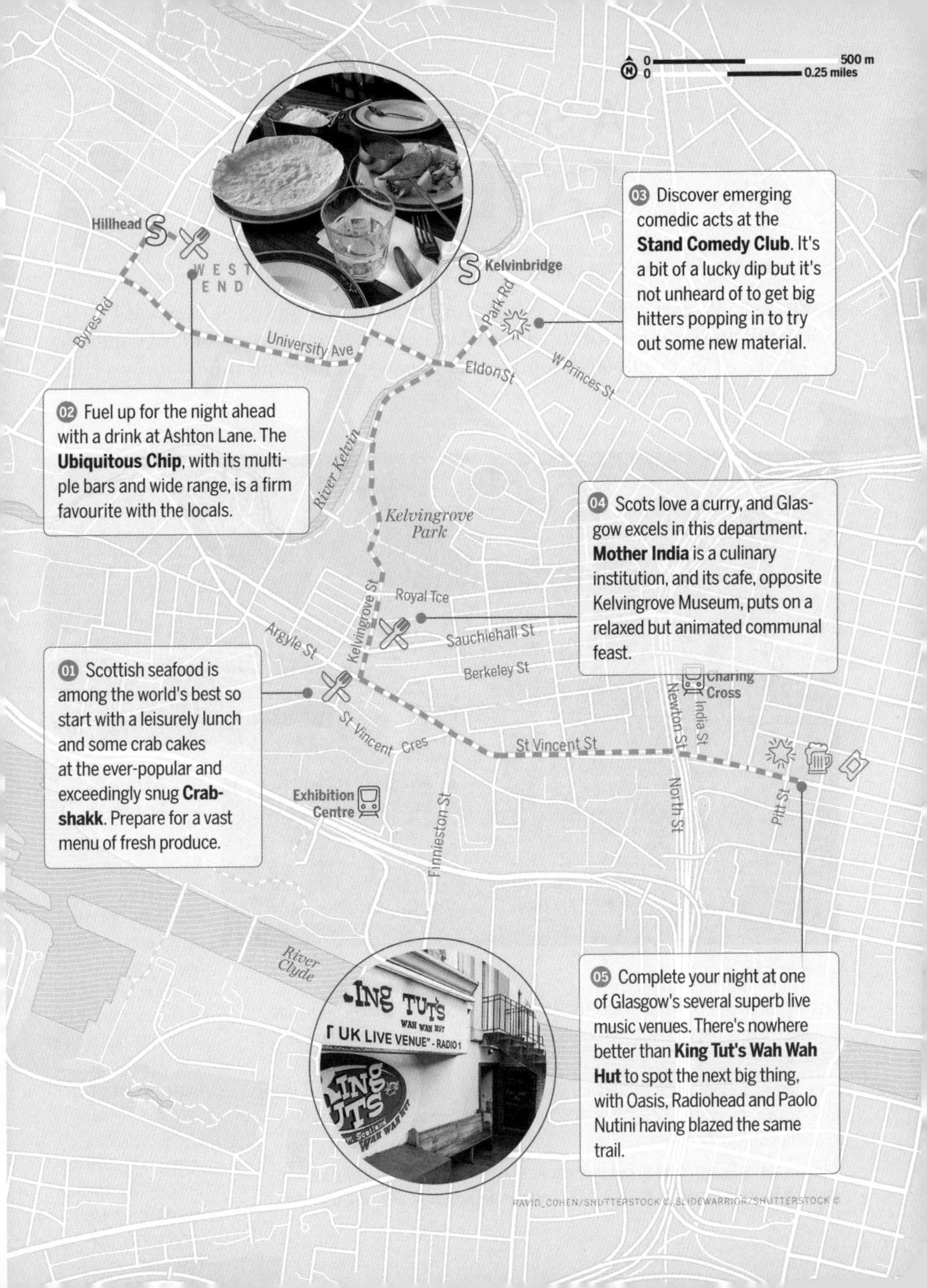

01 Scottish seafood is among the world's best so start with a leisurely lunch and some crab cakes at the ever-popular and exceedingly snug **Crab-shakk**. Prepare for a vast menu of fresh produce.

02 Fuel up for the night ahead with a drink at Ashton Lane. The **Ubiquitous Chip**, with its multi-ple bars and wide range, is a firm favourite with the locals.

03 Discover emerging comedic acts at the **Stand Comedy Club**. It's a bit of a lucky dip but it's not unheard of to get big hitters popping in to try out some new material.

04 Scots love a curry, and Glas-gow excels in this department. **Mother India** is a culinary institution, and its cafe, opposite Kelvingrove Museum, puts on a relaxed but animated communal feast.

05 Complete your night at one of Glasgow's several superb live music venues. There's nowhere better than **King Tut's Wah Wah Hut** to spot the next big thing, with Oasis, Radiohead and Paolo Nutini having blazed the same trail.

08 A Splash of COLOUR

MURALS | STREET ART | WALKING TOURS

Recent years have seen artists from near and far add their own, very colourful, mark to the city streets as Glasgow's lingering spectre of heavy industry is contrasted by magnificent murals that have spread far and wide.

TIM BIEBER/GETTY IMAGES ©

Trip Notes

Getting around The murals selected are located between the city centre and the west end of the city and can be tackled on foot or by hopping on and off the Subway.

A dynamic appeal While the larger murals are here to stay, the street art to be found in all corners of Glasgow is subject to change, with comings and goings keeping fans on their toes.

Guided tours Learn more about the murals and their creators on a tour with Walking Tours in Glasgow. Tours last 90 minutes and cover at least eight murals.

Diversity is Key

The vibrancy of the murals across Glasgow is matched only by its diversity. Street art celebrities like Smug mingle with first-time local unknowns, and bold, photo-like spray paint murals neighbour intricate stencil sketches. Since 2008, everything from the bizarre to the conservative has been raising eyebrows and inspiring chuckles.

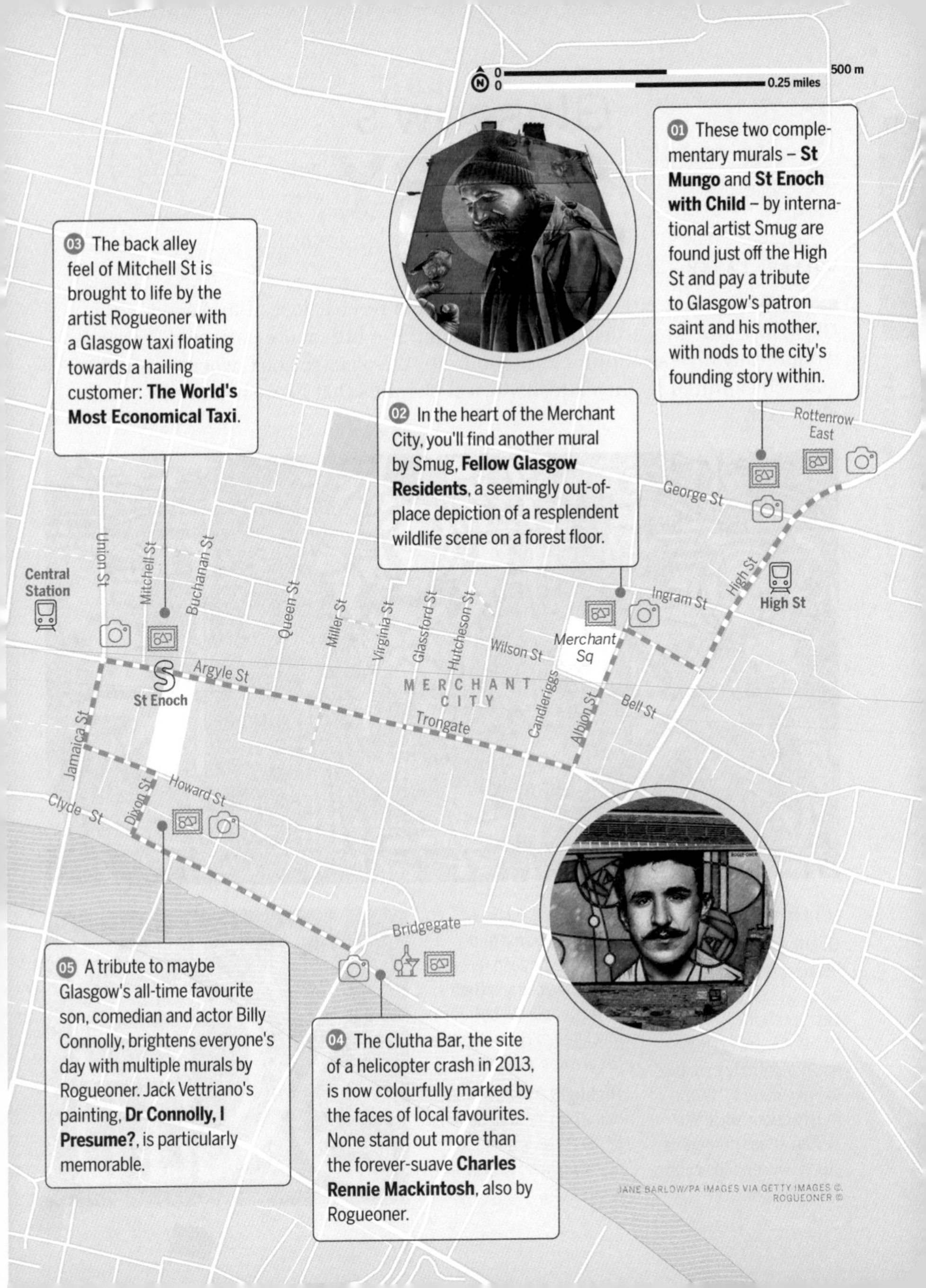

01 These two complementary murals – **St Mungo** and **St Enoch with Child** – by international artist Smug are found just off the High St and pay a tribute to Glasgow's patron saint and his mother, with nods to the city's founding story within.

02 In the heart of the Merchant City, you'll find another mural by Smug, **Fellow Glasgow Residents**, a seemingly out-of-place depiction of a resplendent wildlife scene on a forest floor.

03 The back alley feel of Mitchell St is brought to life by the artist Rogueoner with a Glasgow taxi floating towards a hailing customer: **The World's Most Economical Taxi**.

04 The Clutha Bar, the site of a helicopter crash in 2013, is now colourfully marked by the faces of local favourites. None stand out more than the forever-suave **Charles Rennie Mackintosh**, also by Rogueoner.

05 A tribute to maybe Glasgow's all-time favourite son, comedian and actor Billy Connolly, brightens everyone's day with multiple murals by Rogueoner. Jack Vettriano's painting, **Dr Connolly, I Presume?**, is particularly memorable.

JANE BARLOW/PA IMAGES VIA GETTY IMAGES ©, ROGUEONER ©

09 Glasgow's STORY

CULTURE | ARCHITECTURE | MUSEUMS

While some cities cry out for, and often receive, love at first sight, Glasgow is often regarded as one that requires a little more patience. The city's wonderfully diverse cultural attractions are the place to start, where you'll find yourself captured by the many historical chapters that have shaped Glasgow's character.

MEUNIERD/SHUTTERSTOCK ©

How to

Getting around Get between the attractions on foot or via the characterful 'Clockwork Orange' Subway (that has masterfully managed to hang on to the same musty odour since the 1970s). It has numerous stops between the centre and West End.

How much Glasgow takes ownership and immense pride in its cultural sites being owned by its people. All but the Mackintosh House on this list are free to enter.

Highlight Salvador Dalí's haunting *Christ of St John of the Cross* is a highlight at Kelvingrove Art Gallery & Museum.

LOIS GOBE/SHUTTERSTOCK ©

GLASGOW EXPERIENCES

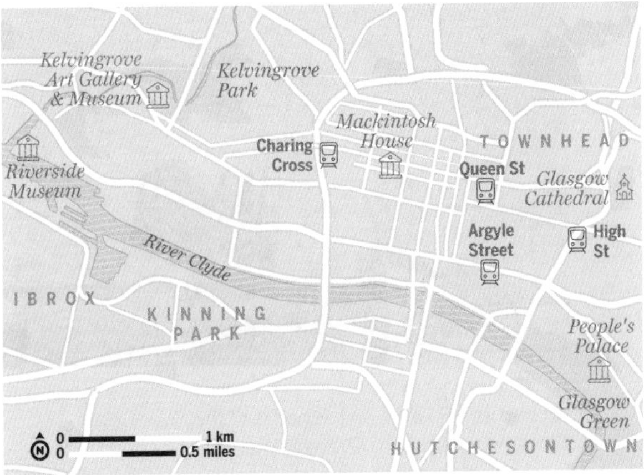

Left Stained glass, Glasgow Cathedral
Below left Art-nouveau brass plate at Glasgow's School of Art

Where it all began Precious little remains of old-world Glasgow, yet 12th-century **Glasgow Cathedral** stands proud as one of the most impressive historic sites in the country. Best viewed from the eerie neighbouring Necropolis graveyard, look down upon what was once the very heart of a fledgling city of trade and gossip.

Glasgow's museums Retrace the social history of Glasgow at the **People's Palace**. Artwork, artefacts and film join forces to open a tenement window on everyday life going back to 1750. It's a quirky, very Glaswegian take on things. Continue with an evocative stroll down the Clyde and you'll be ready to buckle up for a journey through the ages of transport. Set within a stunning modern building, vehicles of all shapes and sizes are on display at **The Riverside**, covering those built for navigating local streets and for taking on the world's high seas. **Kelvingrove Art Gallery & Museum**, meanwhile, is one of Britain's best and you can easily lose yourself in this gigantic Victorian palace. Be sure to check ahead for latest exhibits.

The iconic Charles Rennie Mackintosh The much-loved art nouveau style of Glasgow's most famous artist and architect litters the city in timeless tribute. While his masterpiece, the School of Art, was recently and tragically destroyed by fire, there are plentiful alternatives, including the stylishly immaculate **Mackintosh House**, a reconstruction of his own home in the city.

Behind the Scenes

Our museums – the most visited attractions in the city – stimulate imagination, thought and escapism. The city's collection, which belongs to its people, is an important part of who Glaswegians are as individuals, and a key part of their identity. Visitors delight in discovering what made Glasgow the industrial giant of the past and the creative and cultural force it is today.

Our cultural offering enriches the lives of residents and is a powerful draw for new and returning visitors. We put people at the heart of preserving Glasgow's past and I love watching our visitors being surprised and wowed by what they discover.

Recommended by Stewart Thompson, *Manager at Riverside Museum @riversidemuseum*

What Makes Glasgow So?

THE STORY BEHIND THAT BIG PERSONALITY

Once a noisy, sweaty industrial powerhouse, Glasgow endures today as a sprawl of architectural wonder and gallus (bold, cheeky or flashy) tales. A place of hard hands and soft hearts, it's behind that toothless grin, and layer of soot, that you'll see the complex soul of this great city.

Left Glasgow Transport Museum
Middle Cloisters at the University of Glasgow
Right George Square

MEUNIERD/SHUTTERSTOCK ©

Around its epicentre on the banks of the River Clyde, Glasgow's collection of villages merged and conspired to form one of the most productive examples of industry that the world has ever seen. Revered as the Second City of the Empire in its heyday, Glasgow became synonymous with trade from the 17th to the 20th centuries as tobacco, cotton, sugar, ships and slavery combined to put a once-insignificant settlement on every sailor's map. It was capitalism in its most impressive form, and Glasgow was open for business.

Turning opportunistic eyes firstly to tobacco, by the mid-18th-century Glasgow was the main port of entry into Britain, as the city's canny tobacco lords took full advantage of Scotland's new-found membership of the productive British Empire and links with the American colonies in Virginia. By 1770, it had moved on to become the country's largest linen manufacturer, before then turning to shipbuilding. At its peak, Glasgow was producing as much as 50% of the world's ships. The new Victorian railway networks opened up local access to coal and iron and the sweat-fuelled mechanics of the city grew and grew. Supported further by the likes of furniture and carpet production, brewers, cooperages and electronic manufacturing, heavy industry had made Glasgow a virtual mass factory and economic powerhouse.

Yet behind the multiplying, ostentatious stone mansions and private empires, there was another side to industrial Glasgow. In the smoggy shadows could be found a city's populous too often gripped by poverty, disease and deprivation. Glasgow became too popular for its own good as the city struggled to accommodate the population surge, with workers flocking in from the Highlands, Ireland and

SOLOVIOVA LIUDMYLA/SHUTTERSTOCK ©

PK289/SHUTTERSTOCK ©

further afield. The 19th and 20th centuries saw the development of slums within limited parts of the city, as a lack of sanitation, overcrowding and malnutrition took hold. It's a desperate image that has lingered long in the minds of the people.

It is in these extremes combined that today's visitors can see the enduring identity of Glasgow. The sandstone mansions remain, in almost-majestic leafy neighbourhoods, and its hauntingly evocative, century-spanning architecture stands forever testament to head-spinning wealth generation and mercantile entrepreneurship. The universities – with Glasgow among the first in existence thanks to an early embrace of education – have gifted extraordinary minds to the worlds of engineering, economics, electronics and the arts. But just as important as its successes – and in addition to the grit, earthiness, directness and wicked sense of humour that visitors are sure to encounter – know that its people are still compulsive checkers of their moral compass, valuing fairness above all else. This shows in its politics as a long-standing socialist hub, in its ownership of history (impressive and abhorrent) and its track record in speaking up, often loudly, against injustice.

> Revered as the Second City of the Empire in its heyday, Glasgow became synonymous with trade from the 17th to the 20th centuries

Glasgow has never been one for standing still. Through centuries it has adapted to progressing politics, new horizons and changing markets. It has pioneered and learned, endured and prospered. And through it all, that cheeky smile remains.

A City Made for Entertainment

Glasgow has shone on the world stage in recent decades, winning numerous prestigious awards for its culture, architecture and design.

It was the hosting of the 2014 Commonwealth Games, though, that really endeared the city to the watching world in a new way. The largest event of its kind ever to come to Scotland, Glasgow had a word with the weather forecaster and gleefully welcomed visitors from across the globe to create a carnival atmosphere across town.

With the annual World Pipe Band Championships, Celtic Connections and hundreds of diverse music events each month, the vibe goes on and on.

10 Footsteps of LEGENDS

HISTORY | CASTLES | VISTAS

While few today would associate Glasgow with castles and medieval mystery, there are numerous ruins and former strongholds with long stories to tell dotted around the surrounds of the city. None can better Dumbarton Castle for depth of history and an evocatively dramatic setting, impossibly lodged within a plug of volcanic basalt.

WAYLEEBIRD/ISTOCK EDITORIAL/GETTYIMAGES ©

How to

Getting here Dumbarton is 15 miles northwest of Glasgow and can be reached by car, train or bus from the city centre.

When to visit The castle is open daily from April to September and Saturday to Wednesday from October to March.

Imagine... The castle was where a captive and betrayed William Wallace spent some of his final hours on Scottish soil before being sent south to London for execution in 1305.

MARIUSZ GOLEBIEWSKI/SHUTTERSTOCK ©

Far left Dumbarton Castle and Dumbarton Rock
Below left Stairway at Dumbarton Castle
Left The view from Dumbarton Rock

A famous guest list The Romans, the Vikings, the Luftwaffe, Merlin, William Wallace and Mary Queen of Scots, just to name a few, have all set foot here – and you'll feel the presence of legends in the air as you ascend Dumbarton Rock. Tucked within a divide in the rugged stone sits its castle, one of Scotland's most formidable and ominous defensive structures.

An ancient settlement Dating to the 5th century, this was likely to have been the seat of power of the Kingdom of Strathclyde. The site of a ferocious four-month Viking siege in 871, the castle also witnessed much more clandestine activities. Both a discreet hiding place for royalty and a grim prison, the 73m Dumbarton Rock held no shortage of whispers and prayers. Modern-day adventurers can self-guide their way around the castle's multiple buildings and fortifications, navigating the steep and foreboding stairways between them.

Reinvented as a garrison fortress British Government forces installed themselves here in the 18th century as a strategic base to keep local Jacobites under a watchful eye, and the more modernised version we see today started to take shape. Take a cannon's-eye view from one of the gun batteries and imagine frantic preparations for a naval attack, contemplate devious schemes hatched from within the Governor's House to doom the Jacobites, or look up and picture German WWII bombers dropping their payloads from high above.

Take in the Views

The summits of Dumbarton Rock offer some of the best vantage points in Central Scotland. Its town is backed by the promise of Loch Lomond and the Highlands to the north, while the mighty River Clyde flows by to the immediate south. Traders, warriors and royalty have come and gone, sailing past Glasgow's Gateway for centuries and, for the imaginative, you can just about create the chilling scene of 200 attacking Viking longboats coming screaming up the river. Ascend, passing the castle's primary buildings, to the White Tower Crag for spectacular panoramas.

Listings

BEST OF THE REST

Surprising Tours

Glasgow Central Tour
Delve underground for the story of Glasgow's great Central Station. A wonderful insight into eerily forgotten Glasgow-by-rail thanks to Paul Lyons, one of the best guides in the business.

City Chambers
Take a free tour of the decadent interior of the City Chambers on George Sq and surprise yourself with the staggering opulence on display – its construction used more marble than the Vatican!

Glasgow Museums Resource Centre
An overspill of the many cultural treasures of Glasgow that are not on current museum display, this is a head-spinning Aladdin's cave of over a million objects. Tours available by contacting Glasgow Life.

Legacies, Icons & Relics

Gallery of Modern Art
Set in the city centre town house of a former Tobacco Lord, you'll find Glasgow's dynamic hub of bold, contemporary art.

Burrell Collection
The refurbished personal legacy of the merchant Sir William Burrell is one of the world's largest and most diverse art collections. Find it in Pollok Park in the South Side.

House for an Art Lover
The immaculate implementation of Charles Rennie Mackintosh's 1901 design is a must-visit for all his fans. Set in Bellahouston Park.

Bothwell Castle
The cragged, deep-red ruins of this 13th-century relic are among the most evocative in Central Scotland. Nestled within a curve in the River Clyde near Uddingston, to the southeast of the city.

Paisley Abbey
A rare Gothic masterpiece, founded in 1163. The stained-glass windows and sentinel cloisters give the magnificent interior a tangible atmosphere. In Glasgow's southwest, by the airport.

Live Music & Performances

The Barrowland Ballroom
An East End institution and historic local favourite that is unapologetically all about the music. Well suited to larger gigs, it has hosted a plethora of household names.

The Glad Café
A hipster hub and fantastic all-rounder for an evening in the South Side. Good grub and drinks menu, and an eclectic mix of up-and-coming artists.

The Hug & Pint
A relaxed, cosy place where promising young bands are frequently hosted downstairs. The menu has some excellent vegan options.

City Chambers

Celtic Connections
A world-famous, two-week music festival that always lifts the January blues. There's a focus on traditional Scottish, but also how Celtic music has connected with cultures across the world.

Whisky

The Pot Still
A mouth-watering collection of several hundred malts plus a classic Glasgow pub feel – a successful combination since the 1800s.

The Ben Nevis
Traditional folk sessions are hosted several times per week at this snug bar in Finnieston.

The Clydeside Distillery
Glasgow's very own new distillery sits proudly on the banks of the Clyde, overlooking what was once the heart of the city. Tours are available while we wait for the liquid gold to mature.

Refreshments

Inn Deep
With vaulted roofs and a subterranean, cellar-like feel, this is an excellent, laid-back hang-out alongside the River Kelvin. Superb and extensive beer selection.

Oran Mor
A characterful converted church bar that pulls in the many faces of the West End, from student to pensioner. Also a theatre venue for plays, and a nightclub downstairs.

Brel
A specialist in Belgian beer, it's one of many bars on and around Ashton Lane. Spills out into a beer garden when the opportunity arises.

Mackintosh at the Willow
Break up your shopping marathon with a supremely sophisticated afternoon tea at another classy Mackintosh recreation. Book ahead.

MICK ATKINS/SHUTTERSTOCK ©

Gretchen Peters performing at Celtic Connections

Scottish Grub

Cail Bruich £££
One of Scotland's finest restaurants features local, sustainable food, often with some backup from France. The head chef recently collected a Michelin Star.

The Gannet ££
Fine dining without pretension in Finnieston; the seasonally led menu delves into the best of Scotland's natural larder with impressive results.

Café Gandolfi £££
An institution of the Merchant City, the founding gentle influence of the Hebridean islands still lingers despite the bustle. Seafood fans take special note.

Stravaigin ££
For more casual dining with loads of atmosphere, this popular option on Gibson St is another West End hub to delight drinkers and diners alike.

Scan to find more things to do in Glasgow online

SOUTHERN SCOTLAND

EVOCATIVE | SERENE | HISTORIC

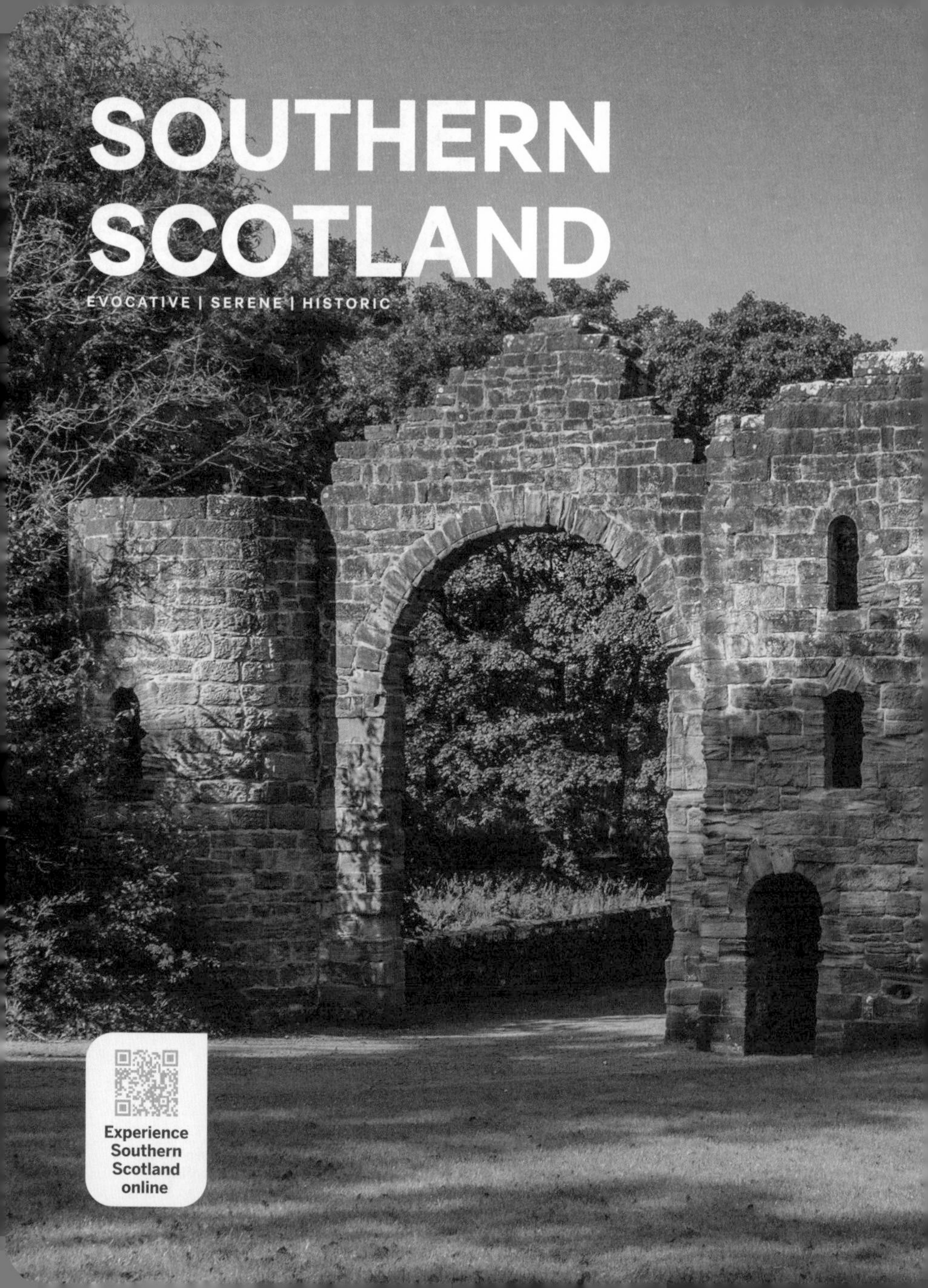

Experience Southern Scotland online

- **Immersion in the Lowlands** (p78)
- **Majestic, Stately Homes** (p80)
- **Land of Sieges & Raids** (p82)
- **Ride to the Sea** (p84)
- **Listings** (p86)

SOUTHERN SCOTLAND
Trip Builder

Seemingly far from the summer crowds, the southern regions of Ayrshire, South Lanarkshire, Dumfries, Galloway and the Scottish Borders hold endless, nature-dominated corners built for quiet reflection and historical exploration. Spectacular ruins meet decadent stately homes and stretching lowland landscapes call for hiking, cycling and wildlife spotting.

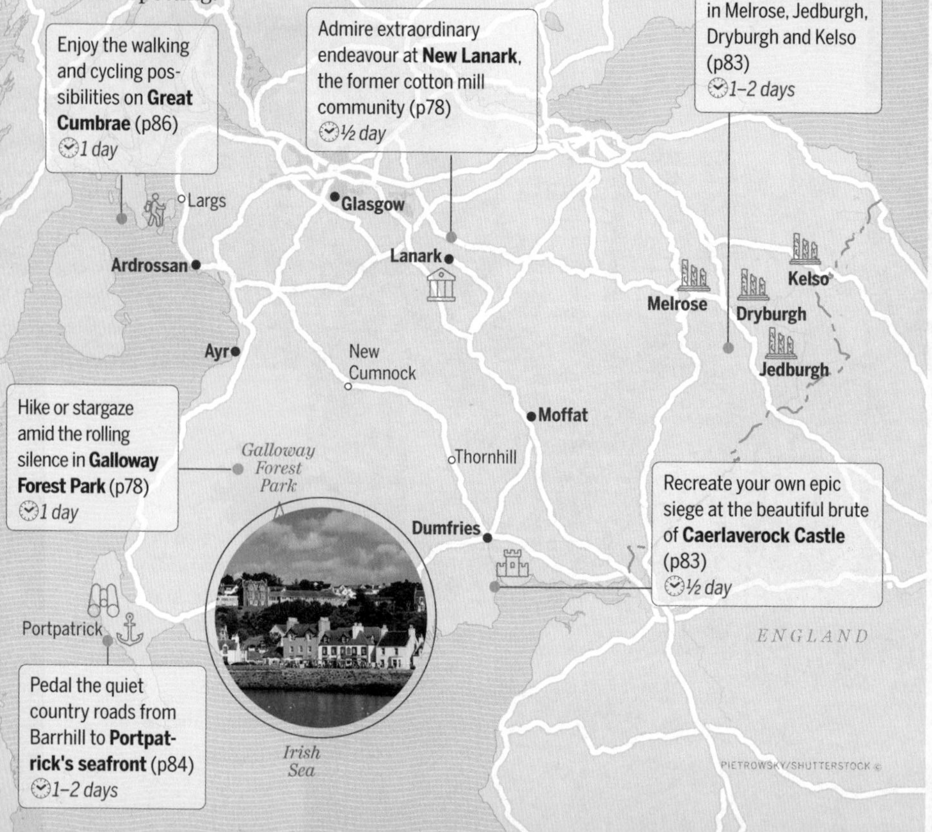
0 50 km
0 25 miles
Enjoy the walking and cycling possibilities on **Great Cumbrae** (p86)
1 day
Admire extraordinary endeavour at **New Lanark**, the former cotton mill community (p78)
½ day
Get lost in the evocative **Borders Abbeys** in Melrose, Jedburgh, Dryburgh and Kelso (p83)
1–2 days
Largs
Glasgow
Lanark
Ardrossan
Melrose
Kelso
Dryburgh
Jedburgh
Ayr
New Cumnock
Moffat
Thornhill
Galloway Forest Park
Dumfries
Hike or stargaze amid the rolling silence in **Galloway Forest Park** (p78)
1 day
Recreate your own epic siege at the beautiful brute of **Caerlaverock Castle** (p83)
½ day
Portpatrick
ENGLAND
Pedal the quiet country roads from Barrhill to **Portpatrick's seafront** (p84)
1–2 days
Irish Sea

PIETROWSKY/SHUTTERSTOCK ©

Practicalities

ARRIVING

Train Hub towns can be accessed by direct trains from Glasgow or Edinburgh.

Bus Other sizeable towns are interconnected to each other and the cities by daily bus routes.

CONNECT

Phone signal can be sporadic in the more rural locations, but wi-fi is generally available at accommodation providers.

MONEY

Quality B&B stays cost upwards of £80 per night. ATMs are available in all sizeable towns, but it's still wise to carry some cash.

WHERE TO STAY

Place	Pro/Con
Melrose	Arguably the most picturesque of the Border towns, with good road access and facilities.
Kirkcudbright	Quaint and timelessly appealing, with proximity to the south coast.
Dumfries	The most accessible and practical base for exploration in the south-west.

GETTING AROUND

Car travel The easiest mode for a thorough exploration of the south. Public transport is not reliable or convenient.

Long-distance walking and cycling Increasingly popular, with terrain and landscapes that are well suited to them. The Southern Upland Way (a little over 200 miles) and the 65-mile trail between the Borders Abbeys are options.

EATING & DRINKING

Local produce and pub grub Produce from surrounding farmlands dominates at all ends of the cost spectrum, with lamb, beef and game featuring heavily. Good-quality 'pub grub' can be found in almost all towns.

Milk and cookies Galloway is particularly famous for its dairy products, while Border Biscuits, based in South Lanarkshire, are among the nation's favourite companion for a cup of tea.

Must try
Cream o' Galloway ice cream

Best whisky
Annandale Distillery (p87)

DEC–MAR
Cold and rainy weather in the tourism quiet season.

APR–JUN
Refreshing and mild spring air with plenty of sunshine.

JUL–AUG
Streching days, warmer temperatures and some rainfall.

SEP–NOV
Crisp days with beautiful colours blanketing the lowland valleys.

11 Immersion in the LOWLANDS

HIKING | NATURE | WILDLIFE

Serenity rules in the south and nature is permitted centre stage. From crashing waterfalls to secretive wildlife spotting, spend a few days immersed in the highlights.

CAROLE MACDONALD/ALAMY STOCK PHOTO ©

Trip Notes

Getting around Road travel by car is lengthy but straightforward and beautifully scenic across the southern regions.

When to visit Southern Scotland is a blissful escape during the bustling height of the summer tourism season, while the warming colours of autumn also hold a strong pull.

More choice The plethora of activities, accommodation, restaurants and organised events across the south of Scotland are helpfully explored in more depth on the new Scotland Starts Here app and website.

Look to the Stars

Galloway Forest Park was the first designated Dark Sky Park in the UK, set in a sparsely populated area with extremely low light pollution. Night walking tours with local freelance ranger Elizabeth Tindall can take visitors into the woodlands for some spooky stargazing.

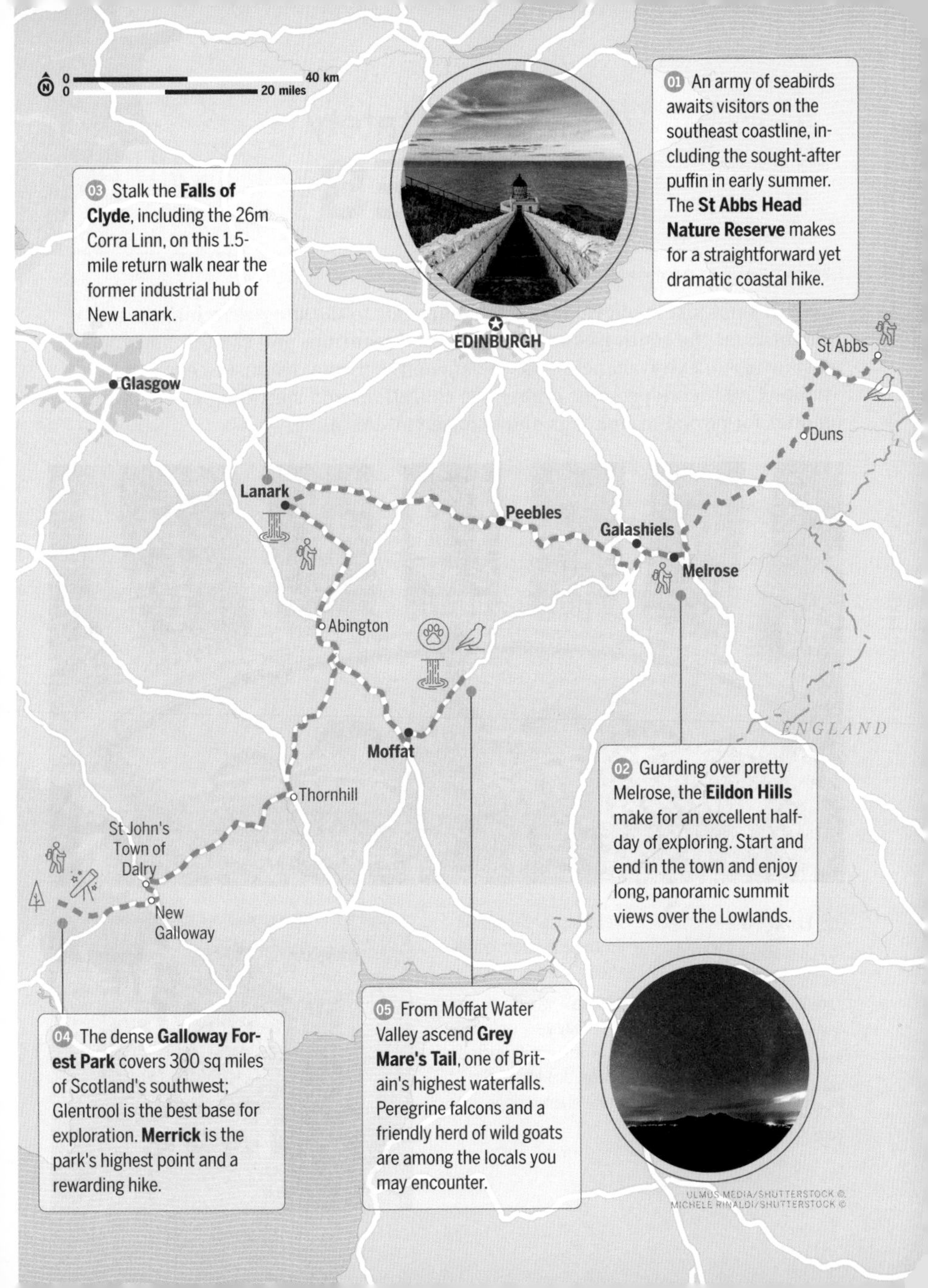

01 An army of seabirds awaits visitors on the southeast coastline, including the sought-after puffin in early summer. The **St Abbs Head Nature Reserve** makes for a straightforward yet dramatic coastal hike.

03 Stalk the **Falls of Clyde**, including the 26m Corra Linn, on this 1.5-mile return walk near the former industrial hub of New Lanark.

02 Guarding over pretty Melrose, the **Eildon Hills** make for an excellent half-day of exploring. Start and end in the town and enjoy long, panoramic summit views over the Lowlands.

04 The dense **Galloway Forest Park** covers 300 sq miles of Scotland's southwest; Glentrool is the best base for exploration. **Merrick** is the park's highest point and a rewarding hike.

05 From Moffat Water Valley ascend **Grey Mare's Tail**, one of Britain's highest waterfalls. Peregrine falcons and a friendly herd of wild goats are among the locals you may encounter.

12 Majestic, Stately HOMES

LEGENDS | HISTORY | ARCHITECTURE

It's not just medieval history that appeals to the story-searching romantics, as the south is studded with grand mansions and estates, housing no shortage of extravagancies and melancholy. Personal whimsies, eye-catching architecture, rich tapestries, impressive collections and sprawling gardens are on offer for period-drama fans and culture vultures alike.

ROB FORD/ALAMY STOCK PHOTO ©

How to

Getting around Getting between the estates, spread across Southern Scotland, is easiest by car.

Access Opening times vary considerably through the calendar year, so consult the websites for the most up-to-date information ahead of visiting.

Top tip The estates are generally very welcoming to all the family, including energetic kids and well-behaved dogs.

CLAUDINE VAN MASSENHOVE/SHUTTESTOCK ©

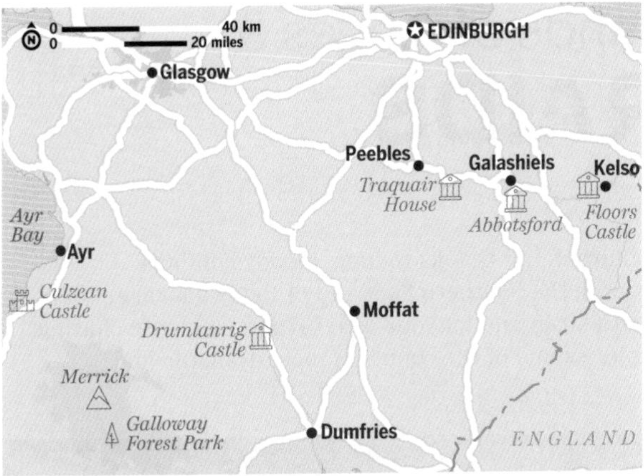

Left Culzean Castle
Below left Drumlanrig Castle

Grand family homes The legendary 19th-century writer Sir Walter Scott lives on as the leading Ambassador to the Borders and his home, **Abbotsford**, is at the centre of various Scott-themed attractions in the region. The homely, yet elaborate, house is packed with Scott's remarkable personal collections and is picturesquely set on the banks of the River Tweed. Romantically steeped in Jacobite melancholy, serene **Traquair** is the oldest continually occupied house in Scotland. The wonderfully musty interior holds a playground for the imagination as secret staircases hide behind delicate, centuries-old furniture. There's an on-site chapel, garden maze and brewery for added entertainment.

Architectural excellence and extraordinary wealth Sitting precariously on the Ayrshire coast amid a vast and luscious country park is **Culzean Castle**. Visionary 18th-century architect Robert Adam had fun with this one, as the palatial exterior is surpassed by a stunning interior oval staircase. Robert Adam learned much from his father, William, and it was the latter that was most responsible for the now-extravagant **Floors Castle**, just outside Kelso. Long-standing home to the Duke of Roxburghe, tours here reveal richly decorated interiors, with a walled garden and various woodland walks on the grounds. Similarly grandiose, **Drumlanrig Castle** in Dumfriesshire is an alluring glowing sandstone structure, with summer tours available. The grounds feature salmon fishing and mountain biking opportunities and were one of many Scottish filming locations used in the successful TV show *Outlander*.

Life Behind the Walls

I feel incredibly privileged to be the 21st generation of the same family living in Traquair – it really is a family home and this is what makes it so special. People often comment on the atmosphere here and I think this comes from having been a continually lived-in house for over 900 years. You can literally feel and touch its history.

The surrounding Borders is a region of Scotland with so much more to discover. Incredible and varied landscapes from a wild coastline to rolling hills and lochs; timeless small towns; extraordinary history and heritage. And a warm welcome wherever you go.

Local insight from Catherine Maxwell Stuart,
21st Lady of Traquair

13 Lands of Sieges & RAIDS

RUINS | CASTLES | HISTORY

Haunted by historic turbulence thanks to long, bloody conflicts between Scotland and England, the Southern Scotland of today has taken on a contrastingly calm air. Breathe it in and let your imagination run loose chasing medieval ghosts as you explore some of the country's most dramatic and evocative ruins.

JAMES MCDOWALL/SHUTTERSTOCK ©

How to

Getting around Southern Scotland is a vast area and getting to and between these attractions is most easily achieved by car, although there are fantastic opportunities for long-distance cyclists.

When to go April to September; most attractions close down over the winter months.

How much All but unstaffed Dunure Castle on this list are owned by Historic Scotland. Tickets range in price but if planning on visiting several of its properties, it's worth purchasing the Explorer Pass.

ESPEDAIR CREATIVE/SHUTTESTOCK ©

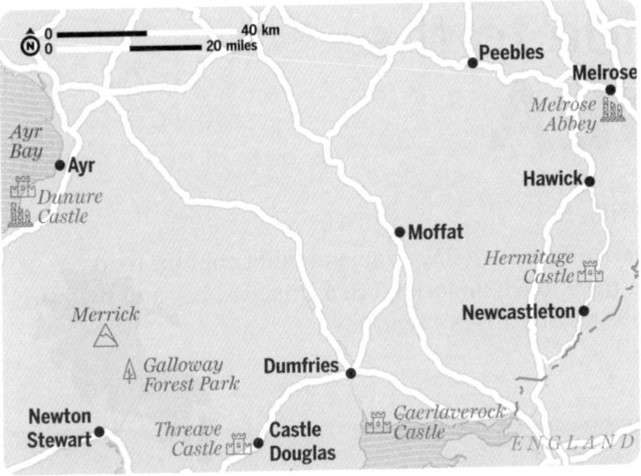

Prepare for attack That a site as idyllically beautiful as **Caerlaverock Castle** should have fallen victim to numerous brutal sieges seems inappropriately far-fetched as you approach the unusually triangular ruin on the Solway coast. Artists and photographers will love its visual romance and rare moat, while kids can play out swashbuckling fantasies in the stone interior.

A clandestine rendezvous Visit the dramatically exposed clifftop ruins of **Dunure Castle** on the Ayrshire coast and the isolated **Hermitage Castle** on the Scotland–England border and eavesdrop on heated discussions past. Dunure was the meeting point, in 1429, of the long-adversarial clans of Campbell and MacDonald. Only the Campbell emerged alive.

Take a tranquil moment There is, however, more to the southern ruins than fury, scheming and backstabbing. **Threave Castle** is set in a wildlife haven near Castle Douglas and involves a short walk – and even shorter boat crossing – to access. The Gothic remains of **Melrose Abbey**, too, are among the most serenely romantic in Scotland, set under the rolling Eildon Hills and the final resting place of Robert the Bruce's heart.

Left Dunure Castle
Below left Melrose Abbey

Plot a Siege of Your Own

Southern Scotland offers so much dramatic history coupled with unspoilt beauty, in an area known for its rich variety of cultures and heritage. Caerlaverock Castle is one of many perfectly unique ruins not to miss. Like so many strongholds in the area, it required sturdy defences from the many English raids during the Scottish Wars of Independence. It's as a result of those nervous times that the incredible atmosphere and unique splendour are still clearly tangible as you wander the staircases and rooms of one of Scotland's most beautiful castles.

Recommended By Mark Turner, *tour guide at Solway Tours*

14 Ride to the SEA

CYCLING | SEASIDE | DAY TRIP

Hop on a train to Barrhill for a cycling utopia of quiet country roads. Your pedal strokes will take you from lonely moorland to a ruined abbey and then to the pastel-coloured cottages of Portpatrick's seafront.

JENNYT/SHUTTESTOCK ©

Trip Notes

Getting here Trains from Ayr to Barrhill take 50 minutes; bicycles are carried free, with no reservation required.

When to go Avoid winter as there are few options for shelter.

Cycling details Recommended for experienced cyclists. The 36-mile route is mainly flat on good-quality roads. The Old Military Rd to Portpatrick avoids the busier A-roads. To rejoin the train, head to Stranraer station, 7 miles from Portpatrick.

The Best of Portpatrick

Portpatrick is a real gem, set among high cliffs with views to Ireland. Walk from the harbour to Dunskey Castle, which sits precariously above the bay. Sitting outside at the Crown Hotel with local seafood and beers, watching the sun go down, is just serene.

Recommended By Mark Turner, *tour guide at Solway Tours*

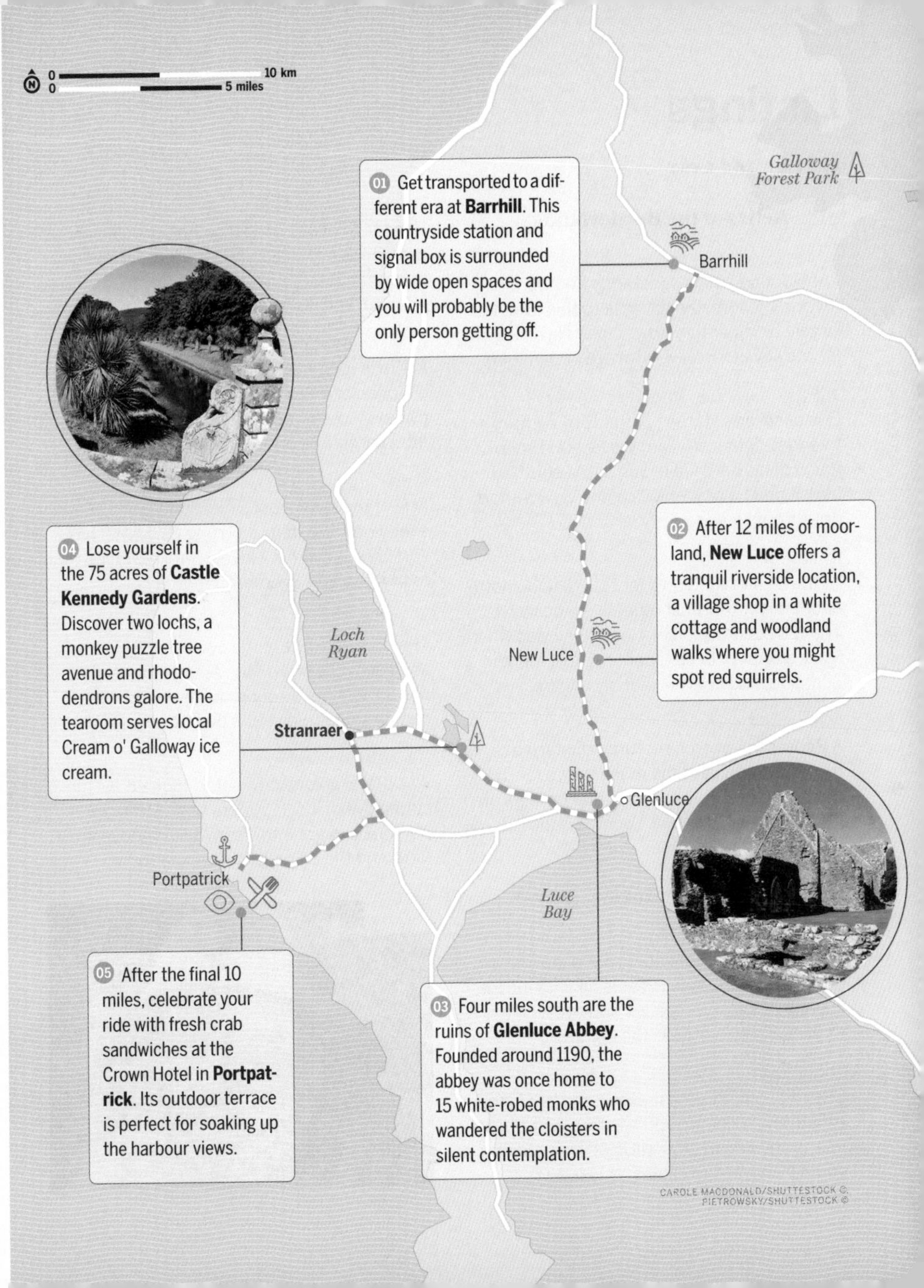

01 Get transported to a different era at **Barrhill**. This countryside station and signal box is surrounded by wide open spaces and you will probably be the only person getting off.

02 After 12 miles of moorland, **New Luce** offers a tranquil riverside location, a village shop in a white cottage and woodland walks where you might spot red squirrels.

04 Lose yourself in the 75 acres of **Castle Kennedy Gardens**. Discover two lochs, a monkey puzzle tree avenue and rhododendrons galore. The tearoom serves local Cream o' Galloway ice cream.

05 After the final 10 miles, celebrate your ride with fresh crab sandwiches at the Crown Hotel in **Portpatrick**. Its outdoor terrace is perfect for soaking up the harbour views.

03 Four miles south are the ruins of **Glenluce Abbey**. Founded around 1190, the abbey was once home to 15 white-robed monks who wandered the cloisters in silent contemplation.

CAROLE MACDONALD/SHUTTESTOCK ©, PIETROWSKY/SHUTTESTOCK ©

Listings

BEST OF THE REST

Relics of the Borderlands

Fatlips Castle

Anticipation builds constantly and wonderfully on the forested hill walk to this remote, largely 19th-century, tower near Hawick. Ask for the key at TB Oliver Garage in Denholm.

William Wallace Statue

One of several statues of the 13th-century freedom-fighter, William Wallace. He spent much of his hard life hiding in the southern forest, and he now enjoys a fine view a short drive from Melrose.

Dundrennan Abbey

To the east of Kirkcudbright you'll find another of Scotland's most reflective hideaways. The 12th-century Cistercian abbey was where Mary Queen of Scots spent her last night in Scotland, and her melancholy lingers.

Mellerstain House

A Robert Adam architectural masterpiece, the house and gardens make for a grand day out on a sunny day. Look up: the ceilings are particularly impressive. Located south of Gordon.

Outdoor Adventures

Go Ape

A treetop adventure course set deep within Glentress Forest, near Peebles. Fantastic for adventure seekers, groups and cyclists; the thrilling 325m zipline is the highlight.

Logan Botanic Gardens

One of Scotland's most exotic corners in the (relatively) mild far southwest near Stranraer. Palms and eucalyptus will have you imagining yourself in warmer climes.

The Mull of Galloway

Head to Scotland's most southerly point for superb views over the Irish Sea and birdwatching opportunities. The lighthouse is perched atop a 79m cliff and is worth the 115-step ascent.

Great Cumbrae

A 4-mile-long island off the Ayrshire coast, this is a popular day trip for west coast walkers and cyclists. Access is by frequent, 10-minute ferry from Largs; hire bikes in the town of Millport.

Coldingham Bay

One of the east coast's nicest beaches, the sandy bay is suited to surfing (the hotel has a surf shop). There's a lovely 3-mile coastal trail to the beach at Eyemouth too.

Ailsa Craig

There's a blue hue to the eye-catching island and gannet colony off the Ayrshire coast that has the distinction of producing world-class curling stones. Sea tours depart from Girvan.

Kitchen Coos and Ewes

A virtual Highland cow safari tour, under the caring eye of local farmers near Stranraer. A personal insight into life on a Dumfriesshire farm and the animals that reside there.

William Wallace Statue

Local Heroes & Tributes

Jim Clark Motorsport Museum

A touching tribute to the racing legend and multiple Formula 1 champion. The museum in Duns features an extensive trophy cabinet, car displays and a driving simulator for kids.

Museum of Lead Mining

A surprisingly family-friendly and fascinating look at the harsh reality of mining in the 18th century, including an eerie tour of an actual mine. Find it in Wanlockhead near Sanquhar.

Devil's Porridge Museum

Just short of the Scotland–England border, this curiously named spot, fuelled by very passionate locals, provides a touching commemoration to the largest munitions factory in the world during WWI.

Festivals & Legacies

Borders and Wigtown

That Scotland's two most celebrated scribblers hailed from the south is surely no coincidence, and modern-day readers and writers flock to the excellent annual festivals in Melrose and Wigtown. Visit festival websites for event dates.

The Common Ridings

Summer in the Scottish Borders sees several horse-led festivals celebrating the equestrian tradition of sending riders to town boundaries to check for thieving raiders. Head to Jedburgh and Hawick for the biggest ones and join the townsfolk in cheering on the costumed cavalcades.

Alloway

The epicentre of Burns-mania, the bard was born and raised in this Ayrshire town. Head first to the excellent Birthplace Museum before strolling to Burns Cottage via spooky Alloway Auld Kirk.

Alloway Auld Kirk

Local Food & Drink

The Hoebridge £££

Top-drawer seasonal dining with great attention to detail. Located in Gattonside, just across the river from the excellent Borders hub of Melrose. Book far (very far) in advance.

The Limetree Restaurant ££

Locally sourced meat, game and fish dominate a minimal menu that wins for quality and value in a cosy setting within the Hartfell Guest House in Moffat.

Auld Alliance ££

In the quaint, coastal setting of Kirkcudbright, local produce is given a supporting hand here from France. Friendly service, big flavours.

Annandale Distillery ££

After 90 years of rest, Annandale Distillery is once again reborn and now producing some very interesting single malts in Annan. Book tours in advance.

Scan to find more things to do in Southern Scotland online

STIRLING, FIFE & PERTHSHIRE

OUTDOORS | FOOD | HISTORY

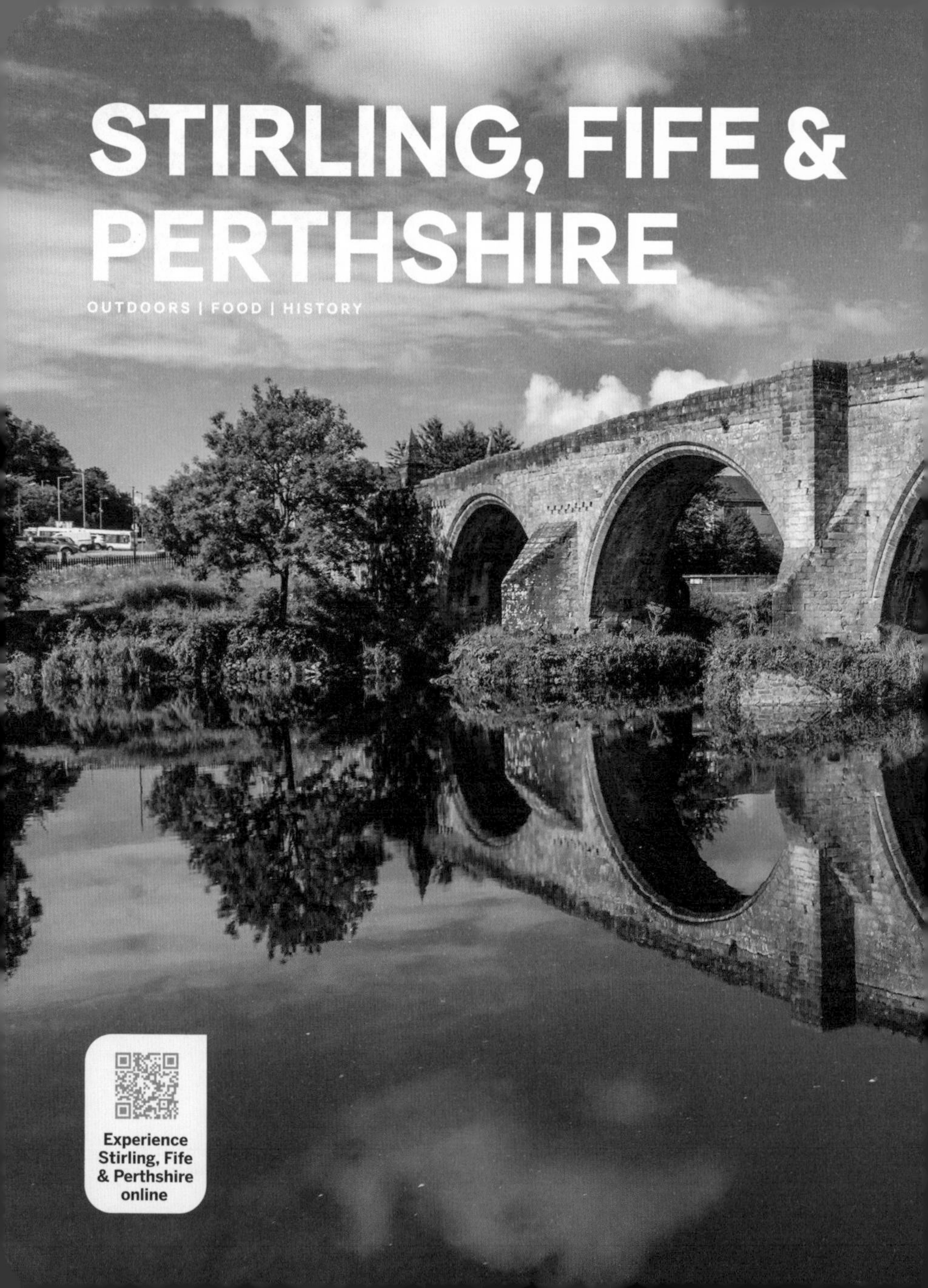

Experience Stirling, Fife & Perthshire online

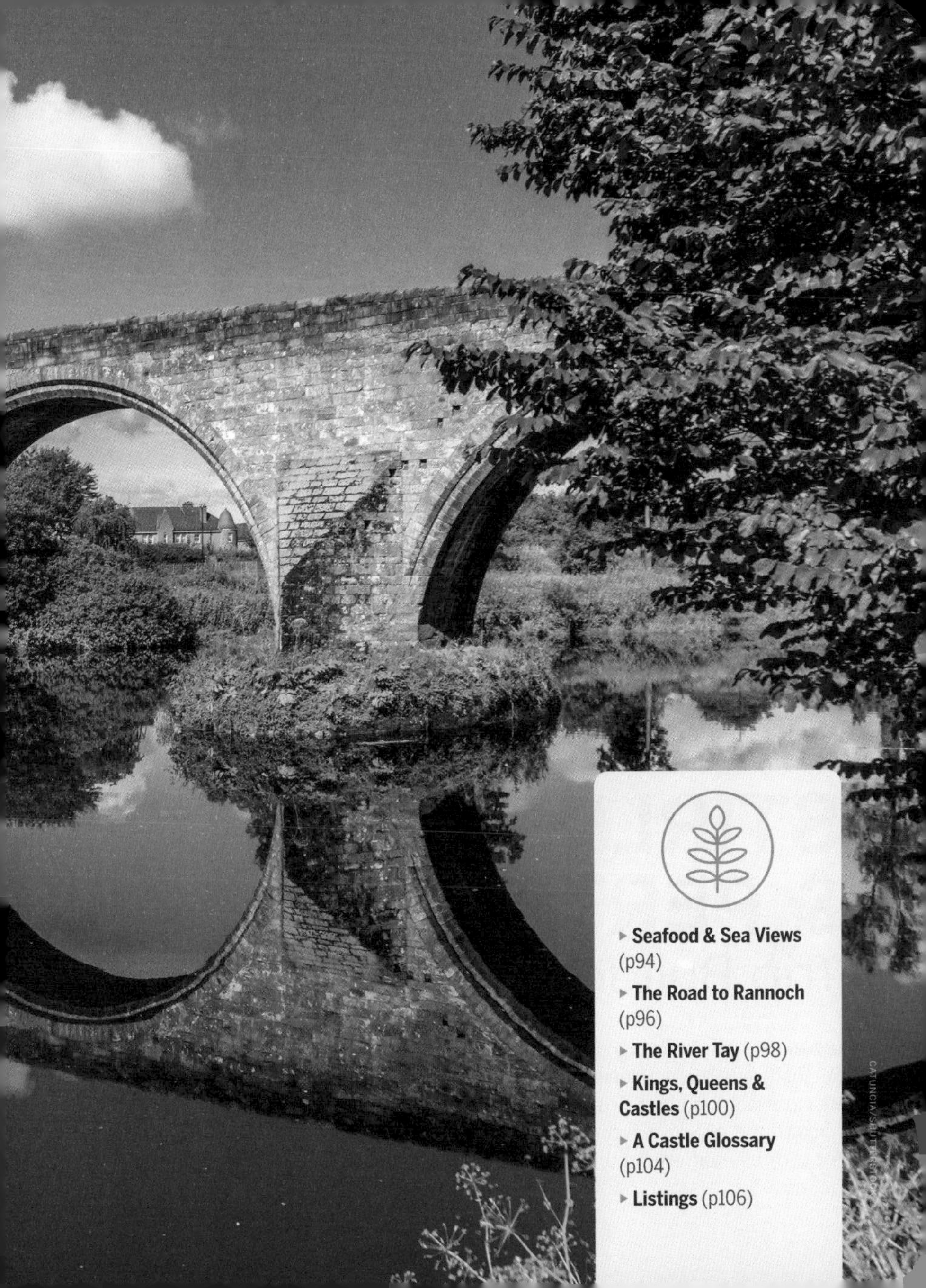

CATUNCIA/SHUTTERSTOCK

▸ **Seafood & Sea Views** (p94)

▸ **The Road to Rannoch** (p96)

▸ **The River Tay** (p98)

▸ **Kings, Queens & Castles** (p100)

▸ **A Castle Glossary** (p104)

▸ **Listings** (p106)

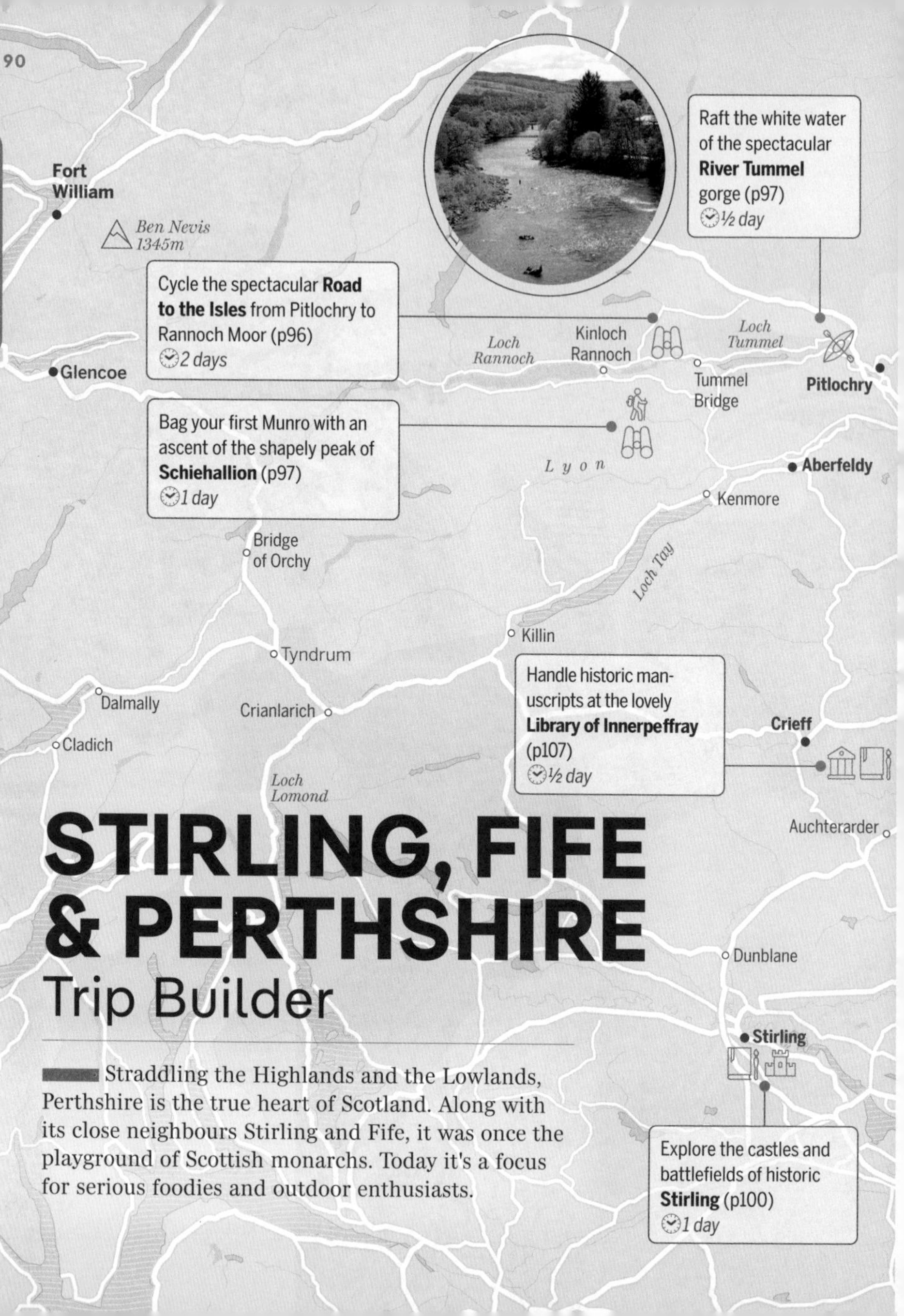
Fort William
Ben Nevis 1345m
Glencoe
Loch Rannoch
Kinloch Rannoch
Loch Tummel
Tummel Bridge
Pitlochry
Lyon
Aberfeldy
Kenmore
Bridge of Orchy
Loch Tay
Killin
Tyndrum
Dalmally
Crianlarich
Cladich
Loch Lomond
Crieff
Auchterarder
Dunblane
Stirling
Raft the white water of the spectacular **River Tummel** gorge (p97) ½ day
Cycle the spectacular **Road to the Isles** from Pitlochry to Rannoch Moor (p96) 2 days
Bag your first Munro with an ascent of the shapely peak of **Schiehallion** (p97) 1 day
Handle historic manuscripts at the lovely **Library of Innerpeffray** (p107) ½ day
Explore the castles and battlefields of historic **Stirling** (p100) 1 day

STIRLING, FIFE & PERTHSHIRE

Trip Builder

Straddling the Highlands and the Lowlands, Perthshire is the true heart of Scotland. Along with its close neighbours Stirling and Fife, it was once the playground of Scottish monarchs. Today it's a focus for serious foodies and outdoor enthusiasts.

Enjoy a picnic on the banks of the River Tay at lovely **Dunkeld** (p98)
½ day

Seek out the elusive Tayside beavers at **Bamff Ecotourism** (p107)
½ day

Delve deep into Scottish history at the enigmatic **Moot Hill** at **Scone Palace** (p101 + p106)
½ day

Indulge in a feast of local produce in the restaurants and farm shops of **St Andrews** (p95)
1 day

Hike between seafood stops on the scenic **Fife Coastal Path** (p94)
2 days

Explore bookable experiences in Stirling, Fife & Perthshire online

Practicalities

CHRISTIAN MUELLER/SHUTTERSTOCK ©

ARRIVING

Stirling and Perth are easily reached from Edinburgh by bus or train (one hour). Stirling train and bus stations are in the centre, within walking distance of the castle and other sights. Perth train and bus stations are on the south side of the centre, about 3 miles from Scone Palace (a one-hour walk); various local buses run past Scone Palace – ask for details at the bus station. An hourly bus service from Edinburgh to St Andrews (two hours) passes through the East Neuk fishing villages.

HOW MUCH FOR A

Serve of fish & chips £8

Lobster dinner from £26

Pint of local IPA £3.80

WHEN TO GO

JAN–MAR

Often cold and wet. Salmon-fishing season kicks off.

APR–JUN

Woods are carpeted with bluebells. Perth Festival of the Arts in May.

JUL–SEP

Busy period of school holidays. Best weather for hill walking.

OCT–DEC

Autumn colours in Perthshire. Good conditions for canoeing.

GETTING AROUND

Driving The best way to visit out-of-the-way places if your time is limited. There are restrictions on parking in certain popular areas, notably the south side of Loch Tummel.

Buses Link most towns and villages in the region. The main operators are Stagecoach East Scotland, First Scotland East, Elizabeth Yule Coaches and Moffat & Williamson. Stagecoach's East Scotland Dayrider ticket (£9) gives unlimited bus travel for one day in Perthshire and Fife.

Bike There is a good network of cycle routes across the region, with a mix of minor roads, cycle lanes and dedicated cycle tracks. Perthshire Gravel offers a wide range of off-road adventure trails.

EATING & DRINKING

Seafood The East Neuk of Fife – from Elie around the coast through Anstruther and Crail to St Andrews – is famous for its concentration of seafood restaurants, from humble fish-and-chip shops to Michelin-starred restaurants – don't miss the local lobster.

Regional produce Inland is some of the richest farmland in the country, and fresh regional produce – including beef, lamb, asparagus, carrots, potatoes and soft fruits – are best sampled at farmers markets, farm shop cafes and country pubs.

Must-try lobster
Crail Lobster Store (p106)

Best fish and chips
Anstruther Fish Bar (p106)

TOP: STEPHEN DOREY/ALAMY STOCK PHOTO ©
BOTTOM: KEVIN GEORGE/ALAMY STOCK PHOTO ©

WHERE TO STAY

The region is popular with tourists, so there's a good range of accommodation from hostels and B&Bs to luxury county house hotels. Best to book ahead in summer.

Town/Village	Pro/Con
Stirling	The region's biggest city has a choice of good-value hotels and B&Bs within walking distance of the castle.
St Andrews	A university town and the home of golf, loaded with upmarket guesthouses and luxury hotels.
Pitlochry	Lively and picturesque, with backpacker hostels and traditional guesthouses.
Aberfeldy	Attractive Highland town, with a campsite, good B&Bs and self-catering cottages.
Perth	More functional than fun, and perhaps a bit old-fashioned.

CONNECT

Wi-fi Easy to find in towns like Perth, Stirling and St Andrews. However, in more rural areas, especially in Highland Perthshire (eg around Loch Tummel and Loch Rannoch), public wi-fi in cafes, hotels and B&Bs can be very slow. Outside towns and away from trunk roads 4G coverage can also be patchy; 5G is nonexistent.

HISTORIC SITES

If you plan on visiting a number of properties owned by Historic Scotland, especially as a family, consider buying an annual membership to save money.

MONEY

There are charges (£2 to £3) for using car parks at tourist hot spots (including Queen's View on Loch Tummel and Braes of Foss at Schiehallion), so keep a supply of £1 coins handy for the ticket machines.

15 Seafood & SEA VIEWS

FOOD | HIKING | VILLAGES

Stretch your legs on the East Neuk segment of the Fife Coastal Path, which strings together a necklace of photogenic fishing villages, packed with places to enjoy the harvest of the sea, from simple fish and chip shops to Michelin-starred restaurants.

IAIN MASTERTON/ALAMY STOCK PHOTO ©

Trip Notes

Getting around You can hike along the Fife Coastal Path from Elie to St Andrews (total distance 25 miles) over two or three days, or link the stops by road, using bike, bus or car, along the signposted Fife Coastal Tourist Route.

When to go Best hiking weather is May to September.

Need to know Check with St Andrews tourist office about the condition of the footpath; sections are sometimes closed due to erosion or high tides.

Fife Foodie Hot Spots

Salt & Pine, Tentsmuir Forest Perfect spot for a walk and a bite to eat.

Jannetta's Ice Cream, St Andrews Favourite place to take the family for a sweet treat.

Balgove Larder, St Andrews Love the farm shop, and you can get lunch at the same time.

Cupar Market Great local produce, especially the Arbroath smokies!

Recommended by Dean Banks, *chef-proprietor of Haar restaurant, St Andrews @haarrestaurant*

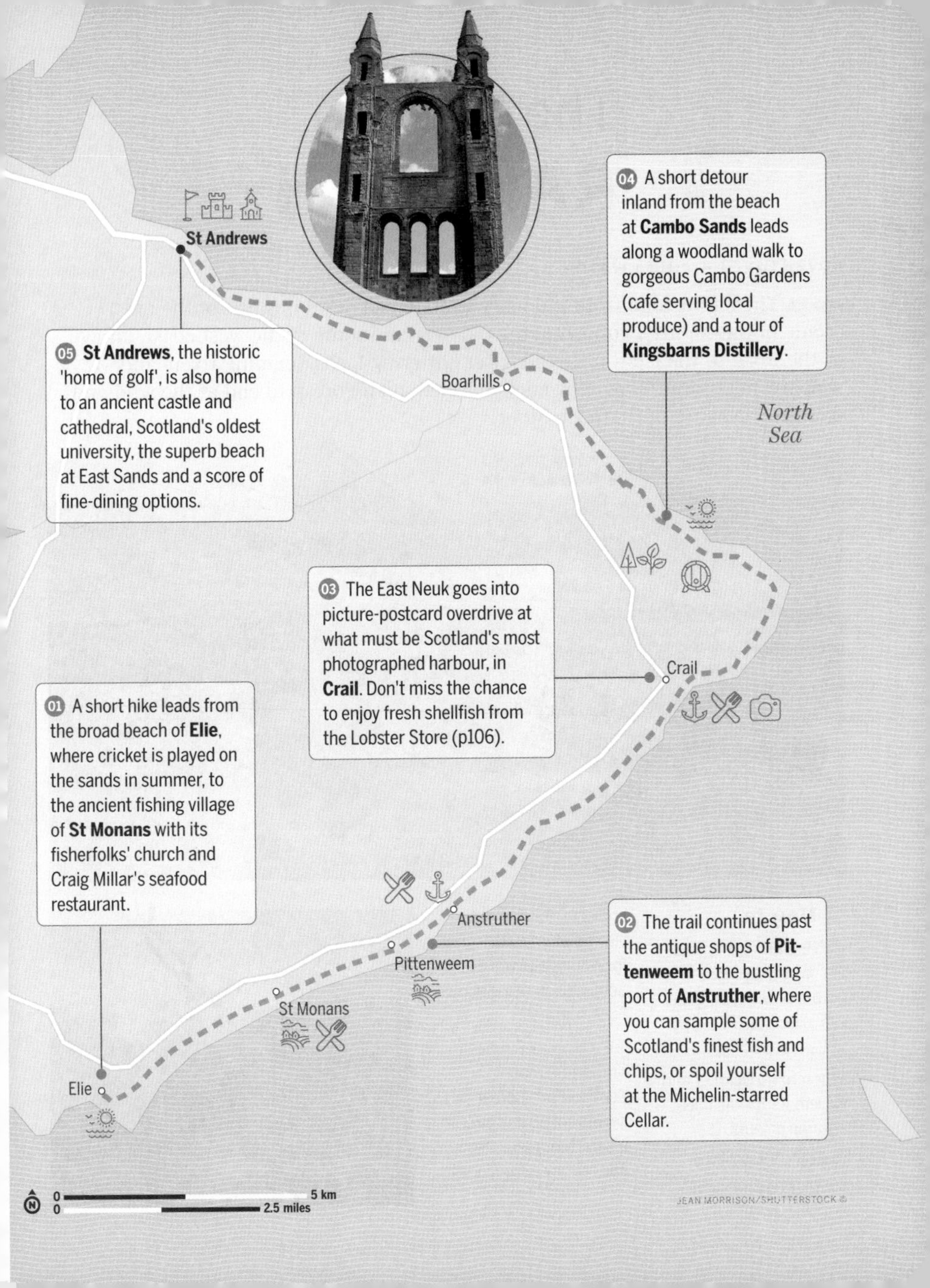

01 A short hike leads from the broad beach of **Elie**, where cricket is played on the sands in summer, to the ancient fishing village of **St Monans** with its fisherfolks' church and Craig Millar's seafood restaurant.

02 The trail continues past the antique shops of **Pittenweem** to the bustling port of **Anstruther**, where you can sample some of Scotland's finest fish and chips, or spoil yourself at the Michelin-starred Cellar.

03 The East Neuk goes into picture-postcard overdrive at what must be Scotland's most photographed harbour, in **Crail**. Don't miss the chance to enjoy fresh shellfish from the Lobster Store (p106).

04 A short detour inland from the beach at **Cambo Sands** leads along a woodland walk to gorgeous Cambo Gardens (cafe serving local produce) and a tour of **Kingsbarns Distillery**.

05 **St Andrews**, the historic 'home of golf', is also home to an ancient castle and cathedral, Scotland's oldest university, the superb beach at East Sands and a score of fine-dining options.

16 The Road to RANNOCH

ADVENTURE | HIKING | WATER

The minor road from Pitlochry to Rannoch Station is one of the most scenic in the country. Following the old overland route to the west coast, known as the Road to the Isles, it threads past glittering lochs, foaming rivers and shapely mountains fringed by ancient Caledonian Forest, to end at the wild and daunting expanse of Rannoch Moor.

JOHN CARROLL PHOTOGRAPHY/ALAMY STOCK PHOTO ©

How to

Getting around A pleasant day trip by car, or a superb two-day cycling tour (35 miles from Pitlochry to Rannoch Station).

When to go October and November for the finest autumn colours.

Queen's View With a car park, visitor centre and cafe, this famous viewpoint is worth a stop for a classic photo of Schiehallion rising above Loch Tummel.

Take a break Rannoch Station Tearoom, Scotland's remotest cafe, serves coffee and cake to hikers, mountain bikers and railway excursionists.

BINSON CALFORT/SHUTTERSTOCK ©

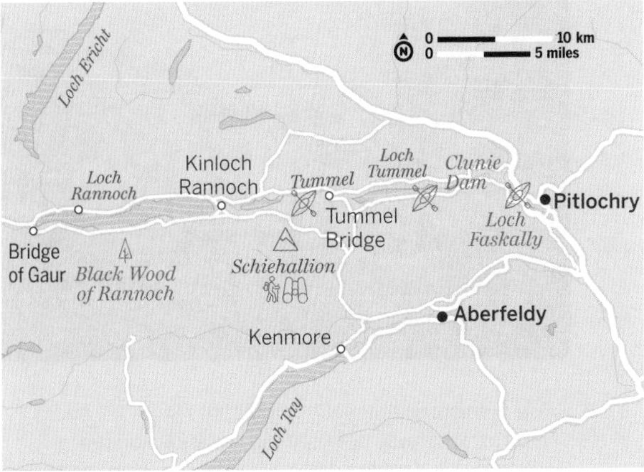

Hike a hill Gaelic for the 'Fairy Hill of the Caledonians', **Schiehallion** is one of Scotland's shapeliest peaks, seen as a perfect pyramid when viewed from the northern shore of Loch Rannoch. It is also one of the easiest Munros (hills of 3000ft/914m in height or over) to climb. A well-made footpath leads from Braes of Foss car park (on the road from Tummel Bridge to Aberfeldy) to the broad, rocky summit ridge, where you'll be rewarded with panoramic views across Rannoch Moor to the peaks of Glen Coe (6.5 miles total; allow four to six hours).

Wander in woods On the southern shore of Loch Rannoch, between Camghouran and Dall, lies the **Black Wood of Rannoch**, a remnant of the ancient Caledonian pine forest. Here in this enclave of native woodland you can lose yourself amid a tangle of twisted moss-draped boughs and gnarled russet bark, a haven for deer, red squirrel, pine marten and rare birds such as Scottish crossbill and capercaillie.

Raft a river The **Clunie Dam** at the east end of Loch Tummel was built in 1950 as part of a hydroelectric power scheme. Regular releases of water from June to September mean that the 2 miles of the **River Tummel** from the dam down to **Loch Faskally** provide some of the most exciting and reliable white-water rafting in Scotland. The river cascades through a rocky, wooded gorge, over Grade II and III rapids to the grand finale – a 6m white-knuckle drop down the Grade IV Linn of Tummel waterfall.

Left Blackmount
Below left Red deer

Rannoch Moor

The motor road ends at Rannoch Station, a lonely outpost where civilisation fades away and Rannoch Moor begins. This is the largest area of moorland in Britain, stretching west for eight barren, bleak and uninhabited miles. Despite the appearance of desolation, the moor is rich in wildlife, with curlew, golden plover and snipe darting among the tussocks, black-throated diver, goosander and merganser on the lochs, and – if you're lucky – osprey and golden eagle overhead. You can take the train to Corrour Station and hike the 11 miles back to Rannoch (allow five hours).

The River Tay

SCOTLAND'S MIGHTIEST RIVER

Rising on the slopes of Ben Lui near the Highland village of Tyndrum, barely 20 miles from Scotland's west coast, and flowing for 117 miles to meet the tide at Perth, the Tay is Scotland's longest and mightiest river – more water flows from its mouth than from the Thames and Severn combined.

Left Loch Tay
Middle An osprey flies above the River Tay
Right Kinclaven Bluebell Wood

RICHARDJOHNSON/SHUTTERSTOCK ©

Since prehistoric times the valley of the River Tay has served as a highway between the lowlands and the Highlands. It's a route now followed by the main road and railway to the north, and by the River Tay Way, a 50-mile walking and cycling route that links Perth to the village of Kenmore at the northeast end of Loch Tay.

Loch Tay – at 15 miles long, the sixth-largest loch in Scotland – was already a centre of population 4000 years ago, when prehistoric people built a series of crannogs – timber-built roundhouses supported on piles driven into the loch bed – along its shores. You can visit a recreation of one of these ancient dwellings at the Scottish Crannog Centre near Kenmore.

For today's canoeists and kayakers, the Tay is a classic river descent, but for thousands of years before roads were built, the river was an important waterway. A log canoe found buried in the mud at Carpow, east of Perth, has been dated to around 1000 BCE (it is now on display in Perth Museum & Art Gallery).

Roman ships sailed up the Tay and legions marched to a line of forts defending the northernmost border of Empire. Ardoch (at Braco, near Stirling) is the best preserved of these, but Inchtuthil, built around 83 CE on the banks of the Tay near Spitalfield, is famous for its 10-tonne hoard of iron nails. They were buried when the Romans abandoned the fort, and only rediscovered in 1960 – samples are held by Perth Museum, and the Royal Scottish Museum in Edinburgh.

The Tay breaches the Highland line at the picturesque village of Dunkeld (whose name means 'Fort of the Caledonians'), a strategic point where the valley narrows. Jacobite clans fighting for the restoration of the Stuart

ANGHARAD TREASURE/SHUTTERSTOCK ©

DALE KELLY/SHUTTERSTOCK ©

monarchy clashed with Cameronian soldiers, who supported William of Orange, at the Battle of Dunkeld in 1689. This event, along with the Battle of Killiecrankie a few weeks earlier, signalled the beginning of 60 years of conflict that only ended with the defeat of Bonnie Prince Charlie at Culloden in 1746.

In an attempt to control the Jacobite clans, General George Wade was charged in the 1730s with building a network of military roads from the lowlands into the Highlands. The first of these followed the valley of the Tay from Dunkeld as far as Ballinluig and is still the route followed by the modern A9 motor road. A second military road crossed the Tay at Aberfeldy via Wade's Bridge (built in 1734), the oldest surviving bridge over the river.

Of course, the river is not just a highway for humans, but also for wildlife.

Of course, the river is not just a highway for humans, but also for wildlife. Eels migrate downstream to the sea to breed, freshwater pearl mussels cling to the river bed, otters forage along the banks, and the European beaver – hunted to extinction in the 16th century – has returned. But the river's most famous wild inhabitant is the Atlantic salmon, whose arduous journey upriver to spawn is the stuff of legend.

Today all salmon fishing on the Tay – one of Europe's premier salmon rivers – is by rod and line, and all fish are carefully released alive after being caught. Old traditions persist, and the opening of the salmon fishing season on 15 January is marked by ceremonies up and down the river, notably at Kenmore, where a pipe band leads a procession of anglers to the river.

Top Tayside Wildlife Experiences

Beaver safari See the amazing wetlands beavers have created, and watch a beaver family swimming, feeding, playing and grooming near their lodge.

Osprey-watching at Loch of the Lowes A webcam ensures you get excellent views of what's going on in the nest.

Dragonflies at Polney Loch, Dunkeld On a hot summer day the edges of the loch come alive with dragonflies and damselflies.

Walk Kinclaven Bluebell Woods Arguably one of the most beautiful bluebell woods in Scotland, full of bird song in spring and summer.

Recommended By Danièle Muir, *owner of Perthshire Wildlife*

@PerthshireWildlife

17

Kings, Queens & CASTLES

CASTLES | HISTORY | ARCHITECTURE

Explore dramatic crag-top castles, elegant aristocratic palaces, romantic island fortresses and the atmospheric ancient crowning place of Scottish monarchs, as you journey around the historic royal heartland of the Scottish nation.

JULIETPHOTOGRAPHY/SHUTTERSTOCK ©

How to

Getting around A car will make the most of your time, as outside Perth and Stirling most sights are poorly served by public transport.

When to go Many smaller castles are closed November to March. Avoid crowds at Stirling Castle by visiting weekdays outside of school holidays (July to mid-August).

Top tip Book lovers shouldn't miss the Library of Innerpeffray (p107). Founded in 1680, it houses a huge collection of rare and interesting books, some of them 500 years old.

AWE INSPIRING IMAGES/SHUTTERSTOCK ©

Scotland's Birthplace & Royal Roots

Climb the ancient mound of **Moot Hill**, which stands beside the lavish 19th-century Scone Palace (p106), and sit on a replica of the **Stone of Destiny**. This is the birthplace of Scotland as a kingdom, where Scottish monarchs – from Kenneth MacAlpin in 843 to Charles II in 1651 – were crowned.

Long before Edinburgh became the Scottish capital, **Dunfermline** was the favoured royal residence. Wander the ruins of the abbey guesthouse, converted in 1500 into a palace for King James VI whose son, Charles I, was born here in 1600, and visit the abbey church, founded by David I in 1128, which houses the tombs of three princes, two queens and seven kings, including Robert the Bruce.

ROBERT COLONNA/SHUTTERSTOCK ©

The Stone of Destiny

Legend has it that the ancient coronation stone of Scottish monarchs was brought to Scone in the 9th century. In 1296 it was captured by Edward I of England, who took it to Westminster Abbey, where it remained for 700 years. It has been displayed in Edinburgh Castle since 1996 but will be moved to a new museum in Perth in 2022.

Top left Scone Palace
Bottom left Dunfermline
Top right The Stone of Destiny

Set in the lush rural heart of Fife, 16th-century **Falkland Palace** was the country residence of the Stuart monarchs. Explore the gardens where Mary Queen of Scots is said to have spent the happiest days of her life, and pop into the world's oldest surviving real tennis court, which dates from 1539. Kings James V, James VI and Charles II all stayed here too on various occasions.

Access by boat trip adds atmosphere to **Loch Leven Castle**, whose 14th-century tower house is one of the oldest in the country. It was visited by Robert the Bruce in 1313 and 1323, and Mary Queen of Scots was held prisoner here in 1567 before being forced to abdicate. Combine a visit with a hike around the lovely **Loch Leven Heritage Trail**.

Who Holds Stirling, Holds Scotland...

The dramatic setting of **Stirling Castle** atop a crag commanding the broad valley of the River Forth – the ancient invasion route into Central Scotland – makes it arguably the country's finest fortress. Patrol the ramparts

History off the Beaten Track

Perthshire has a lovely selection of small churches – St Serf's in Dunning, with the magnificent Pictish carvings of the Forteviot Stone; Tibbermuir near Gleneagles; and two St Mary's, both 16th century – Grandtully with a wonderful painted ceiling, and one next to Innerpeffray Library itself. (Another amazing book collection can be found in Dunblane near the cathedral – Bishop Leighton's Library is a tiny treasure.) And then there's Abernethy Tower, southeast of Perth – a historical enigma, it's one of only two of this style in Scotland and is thought to be almost 1000 years old.

Recommended by Lara Haggerty, *Keeper of Books at the Library of Innerpeffray @Innerpeffray*

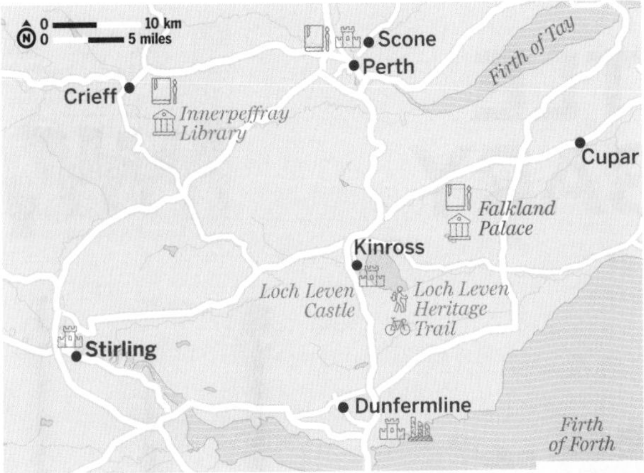

Left Abernethy Tower
Below Dupplin Cross in St Serf's Church, Dunning

to take in the stunning views before exploring its centrepiece – the magnificent royal palace built in Renaissance style for King James V in the 1530s.

From the castle you can wander downhill to **Stirling Bridge**, site of a decisive battle in 1297 when William Wallace (of *Braveheart* fame) defeated an English army and set the scene for Scottish independence. Rising on another crag to the north is the Gothic tower of the **Wallace Monument** – climb to the top for fantastic views of Stirling Castle.

Scotland's independence was clinched in 1314 at the Battle of Bannockburn, when Robert the Bruce decisively trounced the forces of Eng-land's Edward II. You can experience a digital re-enactment of the clash of armies at the National Trust for Scotland's Bannockburn Visitor Centre (p107), before taking a stroll across the actual battlefield.

More castles litter the countryside around Stir-ling, notably spectacular **Castle Campbell** (near Dollar), perched high on a wooded cliff (approach from the lower car park via a woodland walk), and **Doune Castle**, made famous as a film location for *Monty Python and the Holy Grail,* and more recently as Castle Leoch in the TV series *Outlander* (be sure to take the audio tour).

A CASTLE GLOSSARY

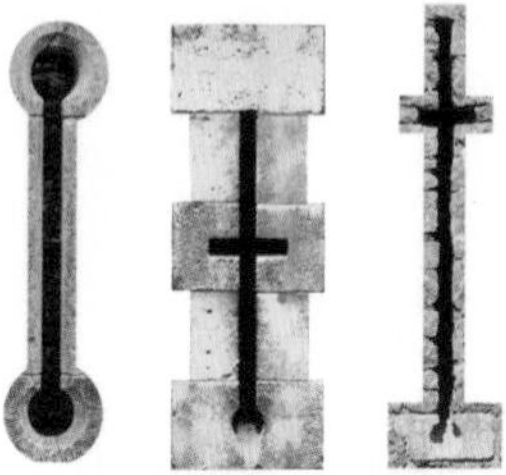

01 Crenellation

The tops of the walls were provided with raised sections that defenders could take cover behind while firing arrows or projectiles through the gaps.

02 Curtain Wall

The main requirement of any defensive castle was a lofty curtain wall at least 3m in thickness that wrapped around a central courtyard.

03 Machicolation

Some castles had projecting corbels, or machicolations, at the top which allowed defenders to drop rocks or boiling pitch between them onto attackers below.

04 Arrow Slit

Arrow slits were narrow on the outside, to make a small target, and widened inside to allow the archer a wide range of fire.

05 Portcullis

This was a heavy metal gate that was

hoisted up and down in parallel grooves either side of the castle entrance. It could be dropped rapidly in an emergency.

06 Sentry Post

A small tower at the corner of the castle walls, providing shelter for soldiers on lookout duty.

07 Murder Hole

A hole in the roof of the entrance passage allowed defenders to pour boiling oil or pitch onto attackers who had breached the gate.

08 Drawbridge

A bridge across an outer moat or ditch that could be raised during an attack to make the castle entrance more secure.

09 Barbican

Extra fortification built around or on either side of the castle entrance to improve its defence.

Listings

BEST OF THE REST

Seafood & Steak

Haar £££
Masterchef finalist in 2018, Arbroath-born Dean Banks has established Haar as one of Scotland's top restaurants. Don't miss his signature grilled lobster in mirin butter.

Balgove Larder & Steak Barn ££
This farm shop on the edge of St Andrews is a treasure trove of locally produced food and drink while the Steak Barn is a top spot for a barbecue lunch or dinner.

Cellar £££
Two of Scotland's Michelin-starred restaurants are in Fife, including the cosy, cottage-style Cellar where seasonal tasting menus highlight the best of Scottish seafood.

Anstruther Fish Bar £
Join the queue that regularly forms outside this award-winning takeaway and sample some of Fife's finest fish and chips. It's also committed to sustainability and recycling.

Lobster Store ££
Seafood doesn't get much fresher than the locally landed crab and lobster at this tiny hut above Crail Harbour. Get your handpicked shellfish to order here (no indoor seating).

Craig Millar @ 16 West End £££
Choose a sunny summer day, book a table for lunch on the outdoor terrace, and enjoy a platter of shellfish or a juicy steak with a view over pretty St Monans harbour.

Historical Highlights

Perth Museum & Art Gallery
A cornucopia of local history, from a prehistoric log boat and a cache of Roman artefacts, to the British record rod-caught salmon and the impressionistic art of the Scottish Colourists.

Crannog Centre
Try your hand at making fire (using just two pieces of wood) and other prehistoric skills at this recreation of an Iron Age lake dwelling on Loch Tay.

Scottish Fisheries Museum
Watch skilled boatbuilders at work restoring historic wooden fishing vessels, and learn about the coastal communities who earned a living from the harvest of the sea.

St Andrews Castle
This storybook castle is a great place for kids to explore, complete with bottle-shaped dungeon and countermine – an underground passage hacked through solid rock during a 16th-century siege.

Scone Palace
With a beautiful setting on the banks of the Tay, this elegant aristocratic palace is one of Scotland's most impressive stately homes. Nearby is the Moot Hill, the ancient crowning place of Scottish monarchs since the 9th century.

St Andrews Cathedral, St Andrews

STIRLING, FIFE & PERTHSHIRE LISTINGS

Library of Innerpeffray
Bookworms can easily spend half a day in this 16th-century library, where voluntary guides will let you leaf through 300-year-old tomes, and seek out ancient books on any subject that interests you.

Battle of Bannockburn Visitor Centre
Re-enact this pivotal 14th-century clash between Scottish and English armies on a digital battlefield.

A Drink & a Snack

Loch Leven's Larder ££
Locals take a break from hiking or biking around the Loch Leven Heritage Trail at this popular farm shop and cafe, whose family-friendly facilities include outdoor tables, a play park and a sensory garden.

Taybank ££
Top choice for a sun-kissed pub lunch by the River Tay in Dunkeld, serving ales from the local Strathbraan Brewery. Live music several nights per week, and a menu featuring local produce.

Inn at Loch Tummel ££
Tote your pint across the road and bag a picnic table in one of Perthshire's best beer gardens, and soak up the glorious views over the sheep-dotted fields to lovely Loch Tummel.

Kingsbarns Distillery
Treat yourself to a leisurely two-hour tour of this rural distillery, where your guide will lead you through the whisky-making process before conducting an in-depth tasting session.

Water & Wildlife

Splash
This outfit offers exhilarating white-water rafting on the Rivers Tummel and Tay, as well as kayaking, canyoning and stand-up paddleboarding.

LUCENTIUS/GETTYIMAGES ©

Canoeing the River Tummel

Perthshire Wildlife
Join an evening walking tour or guided canoe safari to go in search of the European beavers that have spread throughout the backwaters of the River Tay system in the last two decades.

Outdoor Explore
Learn to canoe or kayak, join a guided half- or full-day canoe trip on Loch Tummel or Loch Rannoch, or go sea-kayaking in the Firth of Tay.

Bamff Ecotourism
A private estate near Alyth dedicated to rewilding, with a network of short walking trails through native woods and wetland crafted by the local beavers. The Cateran Trail long-distance footpath passes nearby.

Pitlochry Dam Visitor Centre
An architecturally stunning visitor centre perched above the dam on the River Tummel houses an exhibition recounting the history of hydroelectricity in Scotland, alongside the life cycle of the Atlantic salmon.

Scan to find more things to do in Stirling, Fife & Perthshire online

THE NORTHEAST

WHISKY | CASTLES | COAST

Experience Northeast Scotland online

▸ **A Coastal Trail** (p114)
▸ **Whisky Tour of Speyside** (p118)
▸ **Dundee Design Trail** (p120)
▸ **Listings** (p122)

Explore bookable experiences in the Northeast online

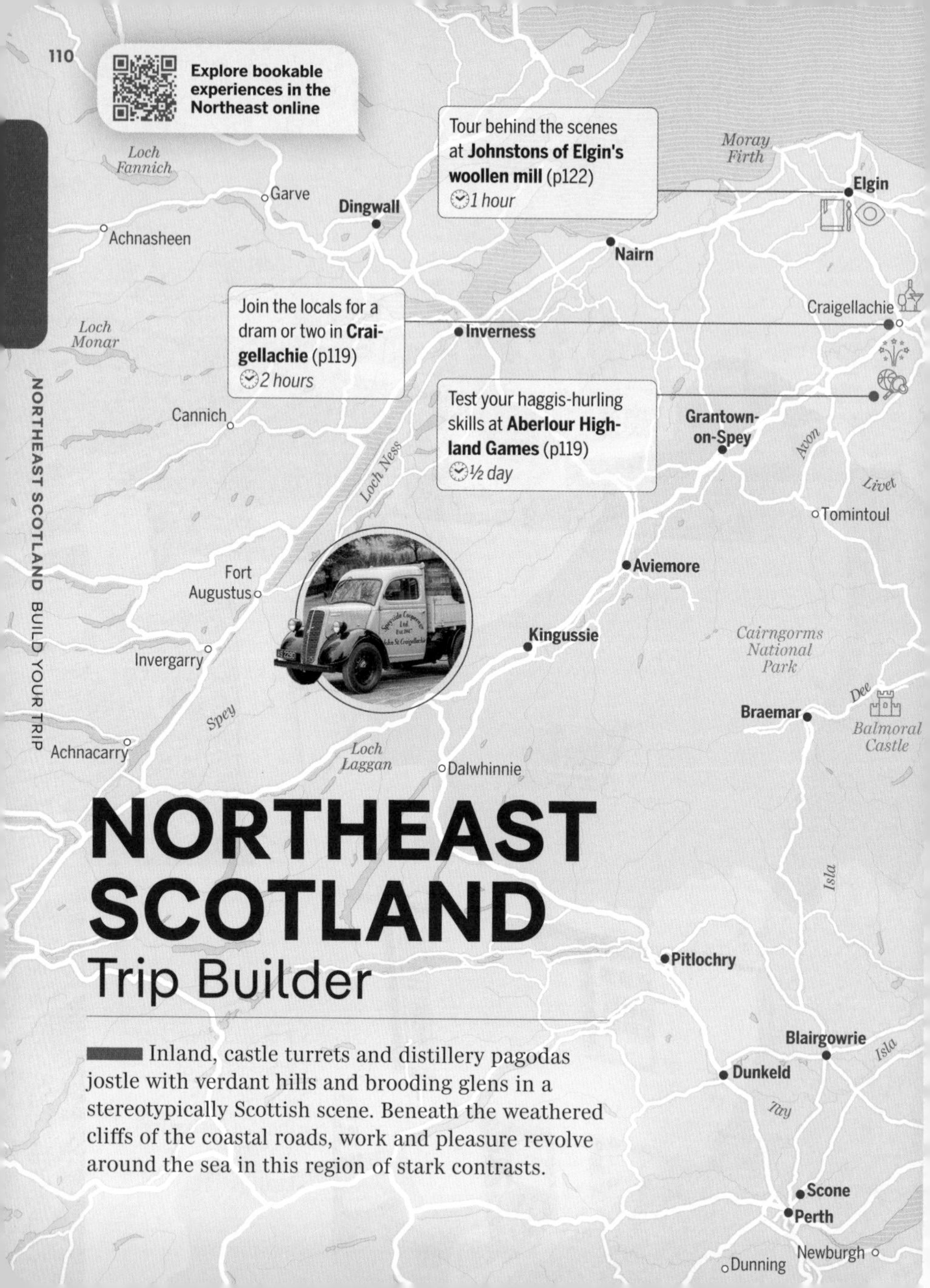

NORTHEAST SCOTLAND

Trip Builder

Inland, castle turrets and distillery pagodas jostle with verdant hills and brooding glens in a stereotypically Scottish scene. Beneath the weathered cliffs of the coastal roads, work and pleasure revolve around the sea in this region of stark contrasts.

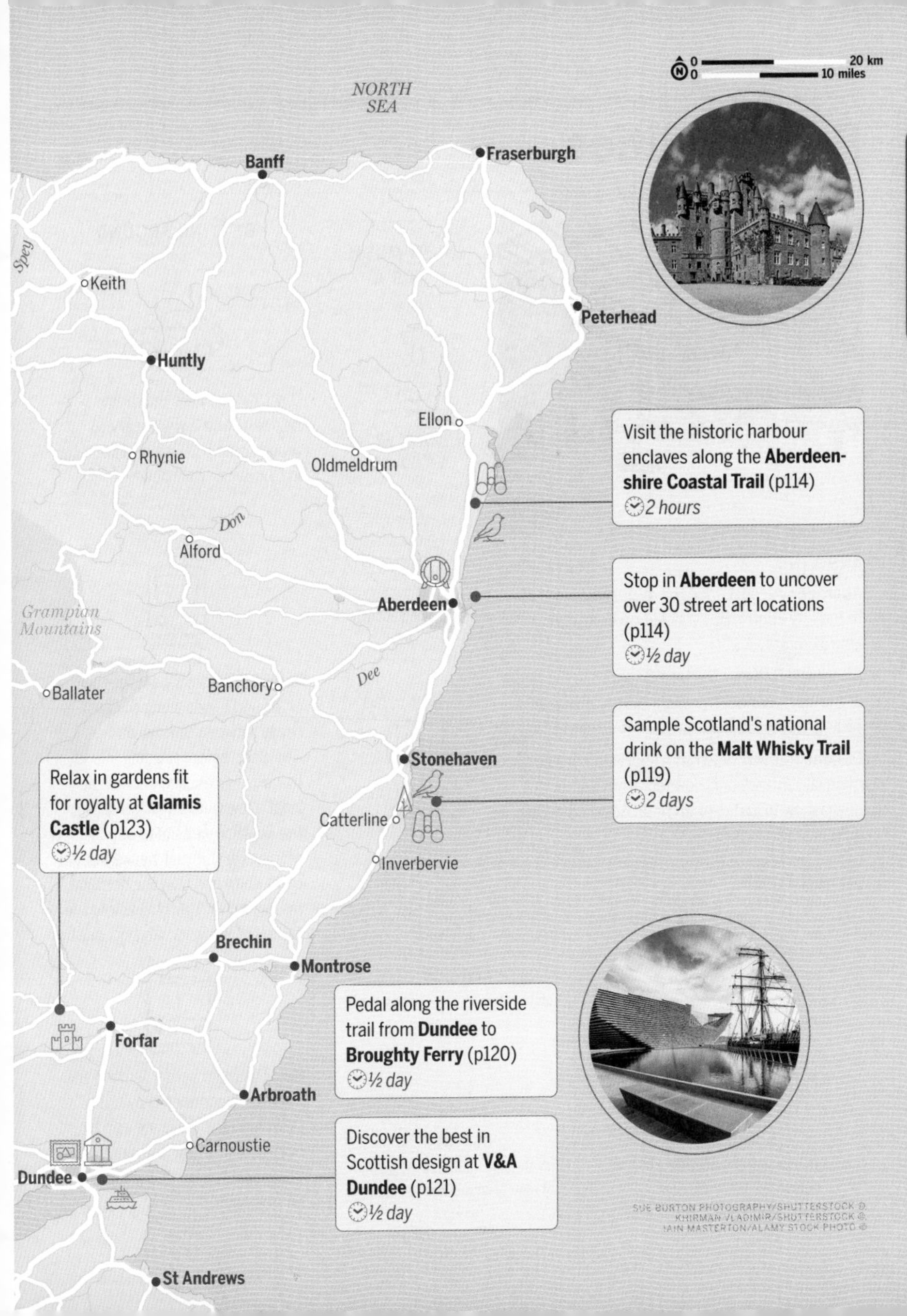

Visit the historic harbour enclaves along the **Aberdeenshire Coastal Trail** (p114)
2 hours

Stop in **Aberdeen** to uncover over 30 street art locations (p114)
½ day

Sample Scotland's national drink on the **Malt Whisky Trail** (p119)
2 days

Relax in gardens fit for royalty at **Glamis Castle** (p123)
½ day

Pedal along the riverside trail from **Dundee** to **Broughty Ferry** (p120)
½ day

Discover the best in Scottish design at **V&A Dundee** (p121)
½ day

Practicalities

ARRIVING

Aberdeen Airport Take the airport bus 7 miles to the city centre. Buy a ticket on board for approximately £3.50.

Aberdeen Railway Station Situated in the heart of the city, connect from Edinburgh or Glasgow. Tickets purchased online start at around £15.

Dundee Railway Station A short walk from the main city attractions, connect from Edinburgh or Glasgow in just over an hour. Advance online tickets start from £11.50.

WHEN TO GO

JAN–MAR
Cold with the possibility of snow; attractions are at their quietest.

APR–JUN
Milder temperatures and mixed conditions.

JUL–SEP
Temperatures are at their highest; perfect for outdoor activities and beach walks.

OCT–DEC
Chilly temperatures; keep warm at winter festivals and Christmas markets.

HOW MUCH FOR A

Dram of whisky
£4 upwards

Cullen Skink
£6

Castle tour
£14

GETTING AROUND

Car Driving offers the most flexibility and is necessary to reach some rural areas. Hire a car in Dundee or Aberdeen.

Train Services connect the main cities and towns along the east coast between Dundee and Aberdeen before heading inland towards Forres. Book tickets at least a few weeks in advance on the ScotRail website or app to save money. On summer weekends, get off at Keith and take the heritage railway to Dufftown to explore the capital of Speyside whisky country.

Bus The main settlements in the region are connected by bus. Download the Traveline app to plan your journey, and search the Stagecoach website for discounted tickets.

EATING & DRINKING

Arbroath Smokie Only haddock smoked in the east-coast town using traditional methods can be called an Arbroath Smokie. Best eaten with your fingers, hot from one of the local smokehouses.

Cullen Skink Originating in the fishing village of Cullen, smoked haddock, potatoes, onions and milk are combined to create a hearty soup. Ideal as a lunchtime filler or a winter warmer.

Aberdeen Rowies/Butteries A savoury snack with a unique consistency similar to a croissant; pick up this local speciality from any Aberdeenshire bakery.

Must-try local treat

Portsoy Ice Cream (p122)

Best Cullen Skink

Rockpool Cafe (p122)

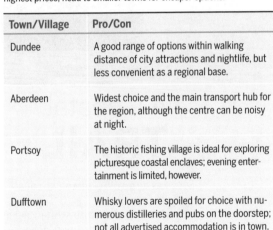

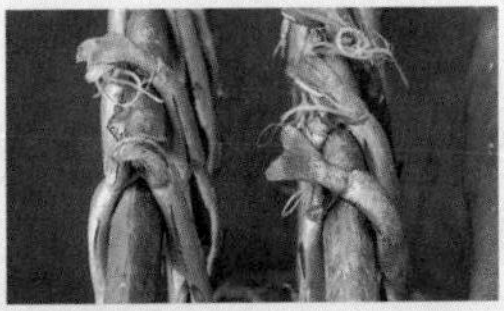

WHERE TO STAY

There are accommodation choices for every budget, from inexpensive hostels to luxury castles. City and sea-view properties command the highest prices; head to smaller towns for cheaper options.

Town/Village	Pro/Con
Dundee	A good range of options within walking distance of city attractions and nightlife, but less convenient as a regional base.
Aberdeen	Widest choice and the main transport hub for the region, although the centre can be noisy at night.
Portsoy	The historic fishing village is ideal for exploring picturesque coastal enclaves; evening entertainment is limited, however.
Dufftown	Whisky lovers are spoiled for choice with numerous distilleries and pubs on the doorstep; not all advertised accommodation is in town.

CONNECT & FIND YOUR WAY

Wi-fi Usually available for free at cafes, restaurants and hotels. Although fast and reliable in urban areas, it can be slow in rural settings.

Navigation Generally easy as major routes and attractions are well signposted. In countryside locations, enter the exact address on a navigation device as postcodes often cover large areas.

WHISKY DISTILLERIES

Find out which of the 50 Speyside whisky distilleries are open to the public and their locations on VisitScotland's interactive map.

MONEY

Buy a Northern Highlights Pass online for up to 50% discounted entry at selected attractions and activities throughout the Northeast. A two-/five-day card costs approximately £15/30.

18 A Coastal TRAIL

BEACHES | VILLAGES | WILDLIFE

Packed with whitewashed lighthouses, pristine beaches and cliff-hugging fishing villages, the Aberdeenshire Coastal Trail weaves through 165 miles of gratifying saltwater scenery. But expect a few surprises along the way – touring a Victorian prison is one of the top attractions.

DENNIS BARNES/SHUTTERSTOCK ©

How to

Getting around A car is essential for this trip from St Cyrus to Cullen. Hire a car in Dundee, a one-hour drive from the start of the trail. A map of the route can be downloaded from the VisitScotland website.

When to go Seasonal attractions open May to September.

Puffin stop From April to mid-August, head to Fowlsheugh or Troup Head for a chance of spotting puffins.

WILLIAM GALE/SHUTTERSTOCK ©

Unspoilt Beaches

A striking offshore lighthouse and miles of immaculate powdery sand dominated by giant dunes have established **Rattray Head** as a frontrunner for the most standout beach on the route. However, a worthy rival can be found at the expansive golden sands of **St Cyrus**, bordered by grassland that brims with wildflowers and butterflies in the summer.

Newburgh is a popular location for quietly observing hundreds of local seals resting along the shore, while surfing lessons offer a more energetic beach experience at **Fraserburgh**.

BERNI0004/SHUTTERSTOCK ©

Historic Fishing Villages

The cottages of **St Cyrus**, b are hemmed in so tightly between the cliffs and the sea that the waves are almost within touching

Traditional Boat Building

The art of traditional boat building is kept alive in the coastal town of Portsoy, home of the annual **Scottish Traditional Boat Festival**. Throughout the year, visitors are welcome to watch volunteers creating wooden vessels by hand at **The Boatshed**, or view their time-honoured designs in the 17th-century harbour.

Top left Portsoy harbour
Top right Rattray Head
Bottom left St Cyrus beach

distance of their front doors. With no room for a road or cars, it has preserved a real sense of bygone times. Just along the coast is **Pennan**, Crovie's movie star neighbour. Photogenic white- and pastel-painted homes line the water's edge, although it is the red telephone box made famous by the film *Local Hero* that draws the most attention. **Gardenstown** completes this string of picturesque villages.

Dramatic Viewpoints

Perched theatrically on a rocky outcrop, **Dunnottar** is one of Scotland's most iconic castles. The approach path reveals a heart-stirring panorama of the romantic ruin burdened by a turbulent history.

During summer, the cliffs at **Fowlsheugh Nature Reserve** are transformed into seabird citadels. Observe the spectacle from vantage points along the coastal path. At **Bullers of Buchan**, a deep chasm and natural archway created by a collapsed sea cave are visually impressive.

The Local Language

Tune in to a conversation in Northeast Scotland and you will quickly be exposed to a whole new vocabulary. Doric is the native tongue, a subset of the Scots language, one of three main languages spoken in Scotland. To the untrained ear it can be hard to follow, so here are a few common words and phrases to help you out.

Loon – boy

Quine – girl

Ken – know

Muckle – big

Bosie – hug

Fit like? – How are you?

Far hiv ye bin – Where have you been?

Dinna fash yersel – Don't worry about it.

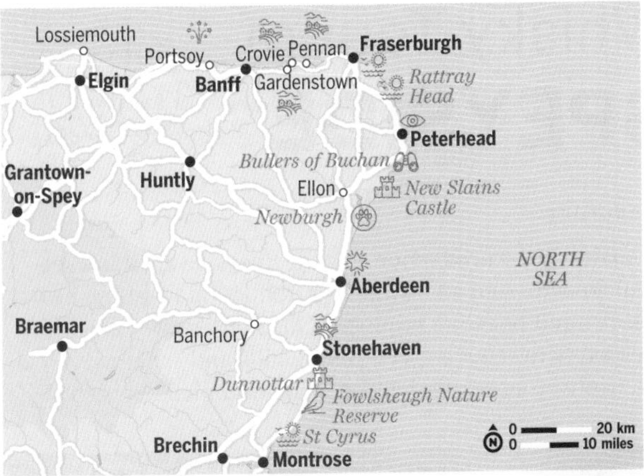

Surprising Stops

The crumbling hulk of **New Slains Castle** is far removed from the stereotypical Scottish fairy-tale dwelling. In fact, if local legend is to be believed, it is the setting for a far more sinister story. After visiting the area, Bram Stoker is said to have used the spooky structure as inspiration for his *Dracula* novel.

This isn't the only building on this stretch of coast with a dark past. Notorious as one of Scotland's toughest jails, **Peterhead Prison** has reinvented itself as a top tourist attraction. The inmates have been moved out and the cell doors permanently opened to allow self-guided tours of the Victorian establishment, which was once stormed by the SAS.

You will be glad you packed a swimming costume when you are floating in the toasty warm seawater at **Stonehaven Lido**. The Olympic-sized open-air pool is heated to a very pleasant 29°C and feels more like the Mediterranean than Scotland.

The 30.5m-high big wheel at **Codona's Amusement Park** affords a unique perspective of Aberdeen Beach. If this sounds too sedate, thrill-seekers are catered for with a range of adrenaline-inducing rides and a state-of-the-art 4D motion theatre.

Left Dunnottar Castle
Below Razorbill, Fowlsheugh Nature Reserve

19 Whisky Tour of SPEYSIDE

DISTILLERIES | HISTORY | CULTURE

The sweet aroma of malt whisky production fills the Speyside air, a bucket-list destination for Scotch aficionados and an excellent introduction for those new to Scotland's national drink. A mind-boggling number of distilleries, over half those in the country, are nestled between the green rolling hills and snaking rivers. Numerous scenic hikes and captivating castles will keep you occupied between drams.

JASPERIMAGE/SHUTTERSTOCK ©

How to

Getting around Buses serve the main Speyside towns but a car is necessary to reach rural distilleries. Car hire is available in Aberdeen. Beware, drink driving is not tolerated; many distillery tours will provide a tasting kit to take away.

When to go Most distillery tours run year-round.

Ride the Whisky Line The 11-mile-long heritage railway runs between Keith and Dufftown.

TIM WRIGHT / ALAMY STOCK PHOTO©

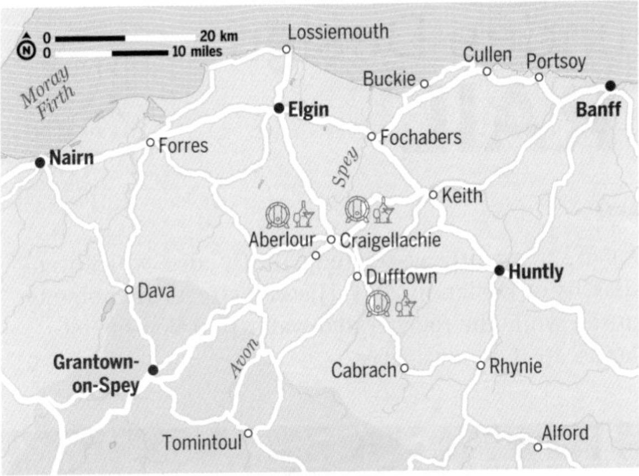

Top left Macallan Distillery, Craigellachie
Bottom left Barrels at Glen Moray Distillery

Malt Whisky Trail If the vast choice of whisky-themed options leaves you feeling a little intoxicated, this curated trail narrows it down to nine locations. Visit the spiritual home of notable names like Glenfiddich or lesser-known labels like Cardhu, the only distillery pioneered by a woman. The Speyside Cooperage makes and repairs over 100,000 casks annually. Take a tour to discover why there would be no whisky as we know it without these wooden barrels.

Spirit of Speyside Festival Each May, whisky fans from around the world descend on Speyside for a celebratory gathering of Scotland's water of life. Village halls, whisky bars and even historic castles open up to welcome the public to an eclectic mix of experiences. For the best part of a week, hundreds of events take place across a wide range of venues. Book tickets online in advance.

Whisky bars Join Craigellachie locals for a dram at **The Highlander Inn** or **Quaich Bar**; ask for recommendations if you're struggling to choose from the extensive malts on offer. In Aberlour, **The Mash Tun** holds exclusive Glenfarclas casks among its ample collection, while **The Still** is lined from floor to ceiling with bottles from every whisky region of Scotland. Order a whisky flight at **The Seven Stills** in Dufftown to compare and contrast a range of malts.

Highland Games

Pair whisky with a day out to one of the region's Highland Games for an iconic taste of Scotland. From the swirling of the bagpipes to the swishing of the kilts and the tossing of the caber, these competitive historic gatherings have been a part of Scottish culture for centuries. Four local communities stage events during July and August that welcome participation from international visitors in a variety of unique events. Compete in uphill whisky barrel rolling at Tomintoul, race on an old message bike in Forres, hurl a haggis in Aberlour or test your speed in the overseas race in Dufftown.

20 Dundee Design TRAIL

HERITAGE | DESIGN | DAY TRIP

'Innovative' and 'cool' are frequently associated with Dundee, which was named the UK's first Unesco City of Design in 2014. Historic streets are home to quirky cafes and vintage stores, while the regenerated waterfront boasts 21st-century architecture and landscaped public spaces.

PHOTOGRAPHICS/ALAMY LIVE NEWS/ALAMY ©

Explore Beyond the City

Take in the surrounding scenery by hiring an e-bike through the city's sharing system (rideondundee.com). To avoid the traffic, start from Slessor Gardens and follow the cycle path alongside the River Tay for 4.5 miles. Stop at the pretty seaside village of Broughty Ferry, home to a 15th-century castle, golden sandy beach and cute cafes.

Trip Notes

Getting around Dundee is a compact city, best explored on foot. Dundee railway station is located opposite V&A Dundee – arrive in under 90 minutes by a direct connection from Edinburgh, Glasgow or Aberdeen. If arriving by car, download a map of public car parks from the Dundee City Council website.

When to go Attractions are open year-round.

Top tip Buy a combined ticket for RRS Discovery and Verdant Works to save money.

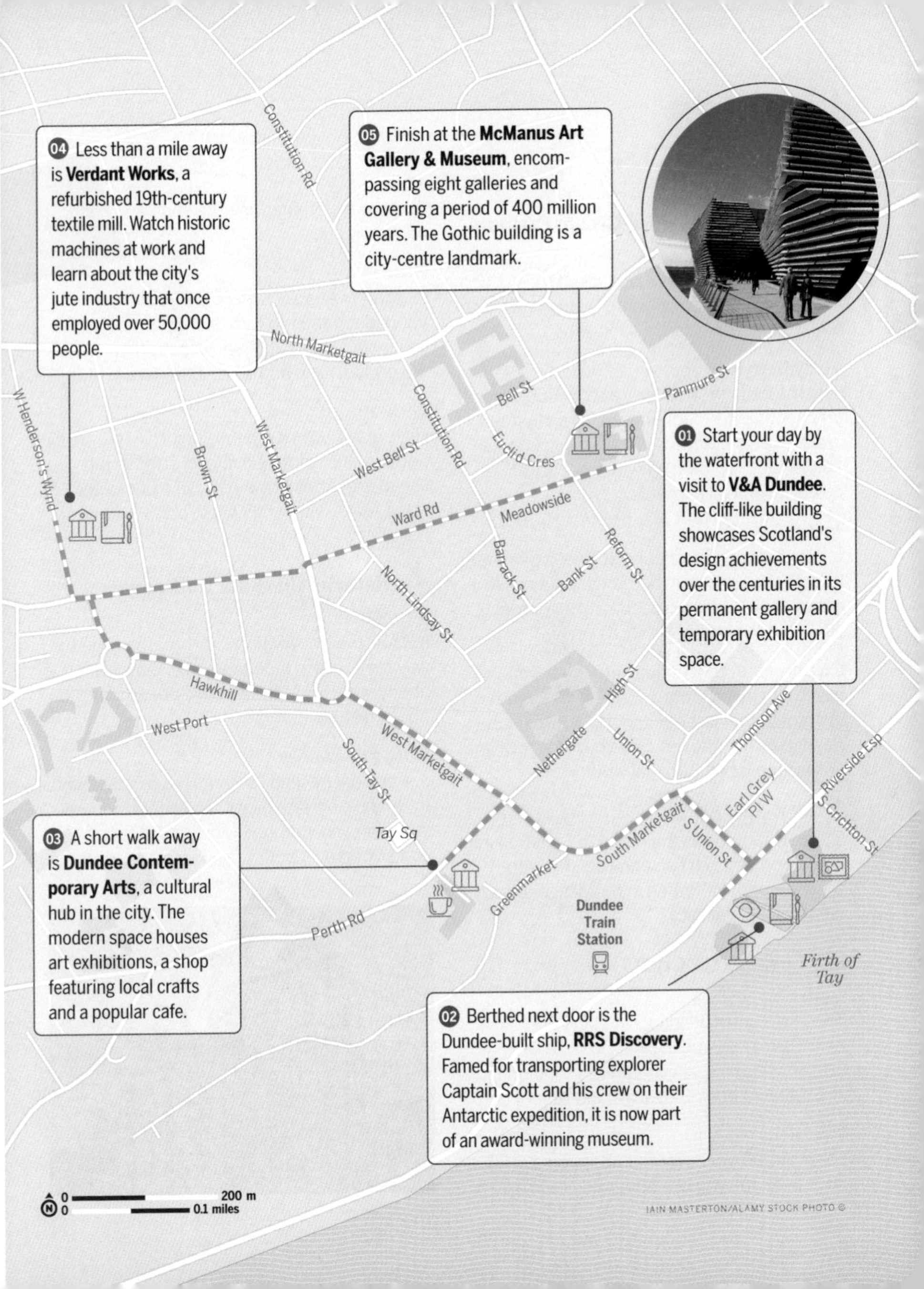

04 Less than a mile away is **Verdant Works**, a refurbished 19th-century textile mill. Watch historic machines at work and learn about the city's jute industry that once employed over 50,000 people.

05 Finish at the **McManus Art Gallery & Museum**, encompassing eight galleries and covering a period of 400 million years. The Gothic building is a city-centre landmark.

01 Start your day by the waterfront with a visit to **V&A Dundee**. The cliff-like building showcases Scotland's design achievements over the centuries in its permanent gallery and temporary exhibition space.

03 A short walk away is **Dundee Contemporary Arts**, a cultural hub in the city. The modern space houses art exhibitions, a shop featuring local crafts and a popular cafe.

02 Berthed next door is the Dundee-built ship, **RRS Discovery**. Famed for transporting explorer Captain Scott and his crew on their Antarctic expedition, it is now part of an award-winning museum.

Listings

BEST OF THE REST

Seaside Cafes & Ice-Cream Parlours

Sweetpea Cafe £
Artisan food served in a rustic setting close to Broughty Ferry train station. Tasty gluten-free and vegan choices are a speciality.

Aunty Bettys £
Join the beachfront queue at this iconic ice-cream parlour in Stonehaven for an Instagram-worthy creation. Pile up the scoops before topping them off with an array of colourful embellishments.

Teas & Seas £
Cream teas are the offering at Teas & Seas near Rosehearty. Indulge in homemade scones in a quirky fishing-themed cabin with sea views.

Portsoy Ice Cream £
Experimental concoctions are the flavour of the day in this award-winning ice-cream shop near the harbour in Portsoy. Previous headliners include hot cross bun, unicorn and cranachan laced with real whisky.

Rockpool Cafe £
Cullen is famous as the home of Cullen Skink, a Scottish smoked fish chowder. Rockpool Cafe is a popular option in the village to sample this local delicacy.

Local Art & Crafts

Logie Steading
The 1920s farm buildings at Logie Steading near Forres have been repurposed as an artisan shopping village. Offerings include secondhand books, local art and whisky.

Johnstons of Elgin
For over 200 years, local craftspeople in Elgin have been turning raw fibre into fine wool and cashmere clothing. Visit the shop and historic mill for a tour.

Hand Pict
A group of Angus crafters and artists have banded together to form a cooperative with a gallery in Letham that showcases their work. A truly local and authentic experience.

The Barn
High-quality contemporary Scottish pieces by both up-and-coming designers and established artists sit side by side in a dedicated retail space within this multi-arts venue near Banchory.

Historic Abbeys & Cathedrals

Arbroath Abbey
In 1320 the Declaration of Arbroath paved the way for Scottish Independence. Sent from the abbey, a copy of the symbolic document is on public display.

Pluscarden Abbey
A scene unchanged for centuries can be found at Britain's only medieval monastery still serving its original purpose. Monks tend to bees and sit in prayer below rainbow glass windows.

Arbroath Abbey

Elgin Cathedral
For fantastic landscape views, climb the tower of the ruined 13th-century cathedral known as the 'Lantern of the North'. A collection of intricately carved stones is a highlight.

Garden Escapes

Glamis Castle
The childhood home of the Queen Mother boasts ornamental gardens fit for royalty. Spooky sculptures depicting scenes from Macbeth lurk in the woodland shadows.

Langley Park Gardens
Lovingly nurtured by the current owners, views extend across the wildflower meadow towards Montrose while a heady scent fills the air in the colourful walled gardens.

Pitmedden Garden
Wander through the recreated Scottish Renaissance garden, inspired by 17th-century designs. The extravagant layout features almost 6 miles of box hedging and over 200 fruit trees.

Gordon Castle Walled Garden
Designed to be as productive as it is beautiful, everything in this 200-year-old kitchen garden in Fochabers is grown with purpose. From gin to beauty products, the home-grown range is inspired.

Johnston Gardens
This small oasis in the west end of Aberdeen is a photographer's dream. The varied palette of colours and textures provides the perfect backdrop for a tumbling waterfall and Japanese-style bridge.

Craft Beer & Gin Tours

Brewdog
Infamous for its irreverent marketing, Brewdog reveals some of their behind-the-scenes secrets in a tour of the original brewhouse and Lone Wolf Distillery in Ellon. The 90-minute 'DogWalk' includes four tastings.

LEE SNIDER/GETTY IMAGES ©
Pitmedden Garden

Brew Toon
This microbrewery with heritage and provenance at its heart has revived a defunct tradition in the east-coast fishing town of Peterhead. Appreciate handcrafted beers in the taproom.

71 Brewing
Street art, industrial architecture and rustic decor are befitting of Dundee's cool city vibe. Sip on a welcome beer before walking through the brewing process and savouring a few more samples.

City of Aberdeen Distillery
A historic railway arch in the city centre provides an unexpected venue for this hip distillery. Take a tour or create your own gin while trains rumble overhead.

Glenrinnes Distillery
View the Highland landscape of the organic estate surrounding the distillery from a mountaintop before a tutored tasting of gin and vodka in a fully immersive half-day experience.

Scan to find more things to do in Northeast Scotland online

SOUTHERN HIGHLANDS & ISLANDS

ADVENTURE | COAST | HISTORY

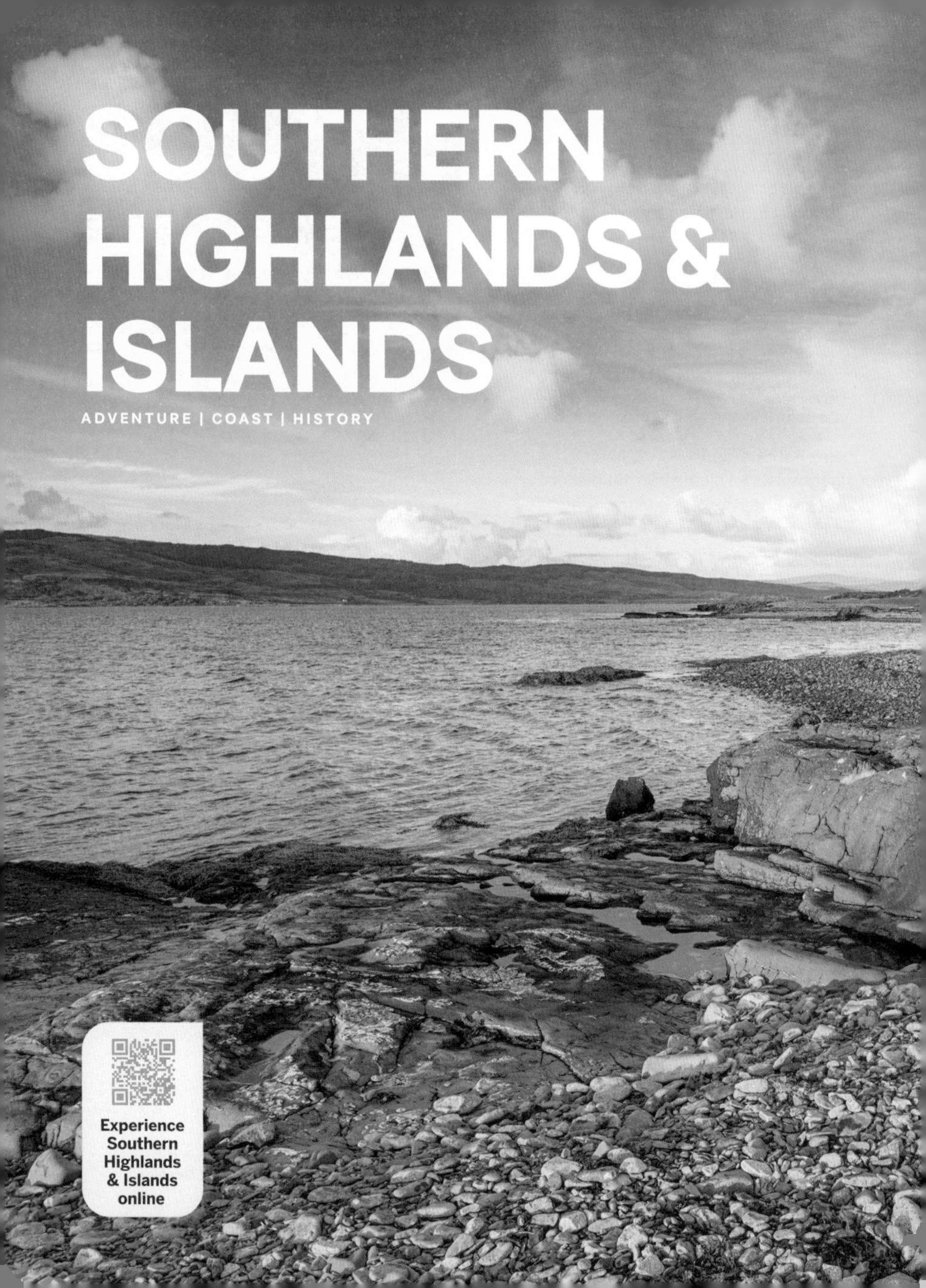

Experience Southern Highlands & Islands online

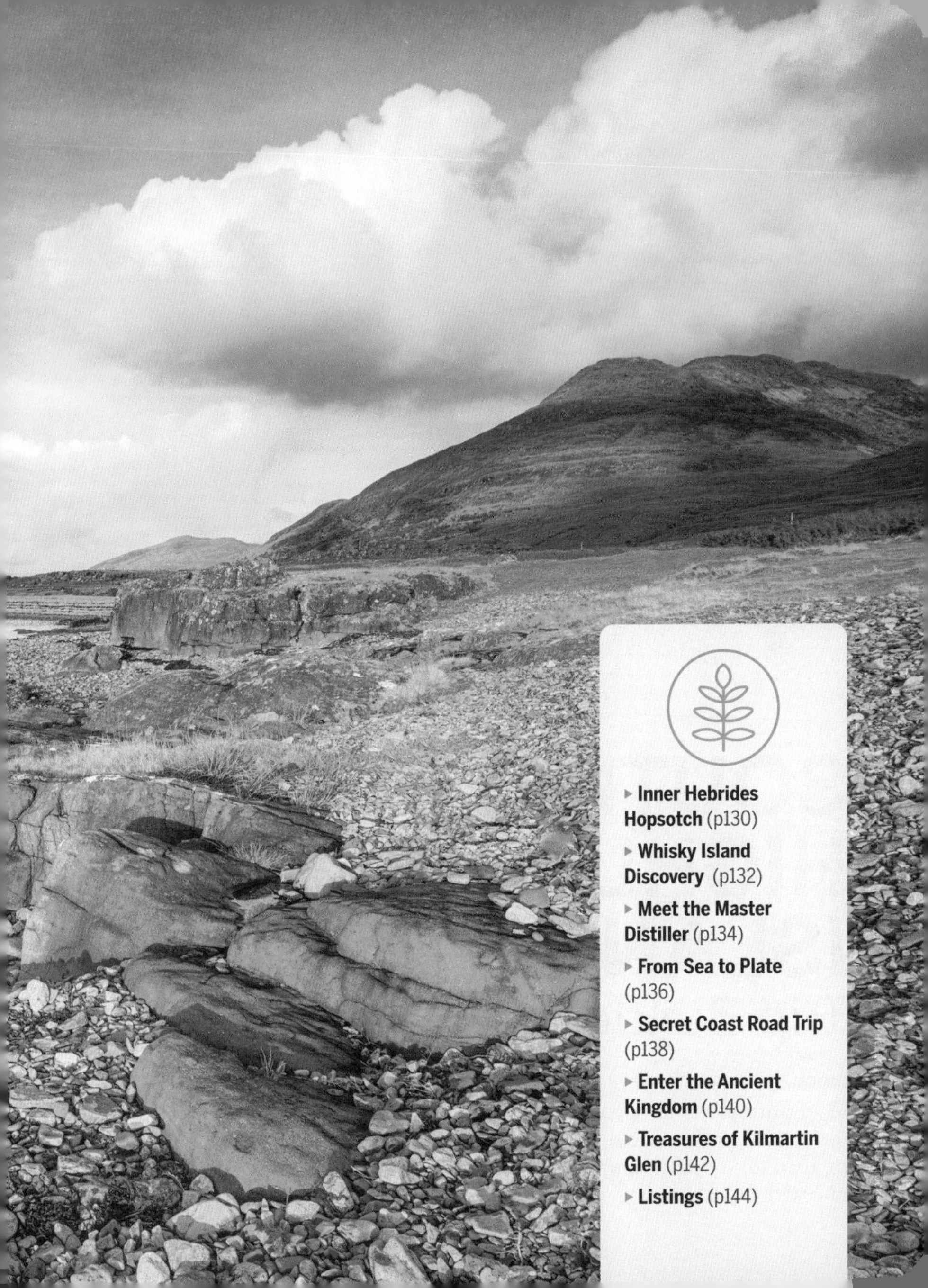

▸ **Inner Hebrides Hopsotch** (p130)

▸ **Whisky Island Discovery** (p132)

▸ **Meet the Master Distiller** (p134)

▸ **From Sea to Plate** (p136)

▸ **Secret Coast Road Trip** (p138)

▸ **Enter the Ancient Kingdom** (p140)

▸ **Treasures of Kilmartin Glen** (p142)

▸ **Listings** (p144)

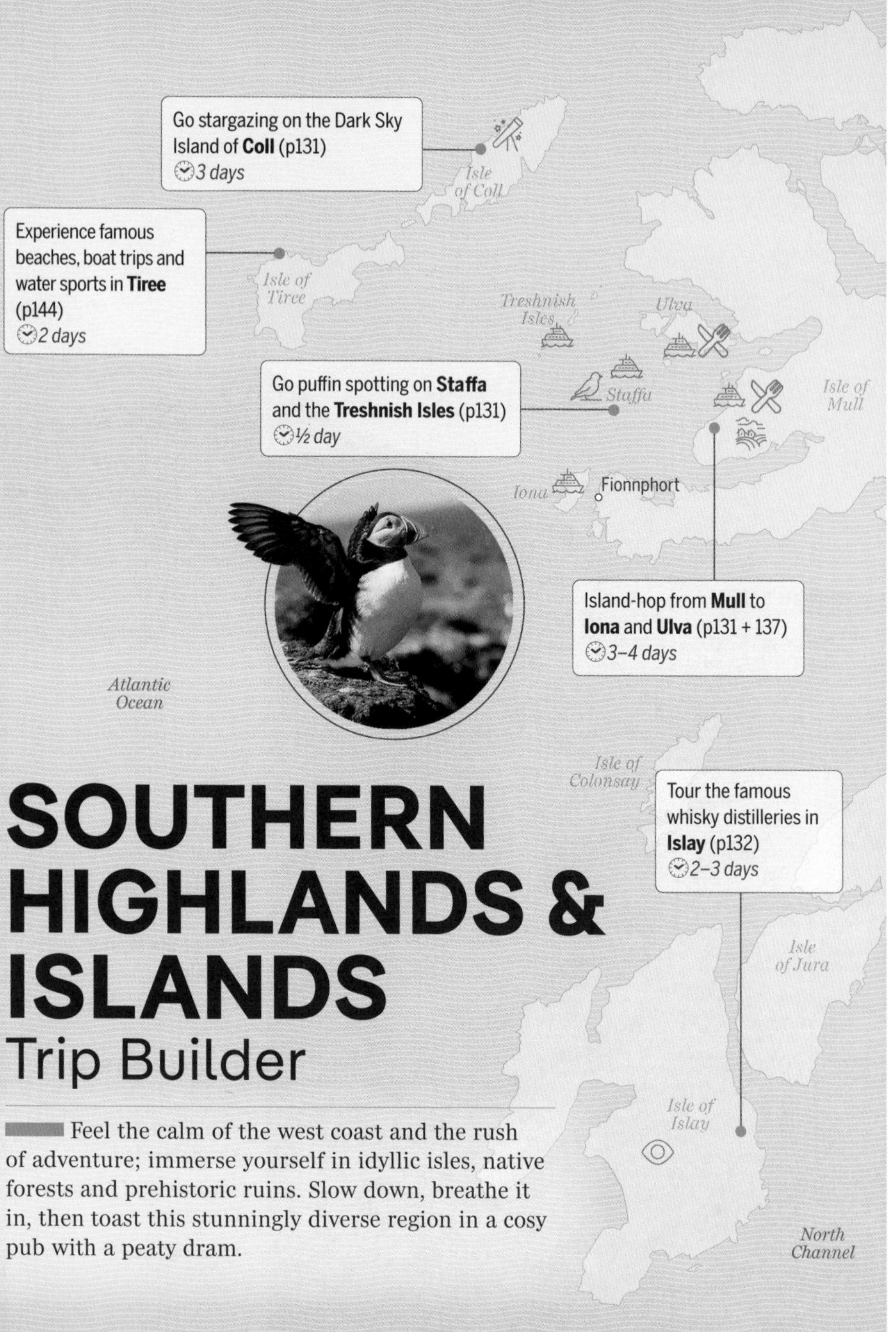
Go stargazing on the Dark Sky Island of **Coll** (p131)
3 days
Isle of Coll
Experience famous beaches, boat trips and water sports in **Tiree** (p144)
2 days
Isle of Tiree
Treshnish Isles
Ulva
Go puffin spotting on **Staffa** and the **Treshnish Isles** (p131)
½ day
Staffa
Isle of Mull
Iona
Fionnphort
Island-hop from **Mull** to **Iona** and **Ulva** (p131 + 137)
3–4 days
Atlantic Ocean
Isle of Colonsay
Tour the famous whisky distilleries in **Islay** (p132)
2–3 days
Isle of Jura
Isle of Islay
North Channel

SOUTHERN HIGHLANDS & ISLANDS

Trip Builder

Feel the calm of the west coast and the rush of adventure; immerse yourself in idyllic isles, native forests and prehistoric ruins. Slow down, breathe it in, then toast this stunningly diverse region in a cosy pub with a peaty dram.

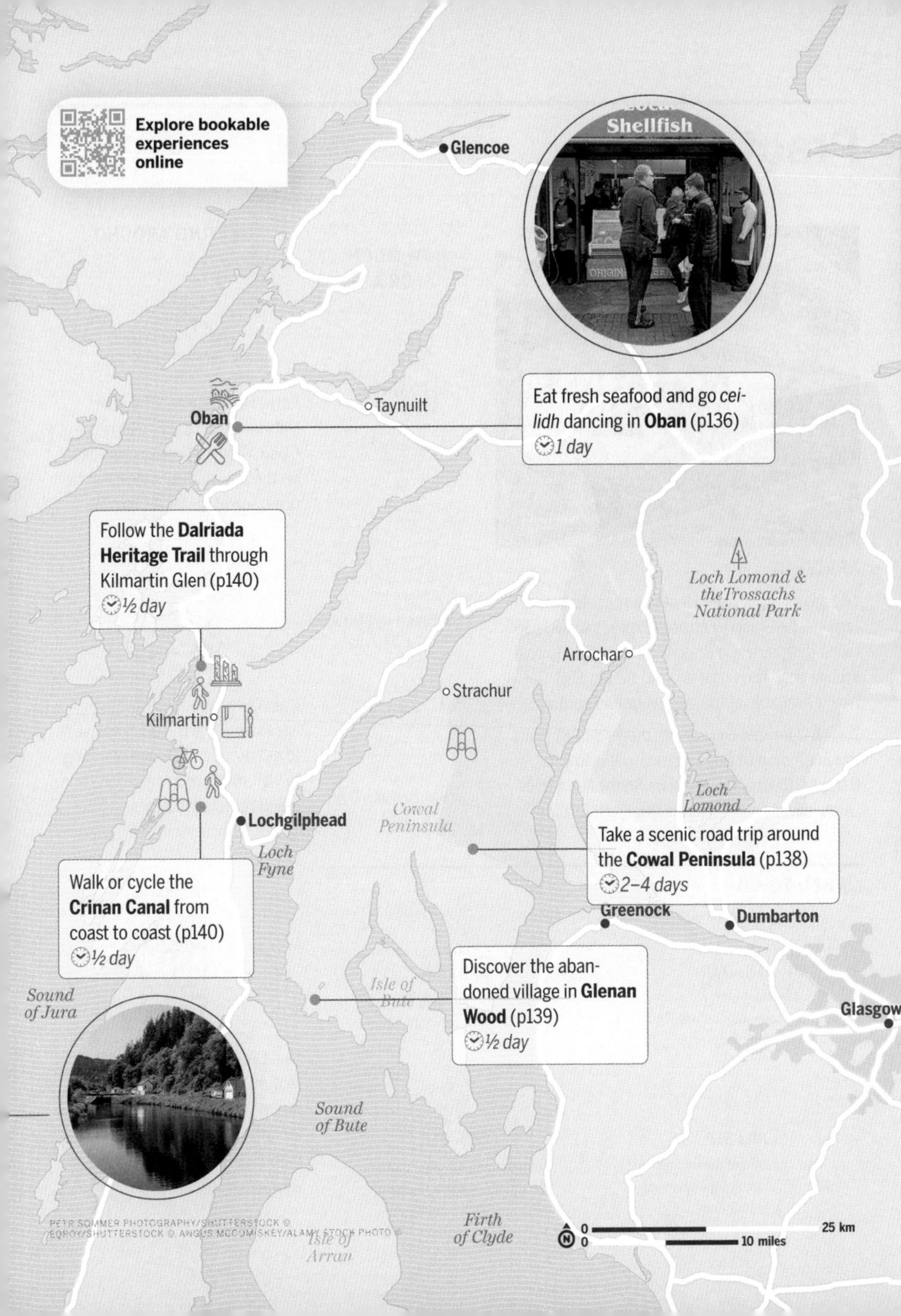

Explore bookable experiences online

- Glencoe

Eat fresh seafood and go *ceilidh* dancing in **Oban** (p136)
⏱ 1 day

Oban
○ Taynuilt

Follow the **Dalriada Heritage Trail** through Kilmartin Glen (p140)
⏱ ½ day

Kilmartin

Arrochar○

Loch Lomond & theTrossachs National Park

○ Strachur

● Lochgilphead

Cowal Peninsula

Loch Fyne

Loch Lomond

Take a scenic road trip around the **Cowal Peninsula** (p138)
⏱ 2–4 days

Walk or cycle the **Crinan Canal** from coast to coast (p140)
⏱ ½ day

Discover the abandoned village in **Glenan Wood** (p139)
⏱ ½ day

Isle of Bute

Greenock

Dumbarton

Sound of Jura

Glasgow

Sound of Bute

Firth of Clyde

Isle of Arran

PETR SOMMER PHOTOGRAPHY/SHUTTERSTOCK ©
/EQROY/SHUTTERSTOCK ©, ANGUS MCCOMISKEY/ALAMY STOCK PHOTO ©

⊕N 0 ——— 25 km
 0 ——— 10 miles

Practicalities

EDINBURGHCITYMOM/SHUTTERSTOCK ©

ARRIVING

Glasgow Airport The closest airport to the region. The Glasgow Airport Express service 500 takes 15 minutes to the city centre; tickets cost £9 one way. Taxis cost around £25 to £30. Car hire is available at the airport or city centre.

Buses Operated by Citylink, buses depart from the Buchanan St Bus Station in Glasgow for Campbeltown and Oban. The ScotRail train to Oban leaves from Glasgow Queen St Station.

HOW MUCH FOR A

Distillery tour
£10

½ dozen oysters
£12

Wildlife boat trip
£60

GETTING AROUND

Ferry Hop between the Inner Hebrides with CalMac ferries from Oban. Foot passengers can pay on the day, but vehicles must be pre-booked for larger ferries.

Car While a car isn't strictly necessary, it is the quickest way to get around if you are planning to visit multiple destinations and reach remote locations.

Bus Citylink and West Coast Motors operate the bus services around the region. Some services are infrequent so advanced planning using the timetables is advised. Book seats in advance.

WHEN TO GO

JAN–MAR
Cold weather, wintry scenery and not busy with tourists. Dark skies for stargazing.

APR–JUN
Flowers, longer daylight hours and the best puffin spotting.

JUL–SEP
Peak season and the warmest weather. All attractions open and lots of visitors.

OCT–DEC
Autumn colours, fewer visitors and drams of whisky by the fire.

EATING & DRINKING

Seafood The west coast is famed for its fresh seafood and Oban is known as the 'Seafood Capital of Scotland'. Order a seafood platter to try a bit of everything. For something hot and more budget friendly, you can't beat fish and chips by the sea.

Whisky Sample Islay's smoky single malt whiskies straight from the source at one of the distilleries or in a cosy local pub.

Must-try seafood platter
Fisherman's Kitchen (p137)

Best coffee & cake
Brambles of Inveraray (p145)

WHERE TO STAY

This region has a wide range of accommodation options to suit all budgets; hostels, glamping sites, B&Bs, guesthouses and hotels. Choose one or two base locations and explore from there.

Place	Pro/Con
Tighnabruaich	A peaceful village on Argyll's Secret Coast, perfect for exploring the Cowal Peninsula. Quiet at night and not touristy.
Oban	Busy port town with great pubs and dining options. Excellent transport links.
Arinagour	Beautiful bay and main settlement in Coll: ferry port, local shop, post office, community centre and hotel-bar are here.
Bowmore	Ideal central base on Islay with shops, restaurants and a distillery. No evening public transport.
Tobermory	Colourful harbour town on Mull with boat trips to Staffa and the Treshnish Isles. Quality accommodation can be expensive.
Iona	Small and serene island, easy to explore on foot. Busy during the day in peak season, always quiet at night.

CONNECT & FIND YOUR WAY

Wi-fi Most hotels, bars, cafes and restaurants have guest wi-fi, and there is free wi-fi on CalMac ferries and at ferry ports. The connection can be slow and temperamental in some locations.

Navigation The region is easy to navigate using road signs, local maps and Google Maps. Do research and download your route in advance in case you can't get online.

TRAVEL DISCOUNTS

Save money with the Citylink Explorer Pass and CalMac Hopscotch tickets. The best ScotRail train fares go on sale 12 weeks in advance.

MONEY

Card payments are widely accepted but it is always advisable to carry cash (including coins) for the honesty boxes and small businesses that only take cash. ATMs can be found in the main towns.

21 Inner Hebrides HOPSCOTCH

FERRIES | BEACHES | WILDLIFE

Feel the buzz of boarding the ferry from Oban, 'Gateway to the Isles', to the dreamy Inner Hebrides. Embrace the slow pace and discover each island's unique traits: the energising activities, postcard villages and paradise shores with a rugged Scottish edge.

Trip Notes

Getting around CalMac operates ferries between Oban and the islands, while Staffa Trips and Staffa Tours sail to Staffa and the Treshnish Isles. Walkers and cyclists are well catered for; to cover more ground, take a car.

When to go Spring for wildflowers; May to July for puffins; August for heather; and autumn for dark skies, vibrant landscapes and fewer crowds.

Top tip Save money with the Hopscotch 19 Coll & Tiree ticket.

Eagle Eye

Sea eagles are often spotted around the sea lochs on Mull's west coast. Look out for their broad plank-like wings and white tails (adults only). They can soar for long periods without flapping their wings and can be seen circling high overhead.

Local tip from Martin Keivers, *owner and skipper at Mull Charters @mull_charters*

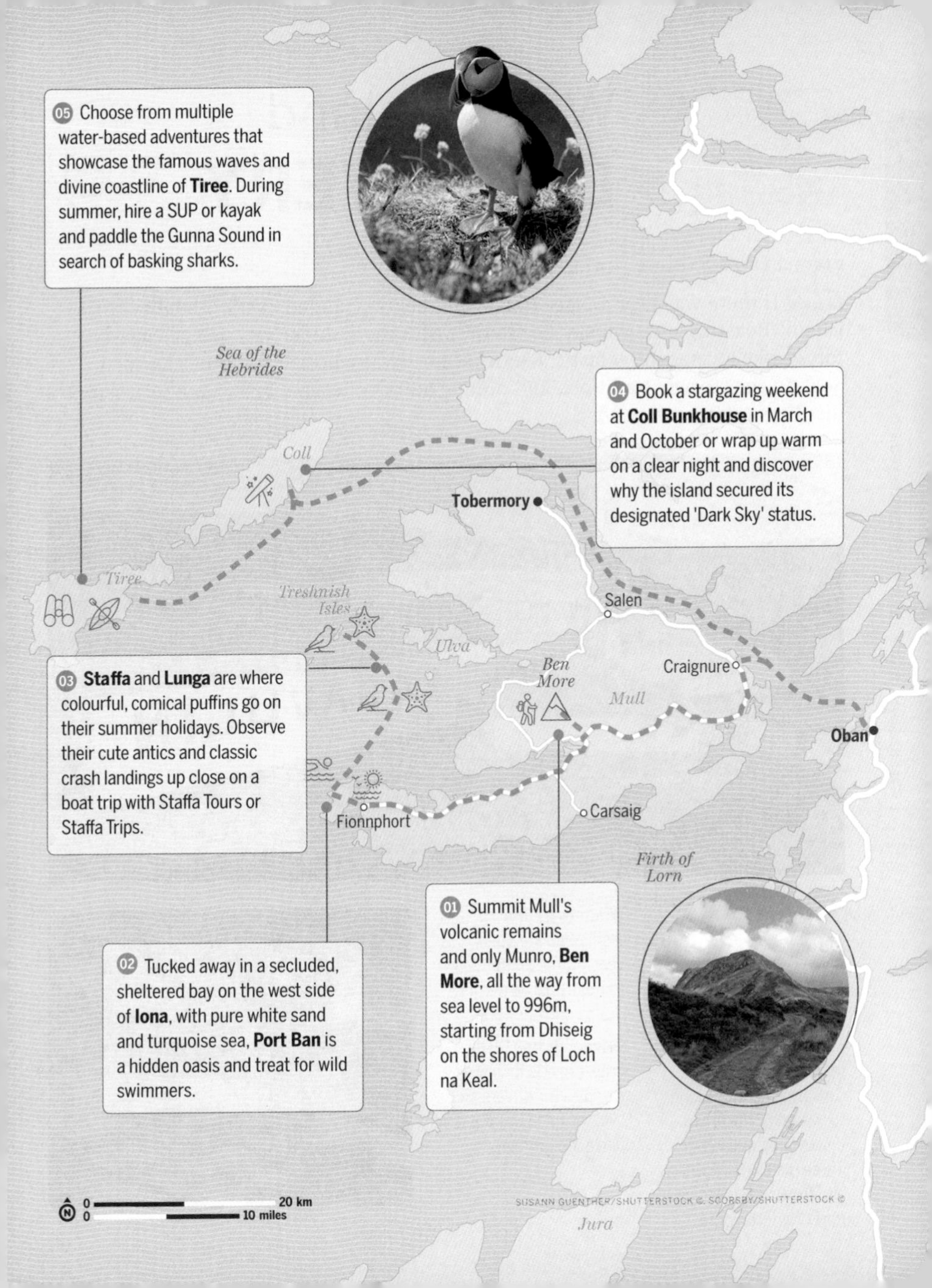

05 Choose from multiple water-based adventures that showcase the famous waves and divine coastline of **Tiree**. During summer, hire a SUP or kayak and paddle the Gunna Sound in search of basking sharks.

04 Book a stargazing weekend at **Coll Bunkhouse** in March and October or wrap up warm on a clear night and discover why the island secured its designated 'Dark Sky' status.

03 **Staffa** and **Lunga** are where colourful, comical puffins go on their summer holidays. Observe their cute antics and classic crash landings up close on a boat trip with Staffa Tours or Staffa Trips.

02 Tucked away in a secluded, sheltered bay on the west side of **Iona**, with pure white sand and turquoise sea, **Port Ban** is a hidden oasis and treat for wild swimmers.

01 Summit Mull's volcanic remains and only Munro, **Ben More**, all the way from sea level to 996m, starting from Dhiseig on the shores of Loch na Keal.

SUSANN GUENTHER/SHUTTERSTOCK © SOORSBY/SHUTTERSTOCK ©

22 Whisky Island DISCOVERY

DISTILLERIES | TOURS | TRADITIONS

If there was ever a place to be voluntarily stranded, it's Scotland's 'whisky island'. Boasting nine whisky distilleries, with more under way, Islay is heaven for whisky lovers, and a fast-track ticket for those who are yet to be charmed. Soak in the stories, traditions and unique quirks of each whisky on a series of distillery tours with a twist.

IAIN MASTERTON/ALAMY STOCK PHOTO ©

How to

Getting here & around CalMac runs ferries from Kennacraig and Oban; Loganair flies from Glasgow. Most distilleries can be reached by bus (Islay Coaches operates Monday to Saturday), local taxi, e-bike or by walking the Three Distilleries Pathway and the Bruichladdich to Port Charlotte route.

When to go The distilleries are open year-round. September for festivals; winter for drams and cosy fires.

Drivers drams Distilleries provide takeaway samples for drivers and cyclists to enjoy later. The perfect nightcap!

BARMALINI/SHUTTERSTOCK ©

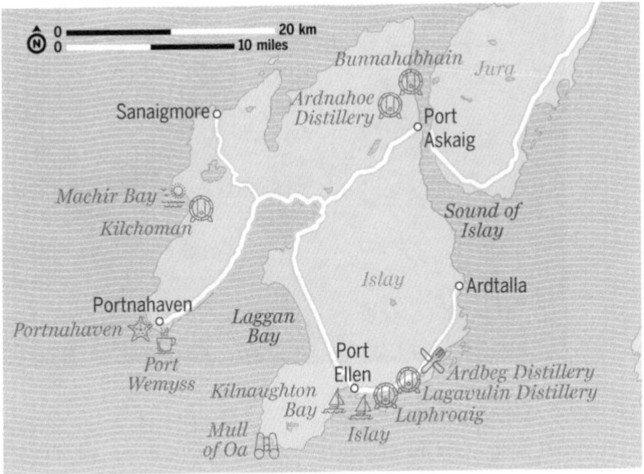

Top left Lagavulin Distillery
Bottom left Tasting single-malt whiskies on Islay

From the cask Start the day with whisky-tinted stars in your eyes, on the Warehouse Experience at **Lagavulin Distillery**. This intimate tasting session includes a series of exclusive drams drawn straight from the cask, courtesy of local 'Lagavulin Legend' and all-round barrel of banter Iain McArthur. **Bunnahabhain** offers a similar, highly acclaimed Warehouse 9 Tasting Experience. This distillery has a stylish visitor centre which commands breathtaking views of Bunnahabhain Bay and the wild Paps of Jura beyond.

Food pairing While the first batch of whisky matures at **Ardnahoe**, Islay's ninth distillery, indulge in a mouth-watering whisky and food pairing session. Islay shellfish, haggis spiced venison and chocolate orange tart, to name a few, are each carefully matched with a Scottish single malt.

On the beach Settle into the sand at Machir Bay and learn all about Islay's only farm distillery on a Beach Tasting with the team at **Kilchoman**. Taste four whiskies from the core range, including a wonderfully fitting dram of Machir Bay. At low tide, watch a shipwreck emerge on the horizon.

The full works Experience the end-to-end journey of **Laphroaig** on an immersive tour: hike to the water source and cut the peat, sample single cask whisky in the warehouse and hand pour your own souvenir bottle. Claim your own plot of peat by becoming a 'Friend of Laphroaig'.

Eat & Explore

Grab a delicious, bistro-style lunch from the new 'Ardstream' trailer at **Ardbeg Distillery** and look out for otters on the hunt for local crab on the pier.

Enjoy an alfresco afternoon tea from the honesty cake cupboard at **Port Wemyss** followed by seal spotting at **Portnahaven**.

Visit the RSPB Nature Reserve on the **Mull of Oa** then watch the sunset at **Kilnaughton Bay** with pizza from Peatzeria or SeaSalt Bistro.

Join **Islay Sea Adventures** for a wildlife boat tour, or paddle the coast with **Kayak Wild Islay**.

Tips from By Emma Clark, *owner at Glenegedale House, Islay @glenegedalehouseislay*

Meet the Master Distiller

JIM MCEWAN, MASTER DISTILLER, ISLAY

Introducing Jim McEwan, the 'cask whisperer' and all-round whisky mastermind, who has dedicated more than 50 years of his life to the industry. From peeking through the windows of Bowmore Distillery as a child, to running the whole operation and putting Islay whisky on a global stage, Jim is a man who certainly knows his drams.

13THREEPHOTOGRAPHY/SHUTTERSTOCK ©

Left Whisky barrels at Bowmore Distillery
Middle Master Distiller Jim McEwan
Right Bruichladdich Distillery

A Dream Come True

Growing up in the village of Bowmore on Islay, Jim spent his childhood playing around the harbour and shoreline, and being chased away from the distillery by the manager. 'The distillery was like a theme park to me; it was so exciting. I always wanted to work there.'

Jim's aspiration was realised in 1963, when he secured his first job in the warehouse at age 15, which later led to an apprenticeship as a cooper, taught by Scotland's longest-serving cooper, David Bell. 'It was a dream come true to build casks; I loved the smell of the oak, the whisky, the burning of the charcoal.'

Never one to stop learning, Jim moved to Glasgow to train as a blender, and after three years was creating perfect blended whiskies for export around the world. He returned to Islay, this time as the manager of Bowmore Distillery, which was an honour for Jim, having started there as a boy.

His next big adventure was as Global Brand Ambassador for Bowmore, during which time he travelled the world extensively, introducing countries to Islay single malt for the first time – heavily peated single malts at that! 'In Asia they thought there was something wrong with the whisky because of the smoky flavour,' he laughs.

Jim thrived on the opportunity to educate people about whisky and his home island. 'When you love a product like whisky, as I do, and you love Islay, it doesn't feel like work. It was a great opportunity and a privilege.'

Bestowed Upon Us

Back permanently on home soil, Jim continued working his magic in the industry, and in 2001 moved to

Bruichladdich Distillery, where he was appointed as Master Distiller. He played a significant role in the revival of this distillery and is responsible for the famous Octomore range, said to be the world's peatiest whisky.

Following his retirement in 2015, Jim was tempted back into the industry to lend his expertise to Islay's newest distillery, Ardnahoe. Now, aside from selling some of his own personal casks, he has stepped back from the business and pursues a quiet life. He enjoys walking with a local group on the island and spending time with his family, including four grandchildren on the mainland.

> There is a great friendship between all the distilleries; it's a spiritual family.

Talking about the industry on Islay today, Jim says, 'I was born and raised here and the island has never been better, nor has the quality of the whisky. There is a great friendship between all the distilleries; it's a spiritual family. Whisky is our global success story and it's a credit to those working in the industry.'

When asked why Scotland is so great at making whisky, Jim answers without a second thought: 'I think whisky reflects our character perfectly: it's warm, comforting, genuine and sincere. It's as if whisky was bestowed upon us. We've cherished it and looked after it, treated it with respect. We've done that as a nation, and that's something to be proud of.'

Quick Facts about Scotch Whisky

Single malt is whisky that has been produced at a single distillery using only malted barley. Blended whisky combines various whiskies from different distilleries and can include grain whisky.

The five main whisky regions in Scotland are the Highlands, Lowlands, Islands, Speyside and Islay. They each have their own unique characteristics.

Whisky is matured in pre-used casks and the type of cask influences the colour and flavour. The most common casks are bourbon and sherry.

Islay is famous for its smoky whisky. This comes from the peat that is used to dry the barley.

23 From Sea to PLATE

SEAFOOD | CULTURE | LOCAL

Serving up some of the finest seafood in the world, Scotland's dazzling west-coast waters are much more than just a feast for the eyes. Follow the Seafood Trail through Argyll on a culinary quest, from bustling harbours and lesser-known islands to sprawling lochs and secluded spots, in search of fresh catch, seafood shacks and high-end hospitality.

How to

Getting around Road-trip the region or take public transport to locations served by bus (westcoastmotors.co.uk) or ScotRail between Glasgow and Oban.

When to go Fresh seafood is available year-round. Some restaurants and eateries close during low season: always best to check.

Top tip If you see squat lobster on the menu, go for it. Not actually lobster, this quirky crustacean is sweeter than prawns and is a lucky find for seafoodies.

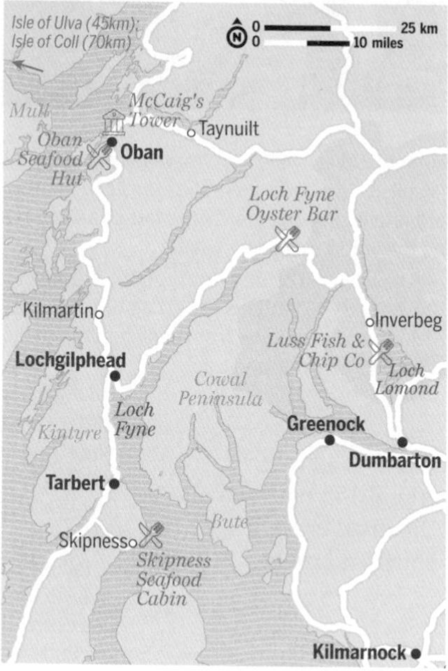

Seafood shacks The rustic-green **Oban Seafood Hut** is a pier-side seafood institution. Budget-friendly seafood is dished out on paper plates, to the sound of seagulls and ferry engines; alternatively, take your prawn-packed sandwich to the peaceful surroundings of McCaig's Tower.

Huddled into a corner of the remote Kintyre Peninsula, with views across to Arran, the family-run **Skipness Seafood Cabin** is where fresh seafood platters are popularly paired with sunshine and a bottle of wine.

Lochside vistas Tuck into a fish supper or grilled lobster and chips on the banks of Loch Lomond, courtesy of new kid on the loch, **Luss**

Above right Seafood from the Isle of Mull
Right Luss Fish & Chip Co, Loch Lomond

Sustainable Shellfish

Seafood is a way of life in Argyll and sustainability is more important than ever. Most shellfish in Argyll are harvested by ethical and environmentally conscious methods, where all undersized and unwanted catch is returned to the sea alive.

Drew Stevenson, *Fisherman's Kitchen, Isle of Seil @thefishermans kitchen_oban_*

Fish & Chip Co. Further west, Loch Fyne is famed for its bounty of oysters. Try them fresh, with grilled smoked cheddar or in panko breadcrumbs at **Loch Fyne Oyster Bar** near Inveraray.

Island eats Operate the low-tech, high-novelty system to summon the tiny ferry from Mull to Ulva for local shellfish at **The Boathouse**; fresh oysters with Guinness is a long-standing tradition. At the Ross of Mull, exceptional, creative dishes at **Ninth Wave** combine seafood caught from the owners' boat that day with foraged ingredients and home-grown produce. Cross to Coll to slurp on delicious homemade spaghetti with creamy lobster or chilli ginger garlic crab at **Coll Hotel** while overlooking Arinagour Bay and the small fishing boats that supplied the goods.

24 Secret Coast ROAD TRIP

SCENERY | PENINSULA | DRIVING

Cradled by the Kyles of Bute and Loch Fyne, Argyll's Secret Coast is just one part of the surprisingly overlooked Cowal Peninsula. Close to the central belt, yet far from the beaten track, these roads less travelled lead to magical woodland trails, hidden beaches, gastronomic gems, and all the wild charm and rich history of the Highlands, without the crowds.

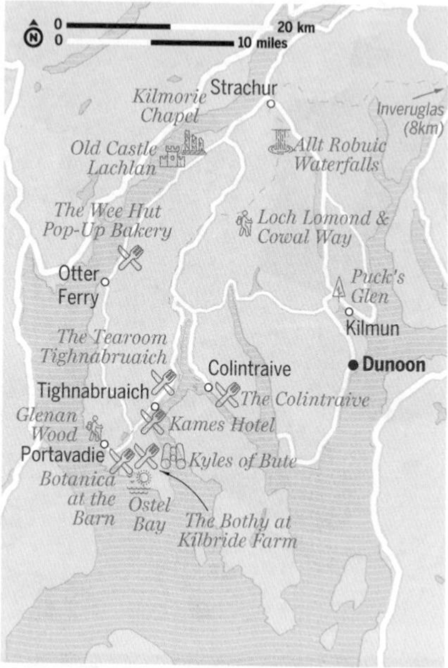

How to

Getting around Hire a car in Glasgow and take the scenic route (A83). Start in Strachur and explore the three-part peninsula.

When to visit Spring for bluebells; September for the Kyles 10 Miles road race; autumn for the beautiful colours.

Relax Finish with a soak in Scotland's largest outdoor heated infinity pool at the luxury Portavadie Spa overlooking Loch Fyne.

Scenic Stops

The enchanting, rocky gorge of **Puck's Glen** is characterised by vibrant moss, inward-slanting trees and crystal-clear pools fed by waterfalls. Tales of frolicking fairies become more believable with every step. Follow the lesser-known Waterfall Trail through Glenbranter to **Allt Robuic waterfalls**.

For jaw-dropping vistas of the undulating coastline, pull over at the **Kyles of Bute viewpoint** on the A8003 near Tighnabruaich.

Ostel Bay is a stunning beach, arched by sand dunes at the end of a farm track.

Right Old Castle Lachlan, Loch Fyne

Across the sea, the shadowy layers of Arran's lofty peaks dominate the horizon.

Discover **Old Castle Lachlan** on Loch Fyne; a ruined fortress draped in ivy. Medieval **Kilmorie Chapel**, a short walk away, is where Maclachlan clan chiefs were laid to rest.

Take a break from driving and walk a section of the **Loch Lomond and Cowal Way.**

Local Eats

Fresh seafood and meat sourced from local farms are served with warm hospitality in the seaside **Kames Hotel** and **The Colintraive**, next to the ferry port for Bute.

The Tearoom Tighnabruaich is famed for its mammoth slices of cake and perfect scones. For more home-baking, **The Wee Hut Pop-Up Bakery** at Evanachan Farm is a charming roadside discovery.

Try the haggis panini from **The Bothy at Kilbride Farm** and visit nearby **Botanica at the Bothy** for the adventure picnic of dreams, featuring freshly baked breads, charcuterie boxes, foraged ingredients and a selection of deli goods.

KAREN APPLEYARD/ALAMY STOCK PHOTO ©

The Deserted Village

Just shy of the modern marina at Portavadie, a rare patch of ancient oakland conceals the hidden remains of a village dating back to 1309. Glenan Wood is an atmospheric and evocative place, owned and protected by the local community. The woodland walk climbs through native forest on a muddy path to the abandoned village. Silence echoes around the lonely ruins, once inhabited for 600 years, and now consumed by nature; strapped into the land indefinitely, as a reminder of the village and its people. Return via the coastal path and savour the peace on the pebbly beach at Glenan Bay.

25 Enter the Ancient KINGDOM

RUINS | NATURE | WALKING

Mysterious standing stones, rock carvings, burial chambers and an ancient hillfort are scattered around Kilmartin Glen like prehistoric treasure. Follow the 7-mile Dalriada Heritage Trail on a journey through human history, spanning 5000 years in just one day.

Trip Notes

Getting there Walk the full route or drive between several well-signposted car parks. West Coast Motors serves Kilmartin and the Crinan Canal on bus routes from Oban and Lochgilphead; both of which are served by train and bus from Glasgow.

When to go The area is crowd-free year-round. Come in late April or early May for bluebells, and autumn for golden light and landscapes.

Rock on Allow extra time to visit Achnabreck for incredible prehistoric stone carvings.

Britain's Most Beautiful Shortcut

Extend your adventure with a walk or cycle along the **Crinan Canal** from Ardrishaig to Crinan for 9 miles of glorious scenery. Look out for osprey, red squirrels, Highland cows and dolphins. Finish with a wander through **Crinan Wood** – a unique patch of temperate Scottish rainforest, bursting with rare plant life.

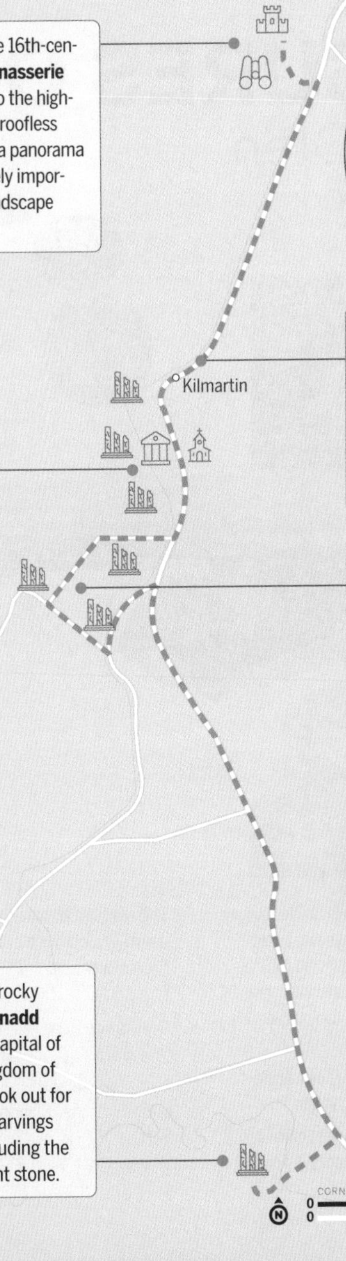

01 Begin at the 16th-century ruin of **Carnasserie Castle**. Climb to the highest point of the roofless tower to reveal a panorama of the immensely important historic landscape below.

02 Follow the path to Kilmartin village for **Glebe Cairn**, used in Early Bronze Age burial rituals, and **Kilmartin Church & Graveyard**, which displays elaborately carved ancient crosses and sculptured stones.

03 Continue along the linear cemetery of burial cairns; all large, circular and unbelievably well preserved. Stop at **Nether Largie North Cairn**, **Nether Largie Mid Cairn** and the chambered **Nether Largie South Cairn**.

04 Step into **Temple Wood Stone Circle**, a site dating from 3000 BCE. Across the fields, the towering **Nether Largie Standing Stones** are freckled with distinctive cup and ring marks.

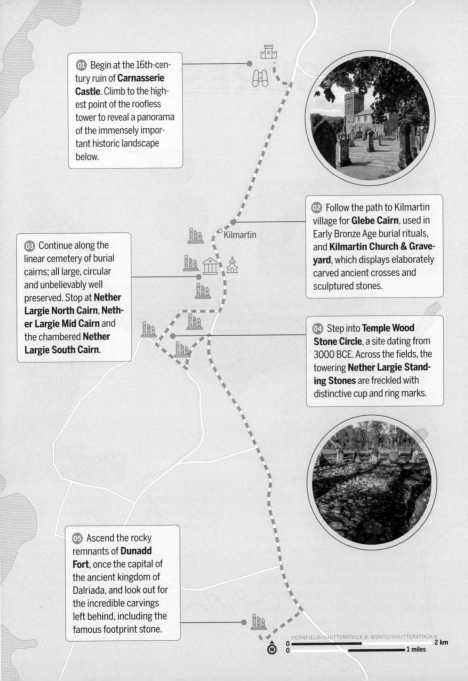

05 Ascend the rocky remnants of **Dunadd Fort**, once the capital of the ancient kingdom of Dalriada, and look out for the incredible carvings left behind, including the famous footprint stone.

TREASURES OF
Kilmartin Glen

01 Footprint Stone

This carved footprint at Dunadd Fort is believed to form part of the inauguration ceremonies for the kings of Dalriada.

02 Achnabreck Rock Art

Otherworldly spirals and cup marks, dating 5000 years; one of the best and most elaborate examples of prehistoric rock art in Scotland.

03 Nether Largie South Cairn

The oldest cairn in the linear cemetery. The central chamber, used in Neolithic burial rituals, was split into four parts.

04 Carved Boar

The outline of a boar on a stone near the summit of the Dunadd Fort.

05 Nether Largie Standing Stones

The large stones, sparking theories of an ancient football pitch or lunar observatory, are freckled with 23 distinctive cup marks.

06

07

08

09

06 Poltalloch Enclosure (Kilmartin Churchyard)

A row of seven grave slabs for the Malcolm family of the Poltalloch Estate, dating from the 1300s to the 1600s.

07 Neil Campbell Tomb (Kilmartin Churchyard)

The lapidarium displays a collection of sculptured grave slabs from the 1200s to 1700s, featuring carved beasts, swords, crosses and warriors.

08 Kilmartin Cross

Kept inside the church to prevent weather damage, this incredibly detailed early Christian cross dates back to 900 CE.

09 Temple Wood Stone Circle

An artistic representation of a ritual or ceremony thought to have taken place within the stone circle.

Listings

BEST OF THE REST

Island Adventures

West Island Way
Rugged coastline gives way to a secluded bay, calm countryside and medieval chapel ruins on the 5-mile Kilchattan Bay Circular: a short and satisfying section of Bute's long-distance trail.

Jura Island Tours
Wild landscapes, 5000 deer, 'Tea on the Beach', and a gin distillery in a converted stable. Step off the ferry from Islay and straight onto this full island tour.

Kiloran Beach
A little slice of paradise on Colonsay. Cycle to the beach and hit the water on a SUP with Colonsay Bikes & Boards. Climb Carnan Eoin for the best views.

Kerrera Tea Garden £
Lunch and cake at a hidden island eatery. Five minutes on the passenger ferry from Gallanach, followed by a 2.2-mile trail of teapots and novelty signs leading to the tea garden.

Explore Lismore
Island sightseeing by Landrover with a Lismore local, including a picnic of delicious handmade treats from The Dutch Bakery.

Boats, Boards & Wildlife

Basking Shark Scotland
Mesmerising marine life encounter. Search for basking sharks and swim with them in the wild, guided by a marine biologist. Group day trips from Coll and private tours from Oban/Tobermory.

Mull Charters
Cruise the west coast of Mull for the chance to spot sea eagles swooping down to hunt fish on the surface of the water.

Tiree Sea Tours
Wildlife spotting and waves of excitement on a high-speed RIB ride around the waters of the Inner Hebrides. Marvel at Skerryvore Lighthouse towering above the sea on a rocky reef.

Seafari Adventures
Witness the famous Corryvreckan whirlpool in full spin on a tour from Easdale, or take a longer tour for whales and wildlife on the Gulf of Corryvreckan.

Castles

Castle Stalker
A picture-perfect medieval tower house, cast away from the shore on a petite tidal island in Loch Laich, near Oban. Stop at Castle Stalker View for coffee and photos.

Inveraray Castle
The ancestral home of the Dukes of Argyll, Chiefs of Clan Campbell, this fairy-tale castle is still very much intact with a grand interior and immaculate waiting to be explored.

Rothesay Castle
A strapping, 13th-century fortress in the middle of a Victorian seaside town on the Isle

West Highland Way

of Bute, complete with a moat and the only circular curtain wall in Scotland.

Bars, Cafes & Cosy Pubs

Food from Argyll at the Pier £

The best comfort food in Oban. Friendly staff, a map on the wall showing where the ingredients are sourced, and the palpable buzz of preparing to board the ferry.

Reef Inn ££

Cold beers and cocktails with relaxed, straight-off-the-beach vibes in Tiree, 'Hawaii of the North'. Unwind in the casual bar and restaurant at this new luxury abode. Non-guests are always welcome.

Ben Cruachan Inn ££

Fireside drams and hearty meals at Loch Awe. Browse the extensive list of single malt whisky, craft beers and Scottish gin, and tuck into big portions of high-quality gastropub fare.

Brambles of Inveraray £

Fancy sandwiches, glorious cakes and freshly roasted coffee, produced by sister company Campbells of Inveraray. Enjoy outside in the charming Secret Garden, down the lane next to the cafe.

Puffer Bar & Restaurant ££

Fabulous fish and chips, local produce and home baking, on Easdale Island; reached by motor boat and home to the World Stone Skimming Championships. Tearoom by day, bar-restaurant by night.

The View

Party like a true Scot, overlooking the harbour in Oban. Live traditional music, Highland dancers, bagpipes and high-energy *ceilidh* dancing, guaranteed to lift your spirits and your heart rate.

DAVID WOODS/SHUTTERSTOCK ©

Rothesay Castle

Gifts, Crafts & Photography

Iona Craft Shop

Buy authentic Iona wool knitwear, gorgeous homewares or handmade jewellery with green Iona marble. The temptation to buy everything will hit you hard. Bike hire and takeaway coffee also available.

Ross of Coll

Colourful clothing and gifts featuring original, Isle of Coll–inspired designs, including the island's famously quirky Highland cow. Purchase from Ross and Chloe's family home in the village of Arinagour.

The Whisky Island Gallery & Studio

Stunning, evocative images of Jura and beyond, available straight from the source, as prints, calendars, books and gifts. Whisky, wildlife and untamed landscapes, sublimely captured by award-winning photographer Konrad Borkowski.

Scan to find more things to do in Southern Highlands & Islands online

CENTRAL HIGHLANDS

ADVENTURE | OUTDOORS | WHISKY

Experience Central Highlands online

▸ **Monster Hunting** (p152)

▸ **On Screen: The Highlands on Film** (p154)

▸ **Up Ben Nevis** (p156)

▸ **Royal Road Trip** (p158)

▸ **Listings** (p160)

CENTRAL HIGHLANDS

Trip Builder

Central to the true Highlands' experience is getting outside, no matter the weather. Be it by boot, bike or boat, Scotland's wild heart is found off-road, in stag-filled forests, salmon-stocked rivers and monster-haunted lochs.

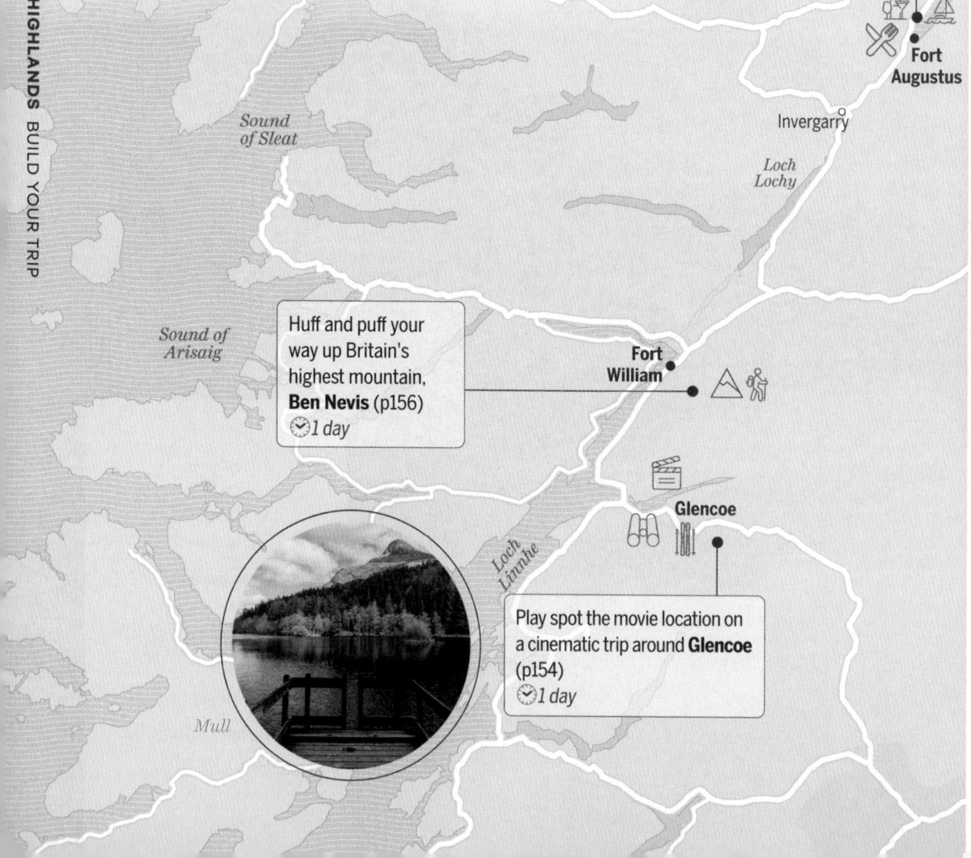
Cruise the **Caledonian Canal**, then stop at floating pubs and canal-side restaurants (p153)
2–3 days
Fort Augustus
Invergarry
Sound of Sleat
Loch Lochy
Sound of Arisaig
Fort William
Huff and puff your way up Britain's highest mountain, **Ben Nevis** (p156)
1 day
Glencoe
Loch Linnhe
Play spot the movie location on a cinematic trip around **Glencoe** (p154)
1 day
Mull

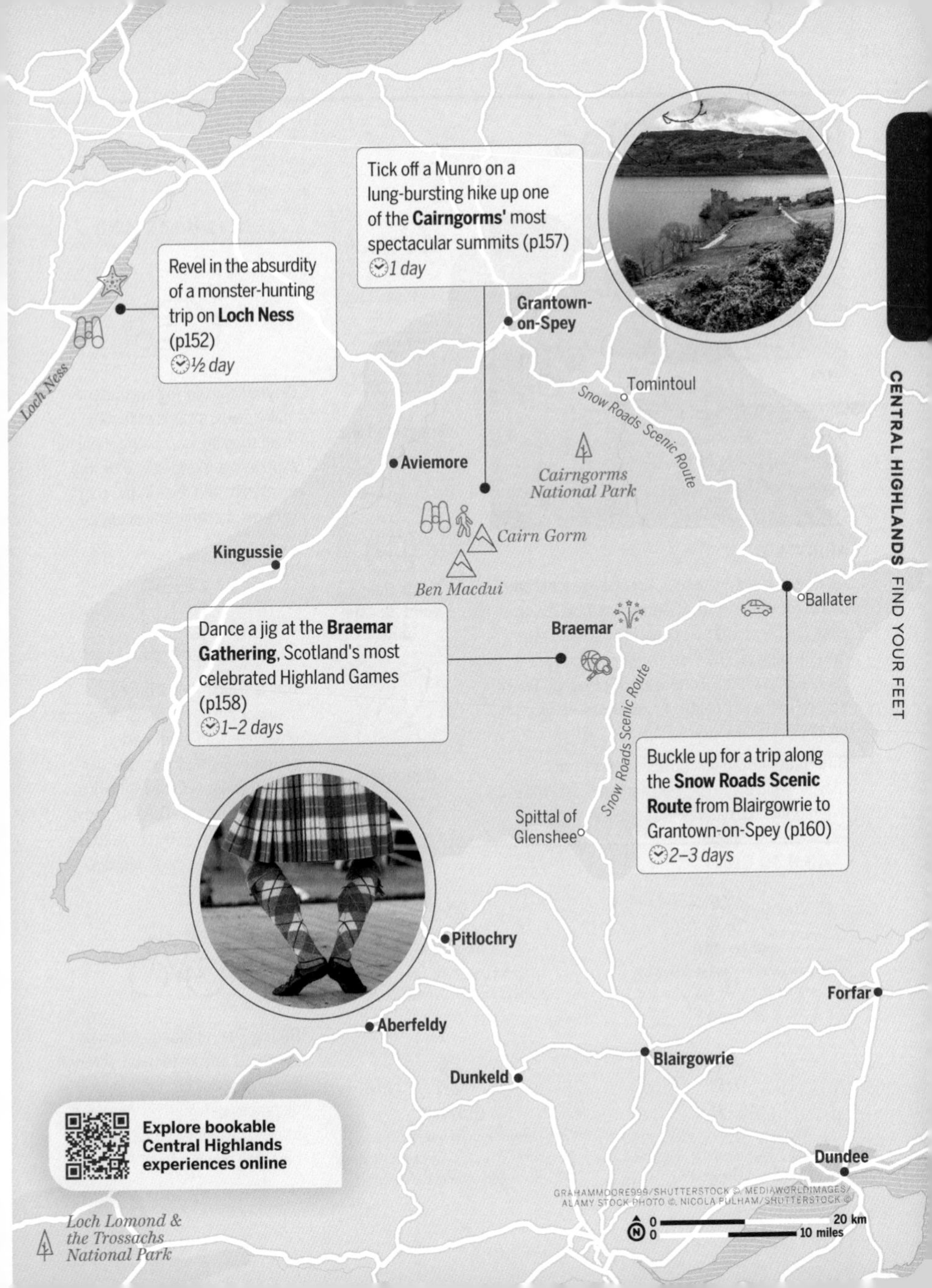

Revel in the absurdity of a monster-hunting trip on **Loch Ness** (p152)
½ day

Tick off a Munro on a lung-bursting hike up one of the **Cairngorms'** most spectacular summits (p157)
1 day

Dance a jig at the **Braemar Gathering**, Scotland's most celebrated Highland Games (p158)
1–2 days

Buckle up for a trip along the **Snow Roads Scenic Route** from Blairgowrie to Grantown-on-Spey (p160)
2–3 days

Explore bookable Central Highlands experiences online

Practicalities

DAVID GOWANS/ALAMY STOCK PHOTO ©

ARRIVING

Air Glasgow and Inverness Airports are ideal entry points for exploring the Central Highlands, with plenty of car-rental companies to save travel into the city centres. The Glasgow Airport Express service 500 costs £9 one-way to Buchanan Bus Station in the city centre. In Inverness, service 11 takes you into the city.

Bus Frequent Citylink buses depart from Glasgow and Inverness for Glencoe, Fort William, Aviemore and beyond. Find schedules online.

HOW MUCH FOR A

Speyside tour
£14

Nevis Range gondola ride
£22

Canoe hire
£55

WHEN TO GO

JAN–MAR
Snow-fuzzed mountains, bracing winds, closed camping sites and few tourists.

APR–JUN
Spring brings snowmelt and some of Scotland's best weather.

JUL–SEP
The busiest time to visit the Central Highlands and the best all-round for weather.

OCT–DEC
From autumn leaves to the Northern Lights, the best season for nature without the crowds.

GETTING AROUND

Driving If exploring beyond the main towns, a car is essential. Road trips are part of the Highland experience, allowing you to stop on a whim and revel in the country's most scenic landscapes.

Bus & train Citylink buses connect the main towns, dropping passengers off at requested stops en route. ScotRail operates services throughout the Highlands: highlights include Britain's most remote station (Corrour) and the West Highland Line to Mallaig.

Biking The Highlands offers up gorgeous terrain to pedal through. Expect serious climbs, long distances between services and lorries travelling so fast they can blow you off your bike.

EATING & DRINKING

Whisky heaven The Central Highlands is awash with world-class single malt whisky. From the foot of Ben Nevis to Speyside to almost every glen in between, there's a sublime whisky experience waiting for you. The Glenlivet (p160), the country's first licensed distillery, or Royal Lochnagar (p159) are memorable starting points.

Pub grub Venison with a view, or salmon with a side of scenery, is the name of the game. The storied pubs in Glencoe and those scattered around the Cairngorms take top billing.

Must eat

A backpack picnic along West Highland Way (p161)

Best pub experience

The Old Forge (p161)

CONNECT & FIND YOUR WAY

Wi-fi Most hotels, bars, cafes and restaurants have guest wi-fi. Mobile phone signal can be hit or miss, so always tell someone your planned route before setting out on an adventure.

Navigation Buy an Ordnance Survey map if hiking, biking or planning any mountain or loch excursions; otherwise, use Google Maps.

WHERE TO STAY

The Central Highlands has a wide range of superb accommodation options to suit all budgets. Wild camping is allowed almost anywhere, but remember best practice: leave only footprints and take everything with you.

Town/Village	Pro/Con
Glencoe	Exceptional views are guaranteed, while adventures by boot, bike or boat are almost compulsory.
Fort William	The outdoors capital of the UK is cradled by epic mountains and sea lochs. Shame the accommodation doesn't match the setting.
Inverness	The de facto Highlands capital with the best selection of accommodation, from dingy hostels to fabulous five-star boltholes.
Aviemore	Postcard mountain town with enviable setting, souvenir shops and plenty of rustic forest lodges and campsites.
Braemar	The Cairngorms' poshest outpost, thanks to nearby Balmoral Castle.
Mallaig	Pretty harbour town with exquisite fish and chips and a ferry schedule for adventures to the Small Isles, Skye or Knoydart.

FESTIVALS

Towns like Fort William and Aviemore see their population swell during events like the Mountain Bike World Cup and the Spirit of Speyside Whisky Festival. Book accommodation well in advance.

MONEY

Main attractions – those stunning mountains, sea lochs and heather-matted glens – are gloriously free, as is wild camping. Banks (and ATMs) are few and far between, so travel with enough cash just in case.

26 Monster HUNTING

HIKING | CYCLING | WATER ACTIVITIES

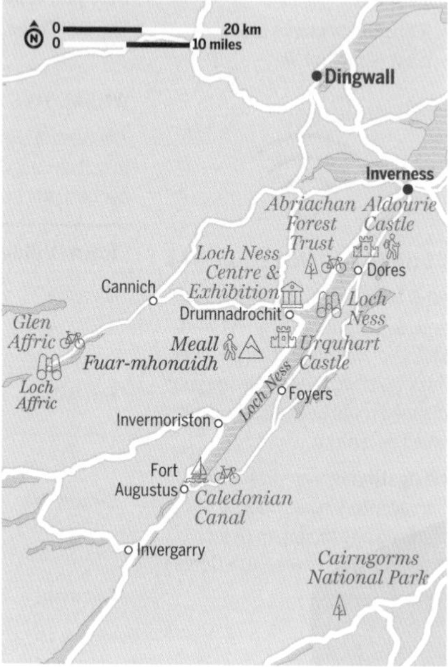

The scenery is spellbinding: rolling moorlands and pine-skirted mountains plunging into clear water where a mysterious and elusive monster hides in wait. This is Scotland's deepest and most famous loch, and whether or not you believe in Nessie – the long-necked cryptid that lurks in its depths – there are multiple ways to discover Loch Ness.

How to

Getting around The north shore of Loch Ness is home to the northernmost section of The Great Glen Way, while the opposite bank offers a mix of activity trails and a military road that make up the South Loch Ness Trail. Together they form the Loch Ness 360° Trail. To walk/cycle the 66-mile circuit takes six/three days.

When to go Year-round. Peak midge season is July and August.

More info The Loch Ness 360° website has interactive trail maps and itineraries.

Boot and backpack Hiking Loch Ness, through ancient Caledonian pine forests and along mighty rivers, offers the best of Scotland's wild terrain in microcosm. Scramble up **Meall Fuar-mhonaidh**, the lochside's highest hill at 699m, or tackle the corkscrew hike between Foyers and Dores. With a good selection of individual two- to three-hour walks, there are also plenty of options for those in a hurry: try the 4-mile **Aldourie Castle** circuit on the south bank.

Shift up a gear The Loch Ness circuit is for seasoned cyclists, but there is also plenty on offer for all ages

Above right Loch Ness
Right Urquhart Castle

NIDPOR/STOCKIMONEWS/ALAMY LIVE NEWS ©

BENNY MARTY/SHUTTERSTOCK ©

From Loch to Lock

Fort Augustus, at the southern tip of Loch Ness, is the start of the historic, hand-dug **Caledonian Canal**, an early-19th-century waterway that cuts south for 60 miles to Corpach near Fort William. Find floating pubs and restaurants serving fresh shellfish and local single malts. Le Boat (leboat.co.uk) has a fleet of self-drive boats.

and abilities. **Abriachan Forest Trust**, 12 miles south of Inverness, has 9 miles of family-friendly loops and gnarly sections, while there are high and low roads to choose from between **Drumnadrochit** and **Fort Augustus**. Fancy a detour? Discover nearby **Glen Affric**, aka Scotland's most beautiful glen. Hire a mountain bike or hybrid at Ticket To Ride in Inverness.

Cruise power Waterfront Drumnadrochit is home to the kitsch **Loch Ness Centre & Exhibition**, and it is also the prime jumping-off point for hourly cruises to spy the world's most famous humpbacked creature. Out on the water, the gimmick is surpassed by views of crumbling **Urquhart Castle**, and there's plenty of fish in the water if you know what to look for. Three companies to sail with are Loch Ness Castle Cruises, Loch Ness Cruises and Loch Ness by Jacobite.

ON SCREEN
The Highlands on Film

01 Highlander (1986)

Christopher Lambert and Sean Connery hammed it up to the extreme when shooting in Glencoe and on the Silver Sands of Morar.

02 Skyfall (2012)

Rannoch Moor and Glen Etive saw Daniel Craig and Judi Dench escaping into the Highlands in 007's Aston Martin DB5.

03 Harry Potter (2001–11)

The Glenfinnan Viaduct was used to speed the Hogwarts Express throughout the wizarding saga, particularly in the Chamber of Secrets.

04 Braveheart (1995)

The Academy Award winner saw a face-painted Mel Gibson cavorting about in his kilt in Glencoe and Glen Nevis.

05 Monty Python and the Holy Grail (1975)

The film's notoriously silly Bridge of Death was shot near the Meeting of the Three Waters near Ballachulish.

06 No Time to Die (2021)

The latest James Bond film recasts the Cairngorms' Ardverikie Estate and Loch Laggan as the backdrop for a madcap 4x4 chase.

07 Mary Queen of Scots (2018)

The Cairngorms' Glen Feshie hosted Saoirse Ronan and Hollywood location scouts to film Mary's armies on the march.

08 The Queen (2006)

Glen Feshie Estate in the Cairngorms was used as a stand-in for Her Majesty The Queen's real-life Balmoral retreat.

09 Rob Roy (1995)

Entirely shot in Scotland, Liam Neeson was in his element when filming around Loch Leven and at Achnacarry's Caig Falls Bridge.

10 Local Hero (1983)

As well as Burt Lancaster and former Doctor Who Peter Capaldi, Camusdarach beach near Morar was the star of this classic.

27 Up Ben NEVIS

HIKING | ADVENTURE | DAY TRIP

Chief among the landscapes to explore in the Central Highlands is Ben Nevis, Britain's highest mountain at 1345m. It towers above every glen, sea loch and mountain and can be tackled in a number of ways from the base camp town of Fort William. Pack a backpack and spend a day scrambling up ridges – just be sure to treat it with the respect it deserves.

JOSEFKUBES/SHUTTESTOCK ©

How to

Getting to the top There are two routes to the summit, both requiring a full day. Factor in covering a distance of 10 to 11 miles. Walk Highlands (walkhighlands.co.uk) has detailed A to B descriptions of both options.

When to go Snow-covered from November to April, the best season is from late May to early October. Crampons, ice axes and experience are a must for a winter ascent.

Festival The Fort William Mountain Festival celebrates mountain culture every February, with films and events.

JOHN A CAMERON/SHUTTESTOCK ©

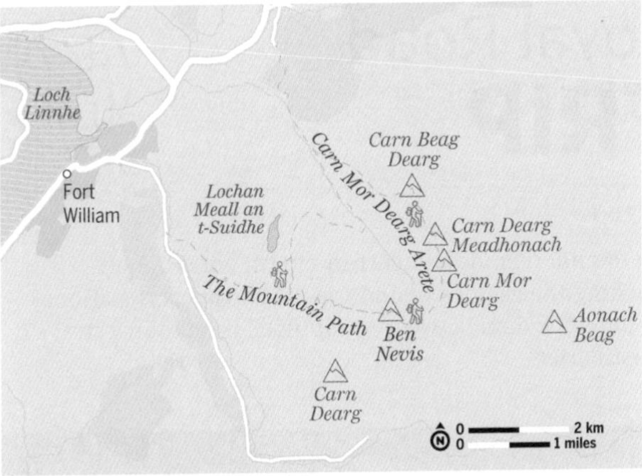

Choose Your Route

The Mountain Path From the Glen Nevis Visitor Centre, the most straightforward ascent begins over the River Nevis bridge before heading up steep terrain with epic views of the Mamores. Further on, the path zigzags up a rocky, if well-worn, scree slope that saw a Ford Model T driven up it to the top in 1911. The summit, crowned by cairns and the ruins of a 19th-century weather station, can be reached in 3½ to 4½ hours. The route attracts around 125,000 hikers a year, so avoid weekends.

Carn Mor Dearg Arete Among Europe's finest mountain and ridge walks, experienced scramblers with a head for heights should consider this alternative. Do not attempt the ascent lightly – at 4½ to 5½ hours to the summit it is both longer and more strenuous, and involves traversing the jagged crest of Carn Mor Dearg and a last push up a steep slope of boulders. The rewards are plentiful: from the spectacular views of Ben Nevis' cliffs, buttresses and gullies to the rocky chutes on the West Face of adjacent Aonach Mor. Start at the North Face car park near Torlundy, don't forget a map and compass, and think twice about attempting the route in misty weather.

Top left Hikers scale Ben Nevis
Bottom left Highland cattle below Ben Nevis

Peak Performance

Munro-bagging in the Central Highlands is an art form. Here are four other heartstring-tugging hikes.

Schiehallion, Pitlochry A broad ridge and storied summit with sigh-triggering views of Loch Rannoch (4–6hr/6 miles).

Aonach Eagach, Glencoe The narrowest ridge scramble in Britain connects Meall Dearg to Sgorr nam Fiannaidh. Not for the timid (7–9hr/6 miles).

Buachaille Etive Mòr, Glencoe The pin-up mountain's iconic rock face is as imposing as they come (7–8hr/8 miles).

Braeriach, Cairngorms Britain's third-highest summit (1296m) and one safeguarded from the crowds because of the long approach or bike in (8–10hr/16 miles).

28 Royal Road TRIP

HISTORY | WHISKY | ROAD TRIP

It doesn't take long to understand the heart-in-mouth potential of Scotland's royal route. Tracking the eastern boundaries of Cairngorms National Park, it is a road trip that joins the dots between sumptuous palace, ancestral clan homes and off-grid distilleries.

BYUNAU KONSTANTIN/SHUTTESTOCK ©

Highland Fling!

September only means one thing in Braemar: caber tossing, tug of war and highland dancing at the **Braemar Gathering**, the annual royal Highland Games. Despite the skirling and whirling, it's a sophisticated affair, attended by the royals since first enjoyed by Queen Victoria in 1848. Buy tickets in advance.

Trip Notes

Getting around This 125-mile route is best discovered over three to four days. While it can be cycled, it traverses Britain's highest public road, with the rolle-coaster section between Blairgowrie and Braemar offering only essential services. Expect single-track roads, tight bends and wayward sheep.

When to go Year-round. September's Braemar Gathering draws the largest crowds.

Top tip Owned by Swiss art dealers Manuela and Iwan Wirth, The Fife Arms in Braemar brims with decadent suites, a restaurant, pub and cocktail bar themed around royal history.

01 Start at Perth's tantalising **Scone Palace**, where Scotland's kings, including Macbeth and Robert the Bruce, were once crowned. Allow enough time for the maze and arboretum.

02 A further 34 miles north along the A9 is **Blair Atholl Castle**, home to the Duke of Atholl and Europe's only remaining private army, the Atholl Highlanders.

03 Drive northeast for 55 miles to see **Balmoral Castle** (pictured left). Built in the wake of Queen Victoria's annual romps to the Highlands, the fairy-tale bastion remains the Royal Family's summer holiday home.

04 Amid the Scots pines and snowy summits nearby is the **Royal Lochnagar Distillery** and the beautiful village of **Ballater**, home to the Rothesay Rooms, a restaurant established by Prince Charles.

05 Finish with a trip on board the Victorian-era **Royal Deeside Steam Railway** at Banchory, 25 miles away. It runs for 1 mile along the River Dee, where the country's finest salmon fishing awaits.

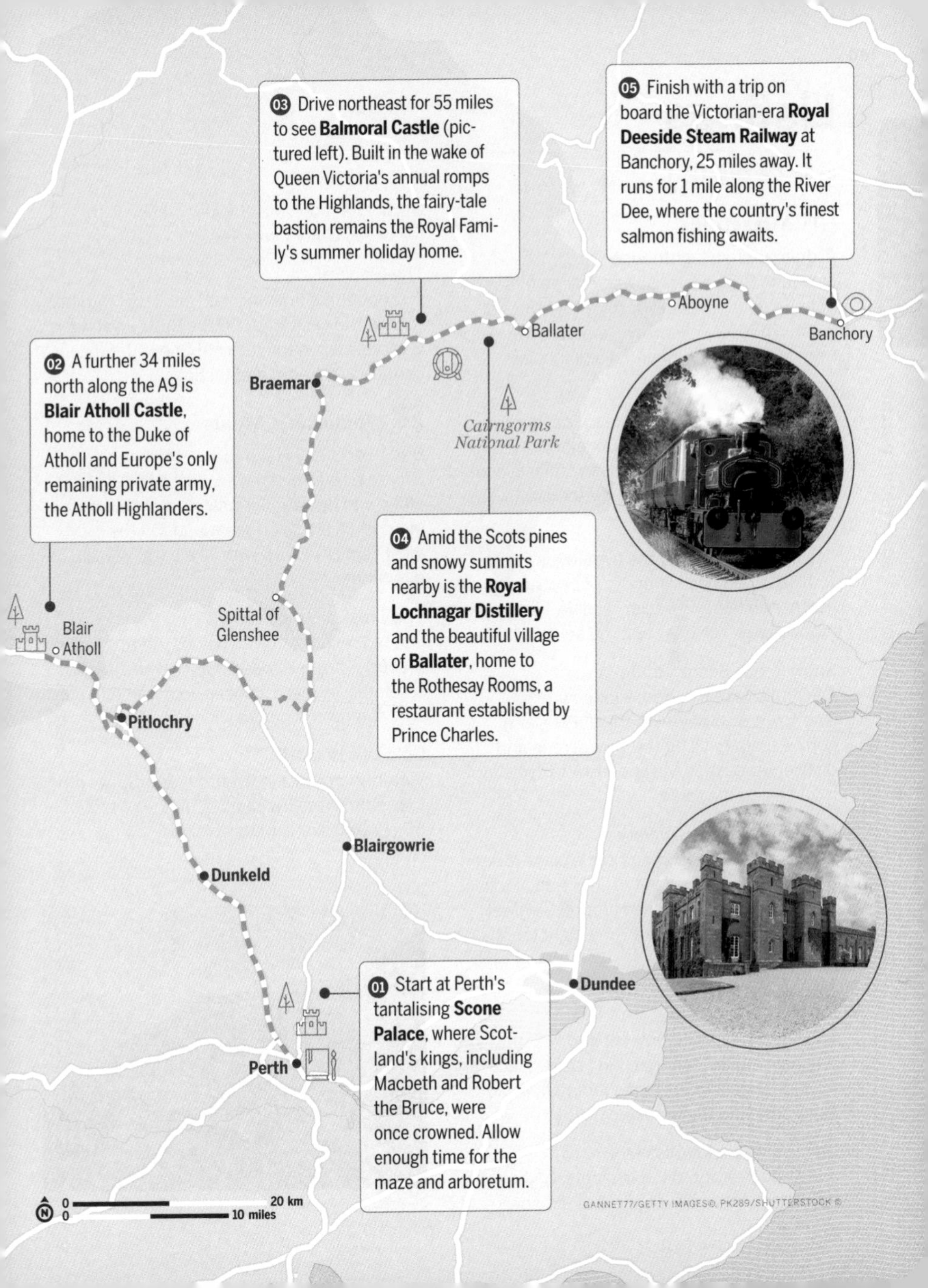

GANNET77/GETTY IMAGES©, PK289/SHUTTERSTOCK ©

Listings

BEST OF THE REST

Attractions

Ardnamurchan Lighthouse
Mainland Britain's most westerly point and a hot spot for cetacean spotting. Sightings of dolphin pods, minke whale and even orca peak from May to September. Take binoculars.

Culloden
Site of Bonnie Prince Charlie's most famous defeat and the bloody last battle of the 18th-century Jacobite Rebellion. rtefacts and an immersive theatre bring it viscerally to life.

Glen Clova
The most beautiful of the five Angus Glens, with secluded Loch Brandy, a spectrum of heathery hikes and easier, wildlife-filled walks (spot eagles, roe deer and red squirrel).

Snow Roads Scenic Route
A 90-mile road trip from Blairgowrie to Grantown-on-Spey, with the finest Cairngorms scenery filling the windscreen and distilleries, castles, viewpoints and cycle trails found along the route.

Cairngorms Dark Sky Park
The Highlands' most memorable place to see the Northern Lights and the Gaelic and Pictish rulers of the stars. Located around Glenlivet and Tomintoul, with events and night tours.

Distilleries

Dalwhinnie Distillery
The highest distillery in Scotland with an original smokestack that can't be missed. Abundant peat in the surrounding bogs adds extra punch to the whisky.

Dewar's Aberfeldy Distillery
A 360-degree approach to single malts, with tours, tastings, a heritage museum, shop, whisky bar and cafe. Slick operation with hands-on whisky courses.

The Glenlivet
The country's first licensed distillery, with history by the cask load. On the River Livet near Ballindalloch in the heart of Speyside whisky country with tours and tastings.

Memorable Meals

Bridge of Orchy Hotel ££
Once a hillwalkers' haven, now a fine-dining affair with house-cured salmon and bowls of Scottish shells on the menu. On the West Highland Way, with lovely walks in all directions.

The Cross at Kingussie ££
Lauded restaurant with rooms offering tasting menus. A former tweed mill, the vibe is now resolutely modern. Loosen your belt for venison, soufflé and paired wines.

Culdearn House ££
Victorian-era villa in Grantown-on-Spey with four-course tasting menus, plus an A to Z of 60 curated single malt whiskies.

PAUL BUTCHARD/SHUTTESTOCK ©

Glen Clova

Brews & Views

Kenmore Inn £
Scotland's oldest inn, dating back to 1572, with views courtesy of the River Tay. Look for a poem scrawled on the Poet's Bar chimney written by Robert Burns.

Clachaig Inn £
Storied Glencoe pub with three bars, including the outdoorsy Boots Bar, home to 400-odd whiskies, 130 Scottish gins, live music, barrel seating and a dusty fire.

The Old Forge £
Mainland Britain's remotest pub in Knoydart. Reached by ferry from Mallaig, or 18-mile walk-in from Kinlochhourn. *Ceilidhs* and local ales, but also Trappist beers from the Belgian landlord.

Black Isle Brewery £
Organic brewery, with an admirable sustainable ethos on its farm and vegetable garden. Tours, a brew shop and overnight stays.

By Boat

Eigg
The island of Eigg was bought in 1997 by the 100-strong community and turned into a sort of sustainable Shangri-La. Home to superb wildlife, beaches and the Lost Map record label.

Kinloch Castle
Architectural masterpiece in red sandstone and the island of Rum's Edwardian time capsule. Guided tours are timed for the arrival of the mainland ferry (April to October).

Nova Spero
Once an entrenched fishing boat, now an overnight adventure cruiser with storm hatches, shipping bell and landing winch. Based out of Kinlochleven, with multi-day trips all year-round.

Isle of Rum, seen from the island of Eigg

Great Outdoors

West Highland Way
Starting in Milngavie and winding 96 miles to Fort William through the Highlands' finest scenery. The ultimate day trip is the knee-crunching Devil's Staircase, from the Kingshouse to Kinlochleven.

Glencoe Mountain Resort
Scotland's first ski centre, with unrivalled snowsports in winter and daredevil mountain-biking trails in summer. Knockout views of Buachaille Etive Mor.

Mountain Bike World Cup
Fort William's steep slopes welcome the Mountain Bike World Cup every year – try the gnarly Witch's Trails at the Nevis Range to tackle gravity head-on.

Loch Morlich
Life-affirming loch cradled by Caledonian pine forest, with the Cairngorms' finest stand-up paddling, kayaking and canoeing from the shore. Spot osprey, red squirrel and capercaillie.

Scan to find more things to do in Central Highlands online

NORTHERN HIGHLANDS

OUTDOORS | HISTORY | ADVENTURE

Experience Northern Highlands online

▸ **Rails to the North** (p166)

▸ **Cape Wrath** (p170)

▸ **On the Clearances Trail** (p172)

▸ **Remote Caithness** (p174)

▸ **Highland Games** (p176)

▸ **Listings** (p178)

HEINZ WOHNER/IMAGE PROFESSIONALS GMBH/ALAMY STOCK PHOTO

NORTHERN HIGHLANDS
Trip Builder

Big skies, dramatic coastlines and vast moorlands: this is the ultimate escape to the wilderness. There is so much space here that it is easy to find yourself alone on the shores of a loch or a pristine beach. And if you tire of your own company there's the spectacle of the Highland Games.

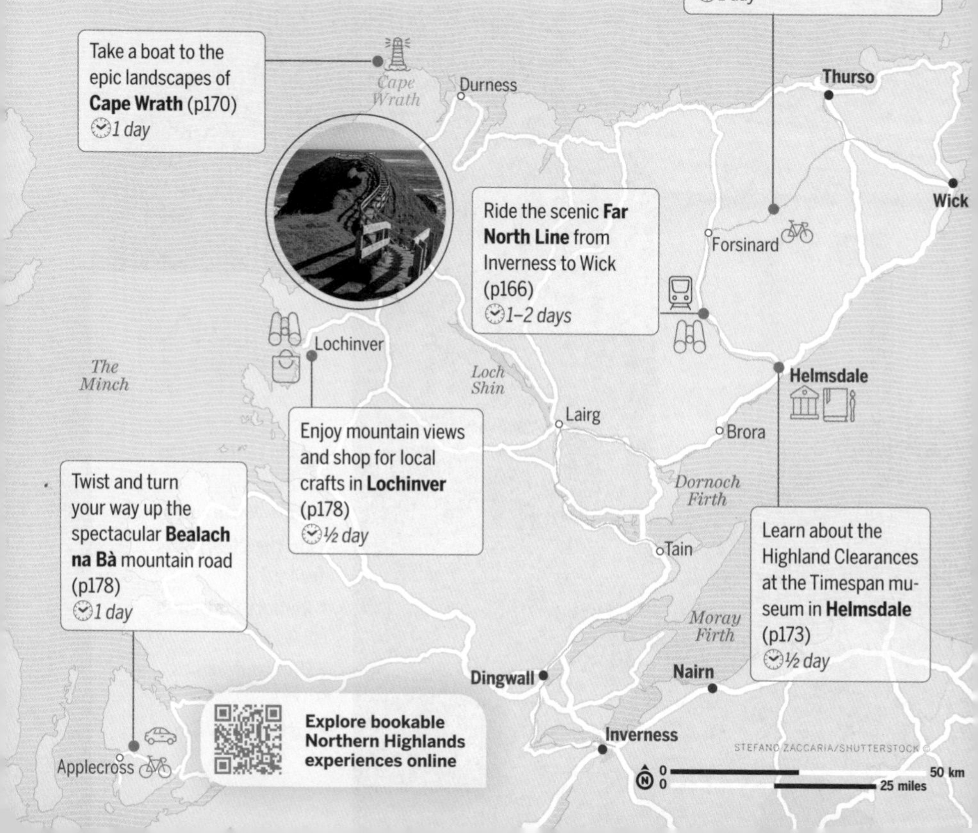

Cycle a remote corner of Caithness at **Altnabreac** (p175) 1 day
Take a boat to the epic landscapes of **Cape Wrath** (p170) 1 day
Cape Wrath
Durness
Thurso
Wick
Ride the scenic **Far North Line** from Inverness to Wick (p166) 1–2 days
Forsinard
Lochinver
The Minch
Loch Shin
Helmsdale
Lairg
Brora
Enjoy mountain views and shop for local crafts in **Lochinver** (p178) ½ day
Twist and turn your way up the spectacular **Bealach na Bà** mountain road (p178) 1 day
Dornoch Firth
Tain
Learn about the Highland Clearances at the Timespan museum in **Helmsdale** (p173) ½ day
Moray Firth
Dingwall
Nairn
Inverness
Applecross
Explore bookable Northern Highlands experiences online
STEFANO ZACCARIA/SHUTTERSTOCK ©
0 50 km
0 25 miles

Practicalities

ARRIVING

Inverness Airport Located 20 miles from Dingwall, the largest town in the south of the region.

Inverness train station Serves the Far North Line and the Kyle Line.

Inverness bus station Has connections including Dornoch and Ullapool.

CONNECT

Wi-fi in towns and villages is good, but away from settlements it is less reliable. Downloading maps or taking a paper map is recommended.

MONEY

Families can save on train travel with 'Kids for a Quid' – a £1 return ticket for children. See scotrail.co.uk.

WHERE TO STAY

Place	Pro/Con
Dornoch	Great variety of accommodation and dining, plus a beach and golf course.
Durness	Good base for Cape Wrath. Hostel, hotels, camping and B&B.
Ullapool	Accommodation to suit all budgets. Convenient for exploring the west coast.
Wick	Large choice of places to stay. Good base for Caithness day trips.

GETTING AROUND

Driving The best way to explore the region's least populated areas.

Trains and buses Serve most towns and villages, but can be infrequent.

Cycling A great way to discover quiet, single-track roads.

TOP: DAVID GOWANS/ALAMY STOCK PHOTO ©
BOTTOM: IAIN MASTERTON/ALAMY STOCK PHOTO ©

EATING & DRINKING

Crowdie cheese This creamy cheese is produced in Tain and goes great on an oatcake.

Smoked fish Fish prepared in traditional smokehouses has a distinctive taste from the wood smoke.

Highland gin distilleries Dunnet Bay and Badachro distilleries use local botanicals, such as gorse blossom and sea buckthorn.

Best hot chocolate
Cocoa Mountain (p179)

Must-try flatbread
Ems & Co Cafe & Bakehouse (p167)

MAR–MAY
Changeable weather, less busy. Spring flowers blossom.

JUN–AUG
Warmest weather; attractions can be busy.

SEP–NOV
Cooler temperatures. Less busy, trees change colour.

DEC–FEB
The coldest months. Some visitor facilities are closed.

29 Rails to the NORTH

TRAIN | SCENERY | EXPLORING

To appreciate the immensity of the north's landscapes, ride a train to the end of the line. The Far North Line offers thrilling coastal vistas, mesmerising wilderness and plenty of places to get off and explore.

LACHLAN1/SHUTTERSTOCK ©

How to

Getting here and around It takes 4½ hours to ride the whole line, from Inverness to Wick. With 24 stations on the line it's worth stopping to explore, but keep in mind that hopping on and off requires careful planning as services are infrequent. See scotrail.co.uk.

When to go Summer for seasonal opening hours and warmer weather, but a snowy winter is spectacular.

Top tip Sit on the right-hand side of the train for a chance to spot seals on the beaches between Brora and Helmsdale.

MIKE KIPLING PHOTOGRAPHY/ALAMY STOCK PHOTO ©

Lineside Experiences

Cake stop Dingwall station, with its impressive canopy, is home to **Ems & Co Cafe & Bakehouse**. Order a Turkish flatbread or cinnamon bun and watch the trains coming and going.

The mural town Invergordon station is covered in murals that depict a 1940s scene of kilted soldiers waiting to go off to war. Many more murals portraying local history are to be found in the town centre.

Into the gorge A mile from Golspie station is the **Big Burn Walk**, a spectacular ensemble of waterfalls, lush foliage and bridges traversing a gorge. Afterwards, grab a takeaway from **Coffee Bothy** and enjoy a stroll down Golspie's seafront promenade.

GEORGE HIGHLANDS/SHUTTERSTOCK ©

Stations Reborn

At **Helmsdale** the former stationmaster's house is a self-catering apartment for those looking for a unique place to stay. Tain has been beautifully converted into **Platform 1864**, a restaurant popular with locals. The dishes feature regional produce and there is a beer garden.

Top left Far North Line train, Dingwall
Bottom left Big Burn Walk
Above right Invergordon Station

Wildlife central Forsinard station is the visitor centre for the **Forsinard Flows Nature Reserve**. A boardwalk takes you to a striking lookout tower where you can survey the expanse of peat bog pools. Birdlife, such as hen harriers, golden plovers and dippers, can be spotted here.

The world's shortest street Celebrate reaching the end of the line at Wick by having a meal on the world's shortest street. The door to the restaurant of **Mackays Hotel** is the only thing on Ebenezer Pl. Locally sourced produce like Scrabster hake makes this a fine place to experience the region's gastronomy. The 1-mile walk to the **Castle of Old Wick** is rewarded with a majestic clifftop ruin; on your way back to town, take a dip in 'The Trinkie', Wick's outdoor pool.

Request Stops

The line has several stations where trains will only stop if you signal to the driver that you

The Passenger's Experience

From fertile fields in the South to the rugged interior around Lairg, I always feel the line gives up more secrets the further north you travel. As the train swings out towards the coast, almost getting its feet wet, the glistening sands near Brora are sometimes for our eyes only. Then it takes you into a magical land: tundra, without the permafrost. This unique landscape, The Flows, is a vast, precious, and humbling place. My home. Then, before you know it, you're back to the world of people.

Niall Laybourne, *photographer from Caithness and regular Far North Line user*

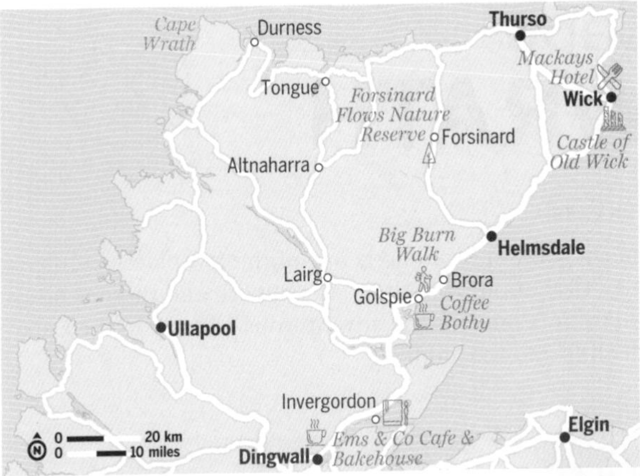

Left Castle of Old Wick
Below Forsinard Flows Nature Reserve

want to get on (or off). Using the request stops is a great way to experience the line.

Sleep in converted railway carriages Spend the night at Rogart station, which has 1960s coaches kitted out with beds and kitchens. They retain many of their original features like the emergency pull cords and no-smoking signs. See sleeperzzz.com.

The castle with its own station Dunrobin, originally a private station for the Duke of Sutherland, is one of the prettiest on the line, with its Arts and Crafts architecture. Use it to visit the castle, where you can feel a peregrine falcon swoop over your head at one of the falconry displays.

Land of gold Birdsong and a flowing river are about the only sounds at Kildonan station, one of the least used in Scotland. In 1869 the area would have been swarming with people trying to cash in on Scotland's gold rush. About 1 mile from the station is Baile an Or (Gaelic for 'town of gold'), the site of the temporary settlement for the prospectors.

LEFT: PETR KLAPKA/SHUTTERSTOCK ©
RIGHT: IAIN SARJEANT/ALAMY STOCK PHOTO ©

30 Cape WRATH

WILDERNESS | TOUR | ADVENTURE

The most northwesterly point of Scotland is one of the few places on the planet that feels untouched. It is cut off from the road network and there is no land between here and the Arctic. Come for the adventurous journey to the Cape Wrath lighthouse, the high cliffs and the wildlife.

SUSIE KEARLEY/ALAMY STOCK PHOTO ©

How to

Getting here and around You cannot drive on Cape Wrath. A ferry takes foot passengers from Keoldale Pier (2.5 miles from Durness) across to the cape, from where you can take the minibus onwards.

When to go The ferry operates April to October, but can sometimes be cancelled due to weather and tide conditions. Access is also dependent on the Ministry of Defence, which owns much of the land and uses it for military training exercises. See visitcapewrath.com.

Top tip Durness has plenty of accommodation options and acts as a good base if the ferry is cancelled.

RICHARD BURDON/ALAMY STOCK PHOTO ©

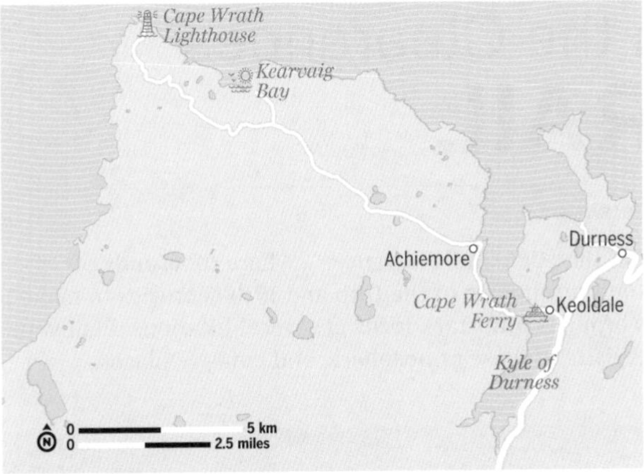

Choose Your Cape Adventure

Ferry & bus Cape Wrath's road is cut off from the mainland by a stretch of water called the Kyle of Durness. **Britain's smallest ferry** crosses it in 10 minutes. A minibus meets the ferry and takes passengers on the 11-mile road to the **lighthouse**. It is a bumpy ride – the road was originally built in 1826 for horse traffic – but the entertaining drivers provide lots of insight about Cape Wrath. Before the return journey, passengers have some time to explore: walk away from the lighthouse to look out on the vast moorland and the highest cliffs in Britain, and stop in at one of the remotest cafes in Scotland, the Ozone.

By bicycle Cycling the road means you can join the **Cape Wrath Fellowship**. All you have to do is take a selfie with your bike in front of the lighthouse and send it to Cycling UK. Bikes must be carried on the ferry; there is no bike rental on Cape Wrath.

A night on the beach Hikers can head to **Kearvaig Bay**, a beautiful sandy beach with a white cottage to spend the night in. This is a bothy with no facilities and a similar experience to camping (see moutainbothies.org.uk). The minibus, by arrangement, can drop off and pick up hikers at the end of the road that leads to the bay.

Top left View from Cape Wrath Lighthouse
Bottom left Cape Wrath Lighthouse

Wildlife of Cape Wrath

Seeing the wildlife on Cape Wrath is a sensual and mental awakening. The remoteness, the high cliffs, the wind, the all-around light from an endless sky, the waves surging below and, of course, the sound of the seabirds and the spectacular plunging dives of many gannets.

Puffins, razorbills and guillemots fly to and from the cliffs in apparently endless succession, fulmars soar in the wind with ease and cackle endlessly from their nests. Further down the cliff face, kittiwakes gather together in separate nest colonies and below them shags dress their cluttered nests with seaweed.

Donald Mitchell, *High Life Highland Countryside Ranger*

31 On the Clearances TRAIL

ROAD TRIP | MONUMENTS | HISTORY

The human tragedy of the Highland Clearances – where thousands of families were displaced from their homes in the 18th and 19th centuries to make way for sheep farming – is brought into stark focus at several locations. Plan your Highland road trip around visits to these atmospheric and emotive places.

ARTERRA PICTURE LIBRARY/ALAMY STOCK PHOTO ©

Trip Notes

Getting here and around Croick Church, the first stop on this trail, is 44 miles from Inverness. Visiting all the locations requires over five hours of driving.

When to go June to August for the better weather, as the sites are mainly outdoors.

Top tip Timespan museum in Helmsdale is excellent for learning more about the Clearances. The cafe is also a great place to taste local – the herbs are from the garden and the crab and salmon caught by local fishers.

Clearance Artefacts

A 'Sutherland Chair' can be seen in Timespan. It was handmade at the time of the Highland Clearances, deliberately designed to be close to the floor so that the sitter would be below the thick peat smoke rising from the fireplace in the thatched longhouse.

Jacquie Aitken, *Heritage Officer @Timespan*

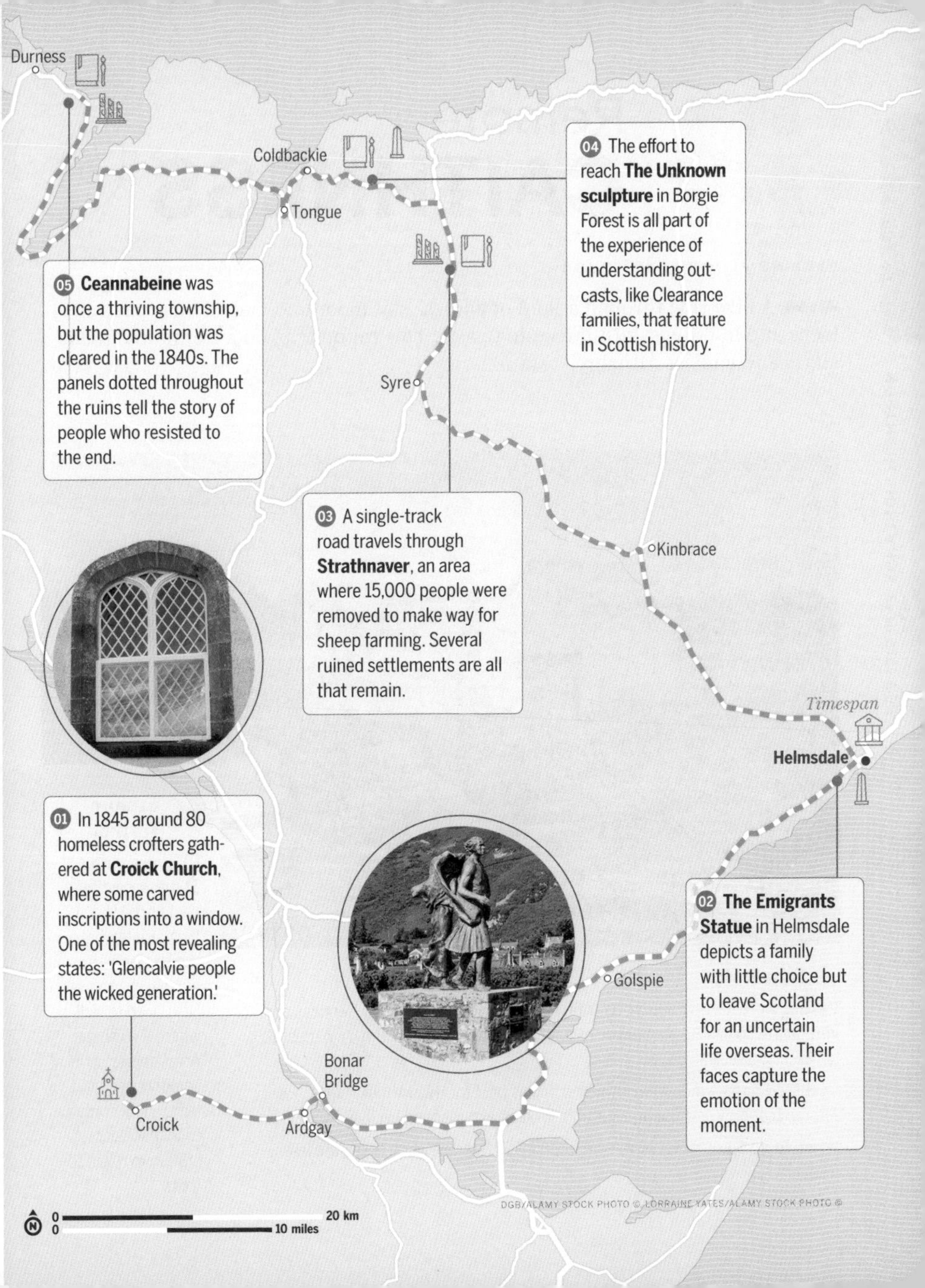
Durness
Coldbackie
Tongue
04 The effort to reach **The Unknown sculpture** in Borgie Forest is all part of the experience of understanding outcasts, like Clearance families, that feature in Scottish history.
05 **Ceannabeine** was once a thriving township, but the population was cleared in the 1840s. The panels dotted throughout the ruins tell the story of people who resisted to the end.
Syre
03 A single-track road travels through **Strathnaver**, an area where 15,000 people were removed to make way for sheep farming. Several ruined settlements are all that remain.
Kinbrace
Timespan
Helmsdale
01 In 1845 around 80 homeless crofters gathered at **Croick Church**, where some carved inscriptions into a window. One of the most revealing states: 'Glencalvie people the wicked generation.'
02 **The Emigrants Statue** in Helmsdale depicts a family with little choice but to leave Scotland for an uncertain life overseas. Their faces capture the emotion of the moment.
Golspie
Bonar Bridge
Croick
Ardgay
0 20 km
0 10 miles
N

32 Remote CAITHNESS

CYCLING | LOCHS | SOLITUDE

A bike ride through a land of endless sky, moorland and silence, passing 11 lochs and buildings with intriguing pasts. This round trip, on a traffic-free road, starts and ends at Altnabreac station.

GARY BRUCE/SHUTTERSTOCK ©

Trip Notes

Getting here It's 30 minutes by train from Thurso to Altnabreac. Services are infrequent, so careful planning is required. Bicycle spaces on the train must be booked. See scotrail.co.uk.

Cycling details A mountain or hybrid bike is best for this 14-mile route. Although bumpy, it is flat and suitable for less-experienced cyclists.

When to go Summer for better weather. Avoid Sunday, when trains are less frequent.

Explore Further

For a longer ride, of 21 miles, continue past Loch More to Westerdale where there is a picturesque old mill by the river. Next head to Halkirk, where the Ulbster Arms serves up local seafood, beef and lamb. Then continue to Scotscalder station to rejoin the train.

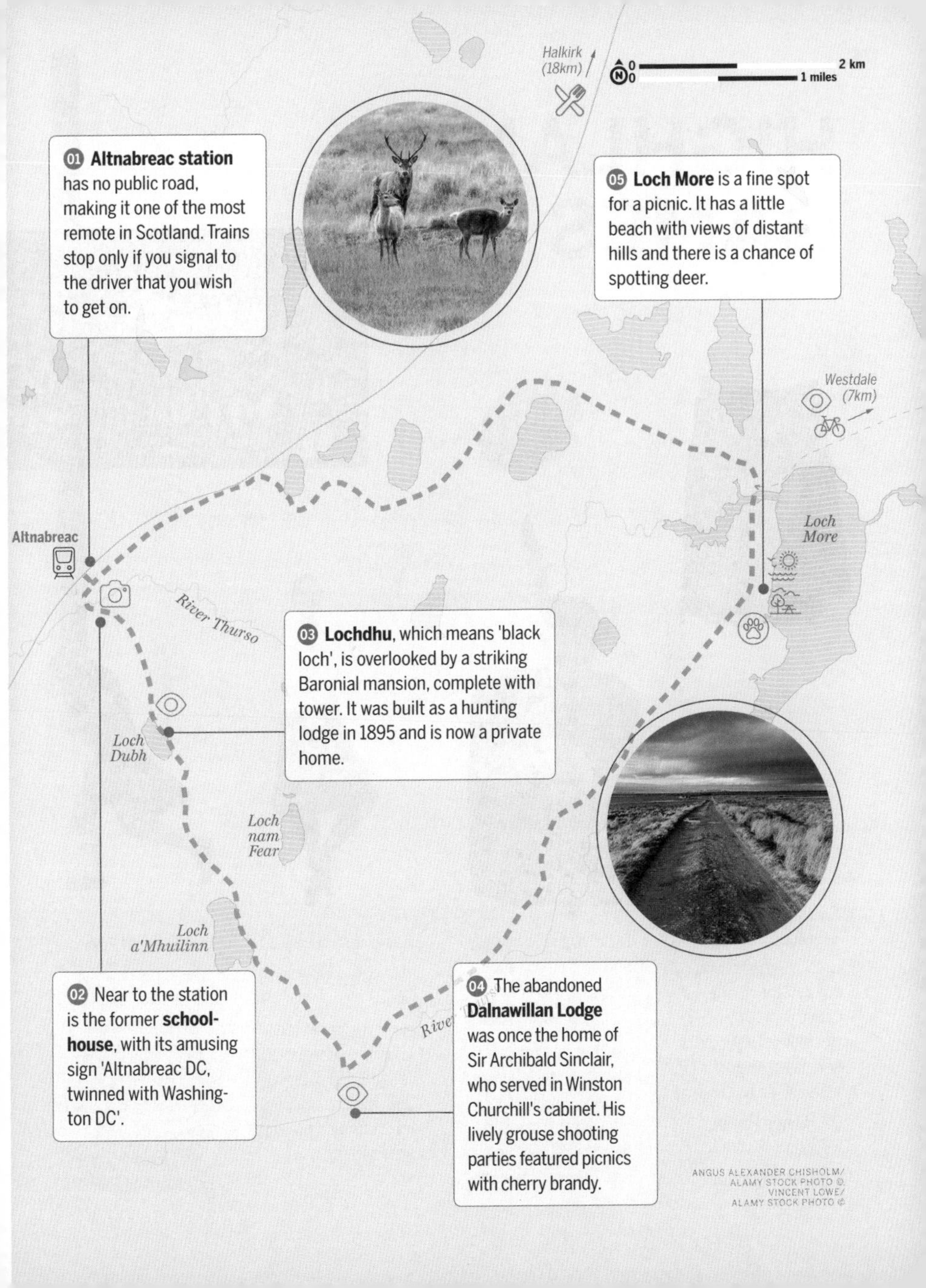

01 Altnabreac station has no public road, making it one of the most remote in Scotland. Trains stop only if you signal to the driver that you wish to get on.

02 Near to the station is the former **school-house**, with its amusing sign 'Altnabreac DC, twinned with Washing-ton DC'.

03 Lochdhu, which means 'black loch', is overlooked by a striking Baronial mansion, complete with tower. It was built as a hunting lodge in 1895 and is now a private home.

04 The abandoned **Dalnawillan Lodge** was once the home of Sir Archibald Sinclair, who served in Winston Churchill's cabinet. His lively grouse shooting parties featured picnics with cherry brandy.

05 Loch More is a fine spot for a picnic. It has a little beach with views of distant hills and there is a chance of spotting deer.

ANGUS ALEXANDER CHISHOLM/ALAMY STOCK PHOTO ©, VINCENT LOWE/ALAMY STOCK PHOTO ©

HIGHLAND GAMES

04

01

02

05

06

03

01 Kilts

Game rules state that competitors in the heavy events must wear kilts. The colours and patterns on the kilt are specific to a clan.

02 Haggis Hurling

A novelty event where competitors stand on top of a whisky barrel and try to throw a haggis the furthest.

03 Highland Chieftain

An honorary role, usually undertaken by a local celebrity. They award prizes to the competitors and lead the opening and closing ceremonies.

04 Massed Pipes and Drums

One of the great spectacles of the games is the sight and sound of hundreds of bagpipers and drummers playing and marching.

05 Highland Fling

Said to be a warrior dance to celebrate victory in battle, or to mimic the antics of red deer.

06 Tossing the Caber

Athletes flip a log, called a caber. It can weigh up to 68kg. The

07

08

10

09

11

goal is to toss it as straight as possible.

07 Livestock Exhibitions

Displays of local breeds, like Highland Cattle, can often be seen at Highland Games.

08 Food and Craft Stalls

Highland Games are a great opportunity to try Scottish produce and street food, or buy something from a local artist.

09 Tug o'War

Two teams pull against each other, with the aim of hauling the opposing team across the line. It involves lots of shouting from the team coaches.

10 Solo Piping Competitions

Musicians are judged on different styles of piping, including pibroch, which is slow and classical.

11 Hammer Throwing

Competitors whirl the hammer around their head as fast as they can and try to throw it the furthest. The hammer can weigh up to 10kg.

Listings

BEST OF THE REST

Whisky & West-coast Seafood

Balblair Distillery

This distillery, 6 miles from Tain, featured in the film *Angels' Share*. The tour ends with a dram of fruit and spice flavours.

Kishorn Seafood Bar ££

A blue log cabin, around 4 miles from Lochcarron, where seafood platters are packed with lobster, mussels, crab, langoustines and scallops.

Shieldaig Bar & Coastal Kitchen ££

The rooftop terrace with loch views is the perfect place to enjoy a scrumptious seafood pizza made in a wood-fired oven. In Shieldaig.

Cliffs, Mountains & Caves

Lochinver

For superb mountain views, head to this town and the surrounding area. Lochinver is the starting point of the hike to Suilven, one of the most distinctive peaks in Scotland.

Duncansby Stacks

Surprisingly few people make the trip to view these spectacular sea stacks, home to vast seabird colonies. They are a 2-mile walk from John O'Groats.

Smoo Cave

Accessed by a long staircase to a 15m-high entrance. A covered boardwalk leads to a waterfall and there are tours to explore further. Located in Durness.

Bealach na Bà

Drive it or cycle it; this steep and twisting road provides outstanding mountain panoramas. The summit is at 626m. Located between Kishorn and Applecross.

Music, Theatre & Highland Games

The Ceilidh Place

Excellent program of Scottish folk music on West Argyll St in Ullapool. There is also a bookshop, art gallery, restaurant, bar and accommodation.

Dornoch Pipe Band

On Saturday evenings, May to September, the band parades in Dornoch's town square. Highland dancers perform to the music.

Lyth Arts Centre

The most northerly arts centre in mainland UK. The program has something for everyone: theatre, comedy, world music, dance and family events. A short drive from Wick.

Halkirk Highland Games

Kilted musclemen tossing cabers, pipe bands, dancers and much more. Held on the last Saturday of July, the Games at Halkirk can attract crowds of 5000.

Lochinver, below Canisp and Suilven mountains

Coast, Beaches & Gardens

North Coast 500

The 516-mile driving or cycling tour starts in Inverness and takes in the best of the region's coastal views.

Inverewe Gardens

Exotic plants, like Himalayan poppies, thrive here, 6.5 miles from Gairloch, because of the Gulf Stream. The plants and the Loch Ewe outlook make this a delight.

Thurso-East

Surfers from around the world descend on Thurso in the winter to ride the waves. The pier at the harbour is a good place to view the action.

Sandwood Bay

One of the most beautiful and unspoilt beaches in the UK, with pink sands, dunes and cliffs. It's a 4-mile walk from the nearest car park at Blairmore.

North Coast Sea Tours

Boat tour to the 60m-tall Old Man of Stoer sea stack, then to the puffins and other seabirds of Handa Island. From Kylesku pier.

Made in the Highlands

The Storehouse

A short drive from Dingwall, the Storehouse has a restaurant and farm shop selling fresh produce, local cheese and bread, plus a brilliant selection of gins, whiskies and craft beer.

Lochinver Craft Market

On selected Fridays stallholders set up in the village hall. Pottery, jewellery, clothing, art, food and more from local producers.

Alchemist Gallery

Located in a historic pharmacy building in Dingwall, this gallery has a great selection of

Sandwood Bay

work from local artists and designers, and hosts regular exhibitions.

Coffee, Cake & Treats

Cocoa Mountain £

Incredible hot chocolate adored by regulars, plus truffles with innovative flavours like whisky caramel cappuccino. Find cafes in Dornoch and Balnakeil Craft Village in Durness.

Secret Tea Garden £

Superb homemade scones and cakes in a gorgeous garden setting in Drumbeg.

Whaligoe Steps Cafe and Restaurant ££

Great selection of loose leaf tea, ramen and pizza, plus picture window with clifftop views. Located 7.5 miles south of Wick.

Highland Farm Cafe £

A modern eco-building with splendid views over the Cromarty Firth. Lovely breakfasts and a great haggis burger. Around 3 miles from Dingwall.

Scan to find more things to do in Northern Highlands online

SKYE & THE OUTER HEBRIDES

HISTORY | HIKING | BEACHES

Experience Skye & the Outer Hebrides online

VINCENT LOWE/ALAMY STOCK PHOTO

▸ **Hiking Trotternish** (p186)

▸ **Driving the West Coast** (p190)

▸ **Skye's Secret Sister** (p192)

▸ **St Kilda: Edge of the World** (p194)

▸ **Cycling South Harris** (p196)

▸ **History on Lewis** (p198)

▸ **Listings** (p200)

SKYE & THE OUTER HEBRIDES

Trip Builder

Adventure awaits off the west coast of Scotland. Skye's jaw-dropping landscapes, time-honoured castles and fine-dining options are popular tourist draws, while those seeking solitude – along with ancient standing stones and stunning sandy beaches – head for the Outer Hebrides.

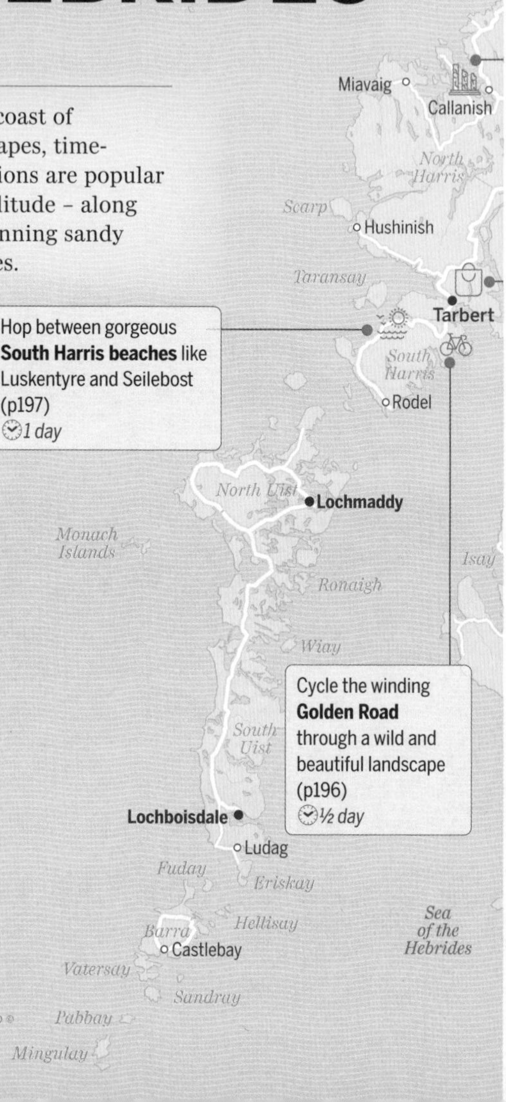

See soaring sea cliffs and rare birdlife on remote **St Kilda** (p194)
1–2 days

Hop between gorgeous **South Harris beaches** like Luskentyre and Seilebost (p197)
1 day

Cycle the winding **Golden Road** through a wild and beautiful landscape (p196)
½ day

Explore bookable experiences on Skye online

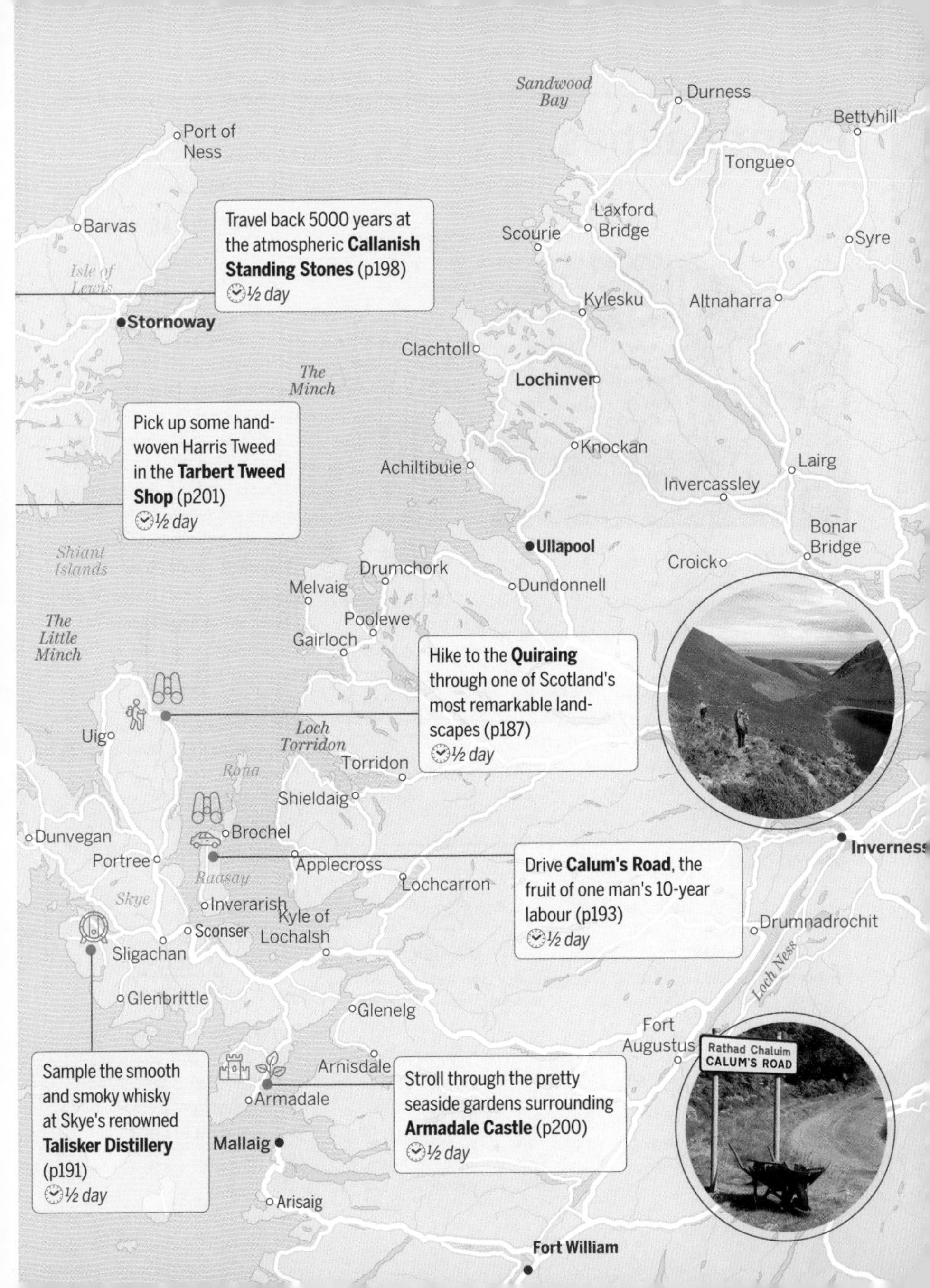
Sandwood Bay
Durness
Bettyhill
Port of Ness
Tongue
Barvas
Travel back 5000 years at the atmospheric **Callanish Standing Stones** (p198)
½ day
Laxford Bridge
Scourie
Syre
Isle of Lewis
Kylesku
Altnaharra
Stornoway
Clachtoll
The Minch
Lochinver
Pick up some hand-woven Harris Tweed in the **Tarbert Tweed Shop** (p201)
½ day
Knockan
Achiltibuie
Lairg
Invercassley
Bonar Bridge
Shiant Islands
Ullapool
Croick
Drumchork
Melvaig
Dundonnell
The Little Minch
Poolewe
Gairloch
Hike to the **Quiraing** through one of Scotland's most remarkable land-scapes (p187)
½ day
Uig
Loch Torridon
Rona
Torridon
Shieldaig
Dunvegan
Brochel
Inverness
Portree
Applecross
Drive **Calum's Road**, the fruit of one man's 10-year labour (p193)
½ day
Raasay
Lochcarron
Skye
Inverarish
Kyle of Lochalsh
Drumnadrochit
Sconser
Sligachan
Loch Ness
Glenbrittle
Glenelg
Fort Augustus
Rathad Chaluim
CALUM'S ROAD
Sample the smooth and smoky whisky at Skye's renowned **Talisker Distillery** (p191)
½ day
Arnisdale
Stroll through the pretty seaside gardens surrounding **Armadale Castle** (p200)
½ day
Armadale
Mallaig
Arisaig
Fort William

Practicalities

MINO SURKALA/SHUTTERSTOCK ©

ARRIVING

Skye Easily reached by bridge from the mainland. Come by car, by train (to Kyle of Lochalsh followed by a local Stagecoach bus service) or by coach tour.

The Outer Hebrides Connected to the mainland, Skye and each other by regular car ferry services run by CalMac. There's also an airport in Stornoway on Lewis – Loganair flights connect to Edinburgh, Glasgow and Inverness – as well as a small airport on Barra.

HOW MUCH FOR A

Fish & chips
£6.50

Distillery tour
£12

Wildlife boat trip
£40

WHEN TO GO

JAN - MAR
Expect chilly and wet conditions, with many attractions closed.

APR - JUN
Ideal time to travel with mild weather and fewer crowds than in summer.

JUL - SEP
Bright but busy. Skye gets very crowded; the Outer Hebrides less so.

OCT - DEC
Wrap up warm against bracing conditions to enjoy sights all to yourself.

GETTING AROUND

Car The easiest and most convenient way to get around the islands is by car. This allows you to visit hard-to-reach spots and stop whenever you like to admire the frequently spectacular scenery. Rent a car on the mainland, in Tarbert (Skye) or in Stornoway (Lewis).

Bus Stagecoach runs regular bus services throughout Skye. A day ticket costs £7.30. In the Outer Hebrides, various local bus services run irregularly during the day, but rarely evenings or on Sunday.

Ferry CalMac ferries link Skye to the Outer Hebrides – and the Hebridean islands to each other. Prices range from £3 to £15 per person and £11 to £70 per car (one way).

EATING & DRINKING

Seafood No trip to Scotland's western isles is complete without tasting fresh, locally caught seafood. Try everything from salmon and scallops to langoustines and lobster.

Spirits From smooth, smoky Talisker whisky to citrusy yet sweet Harris Gin, spirit lovers will be in their element.

Sausages The country's most famous blood sausage comes from Lewis. You'll find Stornoway black pudding on menus across the region, usually as part of a Full Scottish breakfast.

Best seafood

The Three Chimneys (p191)

Must-try whisky

Isle of Raasay Single Malt (p192)

CONNECT

Wi-fi Widely available and generally reliable in hotels and restaurants throughout Skye. There's even free public wi-fi in the main town of Portree. In the Outer Hebrides, things get slower and patchier – and you can't rely on phone signal for data backup. Your best offline sources of information are the VisitScotland iCentres in Portree and Stornoway.

WHERE TO STAY

Most people venture here to get closer to nature. But how close do you want to get? Choose between the comfort of a big town base and a back-to-basics rural stay.

Place	Pro/Con
Portree	Well connected with hotels, restaurants and shops. Gets very crowded in summer.
Sleat Peninsula	Skye's southern tip is green and serene, but a long drive from most of the major attractions.
Stornoway	The Outer Hebrides' main town is a convenient, comfy base, yet lacks the away-from-it-all feel.
West Coast of Harris	Stay in a B&B overlooking the spectacular sandy shoreline. Downside: hard to reach with no car.
St Kilda	Britain's most remote island is a unique option, even if it's a long journey and a basic campsite.

PREPARE FOR RAIN

It doesn't matter when you're visiting: there is always the chance of rain (and usually with very little warning). Always carry a raincoat.

MONEY

Cards are widely accepted, but carry cash to use in small businesses like cafes and independent museums.

33 Hiking TROTTERNISH

HIKING | VIEWS | DAY TRIP

Strap on your hiking boots for a day in the glorious landscapes of Skye's Trotternish peninsula. Start with the spectacular and strenuous Quiraing hike, tackle the short but steep Old Man of Storr, then warm down with the easy-going Scorrybreac circuit.

How to

Getting here Trotternish is the northernmost peninsula of Skye. The hike starting points are easiest to reach by car (drive north on the A855 from Portree), though the infrequent 57A bus will get you close.

When to go Summer is the best time for hiking. Even then, the weather can turn in an instant, so dress appropriately.

Top tip End your day with a slap-up meal overlooking Portree Harbour at the superb **Scorrybreac Restaurant** (scorrybreac.com).

The Quiraing

This epic collection of craggy cliffs, rocky stacks and grassy plateaus is one of Skye's most distinctive landscapes – and one of its most popular hikes. This challenging 4-mile, two-hour loop gets busy in summer, so start as early as possible to avoid crowds and ensure a parking spot; it's particularly spectacular at sunrise. Follow signs off the A855 at Brogaig and drive for around 2 miles to reach the Quiraing car park.

The Prison

From opposite the car park, the hiking trail immediately leads up to a distant, jagged rock formation known as the Prison. The name comes from its resemblance to a fortress, which becomes clearer as you continue along

Rock & Fall

For a spectacular view without the climb, stop at the **Kilt Rock** viewpoint between the Old Man of Storr and the Quiraing. This 90m-high cliff face is made up of basalt columns that resemble the pleats of a kilt. Nearby, **Mealt Falls** elegantly plummets into the foaming ocean.

Top left The Quiraing
Top right Hiking to the Old Man of Storr
Left The Prison

the path, crossing a small stream and climbing a scree slope beside the structure.

The Needle

Continue beyond the Prison and you will come to a series of column-like rock formations, including the wizened and jagged Needle. Beyond this point, the cliff-hugging path winds down into a shallow valley, then instantly climbs back up again. Luckily, the views get better and better with each step.

The Table

As you reach the 540m summit, the view expands into a full panorama. On a clear day, you can see beyond the islands of Raasay and Rona to the mainland. More immediately, you can look down at the Table, a flat glassy plateau that was allegedly used for centuries by locals to hide sheep and cattle from invaders. When you are done, a steep and often muddy path leads back to the car park.

A Different Way Back

Head down Trotternish's attraction-packed west coast for an alternative route back to Portree.

Skye Museum of Island Life A preserved village of thatched cottages offers insight into crofting life.

Grave of Flora MacDonald Nearby is the grave of Flora MacDonald, who helped Bonnie Prince Charlie escape capture.

Fairy Glen An enchantingly strange landscape of rolling green hillocks, *lochans* (ponds) and rock formations just east from the town of Uig.

The Galley Cafe Grab a takeaway snack and drive down to the charming ruins of Caisteal Uisdean for a lochside picnic.

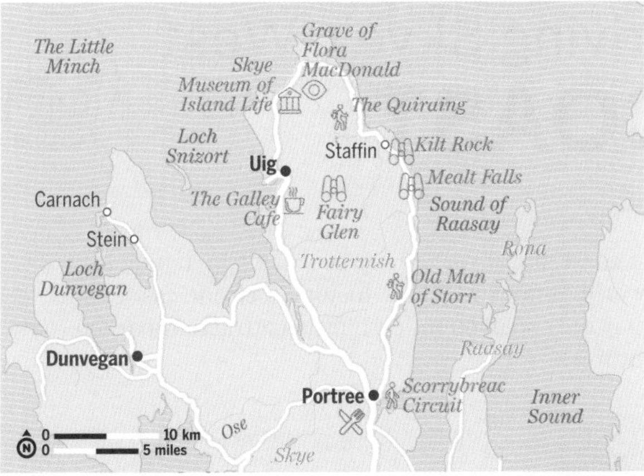

Left Stone circle at Fairy Glen
Below Skye Museum of Island Life

The Old Man of Storr

Another popular Trotternish hike leads to the Old Man of Storr, a 50m-high shard of rock said to be the thumb of a local giant buried in the landscape. A clear gravel path curves up the hill from a car park beside Loch Leathan, just off the A855, although the path soon turns to well-worn rock and dirt. It gets steeper, rougher and muddier as it snakes up to the top, but within just 45 minutes you will be standing at the foot of the Old Man and surveying the landscape below. Head back down the same way you came (30 minutes).

The Scorrybreac Circuit

This gentle, 45-minute shoreside loop is a fine way to round off an active day. Start at the small car park behind the Cuillin Hills Hotel. Signs will lead you past the boathouse and up the hill to the Nicolson Memorial, commemorating one of Scotland's oldest Celtic clans. A nearby viewpoint offers a lovely prospect of Portree Bay. Continue to the tidal Black Rock, a popular sunbathing spot for seabirds, and along the narrowing coastal path past a series of salmon farms. Soon enough, the path climbs inland and winds its way back to Portree.

34 Driving Skye's West COAST

WILDLIFE | WHISKY | ROAD TRIP

Skye's dramatic west coast makes for the perfect road trip, taking in stunning coastal scenery, world-famous whiskies, historic lochside castles and rarely spotted wildlife. It may only span 50 miles, but this attraction-packed route offers a whole day of adventure.

DALE KELLY/SHUTTERSTOCK ©

Trip Notes

Getting here Follow the A87 over Skye Bridge from the mainland. After around 25 miles, you will see signs to Dunvegan (A863): this is the starting point for the driving tour.

When to go Summer offers the best chance of sunshine but also the biggest crowds. If possible, aim for the shoulder months: May or September.

Lunch stop Pick up a seafood snack at the Dunvegan Prawn & Mussel Bar.

Beautiful Beaches

This west-coast route passes several lovely stretches of shoreline. Top picks are **Coral Beach**, an eye-catching arc of dazzling white sand dotted with coralline algae, and **Talisker Bay Beach**, a quiet sand-and-stone bay hugged by dramatic cliffs and a tumbling waterfall.

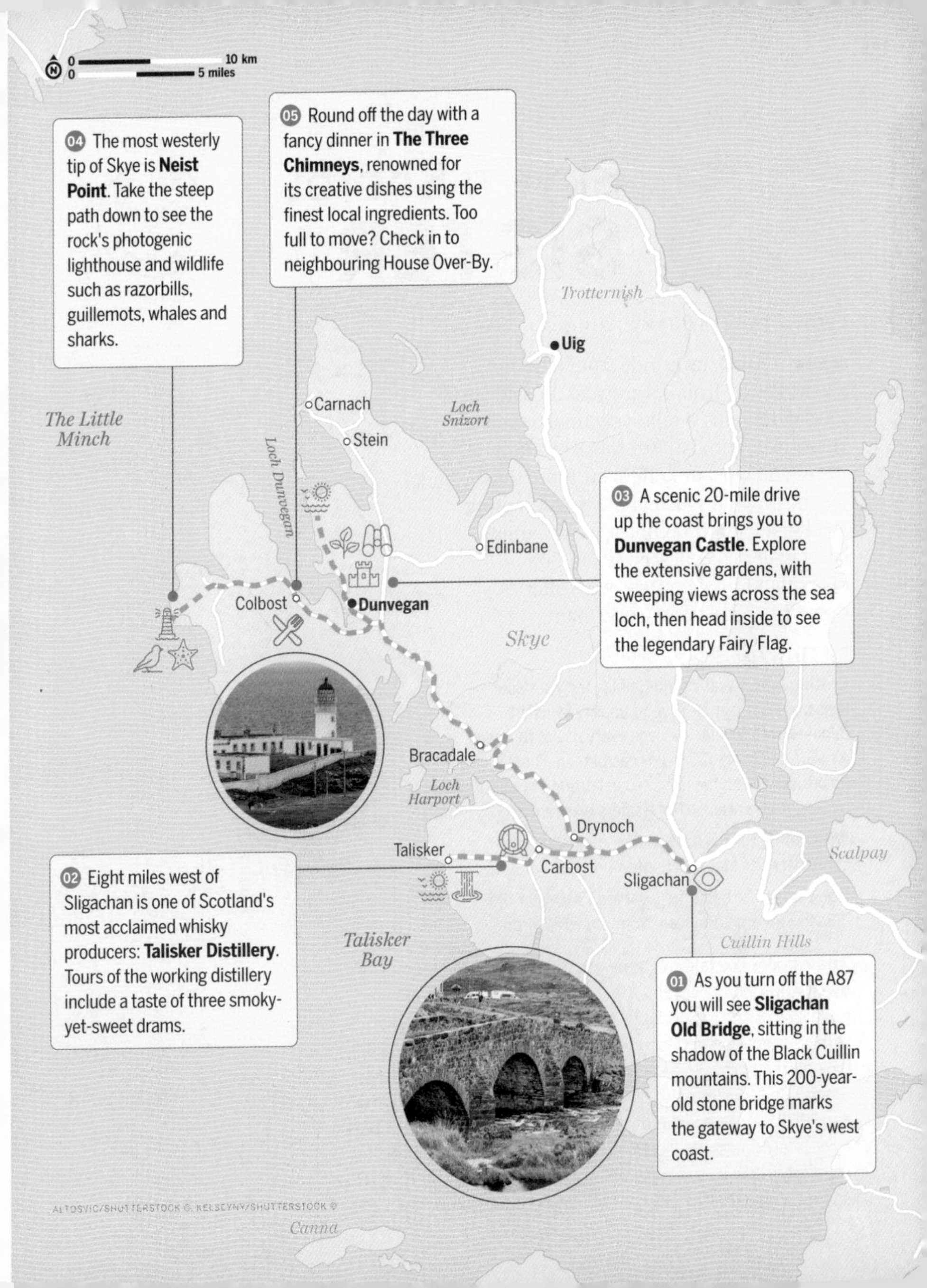

01 As you turn off the A87 you will see **Sligachan Old Bridge**, sitting in the shadow of the Black Cuillin mountains. This 200-year-old stone bridge marks the gateway to Skye's west coast.

02 Eight miles west of Sligachan is one of Scotland's most acclaimed whisky producers: **Talisker Distillery**. Tours of the working distillery include a taste of three smoky-yet-sweet drams.

03 A scenic 20-mile drive up the coast brings you to **Dunvegan Castle**. Explore the extensive gardens, with sweeping views across the sea loch, then head inside to see the legendary Fairy Flag.

04 The most westerly tip of Skye is **Neist Point**. Take the steep path down to see the rock's photogenic lighthouse and wildlife such as razorbills, guillemots, whales and sharks.

05 Round off the day with a fancy dinner in **The Three Chimneys**, renowned for its creative dishes using the finest local ingredients. Too full to move? Check in to neighbouring House Over-By.

35 Skye's Secret SISTER

CROWD-FREE | WHISKY | HIKING

A quick ferry ride from Skye but a world away from its crowds, the Isle of Raasay remains a relatively unexplored Hebridean outpost. But this rugged, 10-mile-long island offers far more than just respite – it's also home to fascinating local history, hilltop hikes, castle ruins, spectacular coastal scenery and one of Scotland's most modern distilleries. Come for a day or stay overnight.

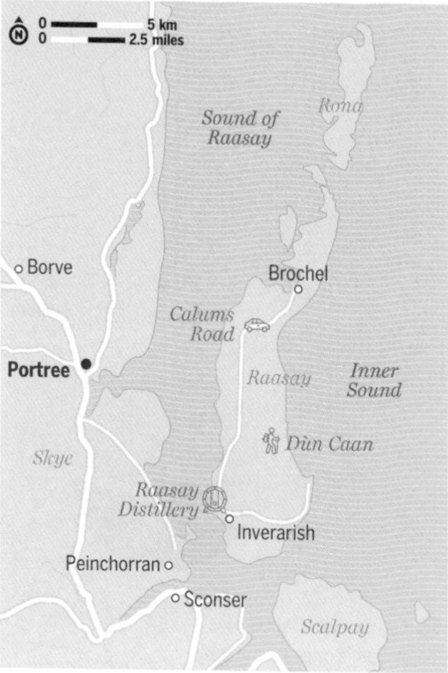

How to

Getting here A year-round CalMac ferry service runs from Sconser on Skye to Raasay in just 25 minutes, with regular services every day of the week. A return trip costs £13/4 per car/person. There's no bus service on the island so get around by car or bicycle; Raasay House Hotel offers bike rentals.

When to go For the best chance of good weather, come between May and September.

Don't miss The beautifully carved 1300-year-old Pictish Stone, a short walk from the ferry terminal.

The whisky The **Isle of Raasay Distillery** has perhaps the best view of any in Scotland, with its glass-covered facade looking out across to Skye's craggy Cuillin Hills. As the first legal distillery on an island once infamous for its illegal production, Raasay released its first single malt in 2021. You can try it for yourself on a tour and tasting, and stay overnight at the distillery's luxurious Borodale House hotel.

The road Raasay's most famous attraction is the work of just one man. After the council repeatedly failed to provide better access to northern Raasay, crofter Calum MacLeod

Top right Barrels at Isle of Raasay Distillery
Below Campervans beside Calum's Road, near Loch Arnish

TOM RICHARDSON SCOTLAND/ALAMY STOCK PHOTO ©

VINCENT LOWE/ALAMY STOCK PHOTO ©

Skye in Miniature

The Isle of Raasay is a well-kept secret. We have all the great things that Skye is famous for: whisky, walks, fantastic food, beautiful beaches, breathtaking views and outdoor activities... But we have it all on this much smaller island, which makes it far easier to fit in everything you would like to do. I suppose you could say that Raasay is Skye's fun little sister.

Carol Anderson, *Raasay Tourism Group*

decided to take matters into his own hands. Over the next 10 years, using only a pickaxe and a shovel, he converted a narrow footpath into a usable, 1.75-mile-long road. Half a century on, **Calum's Road** remains as a lovely scenic drive, starting just beyond the brooding Brochel Castle.

The hill The island's highest peak is the flat-topped **Dùn Caan**, which can be reached with a three-hour, round-trip hike from the ferry terminal. The path winds through historic mining villages, pine forests and loch-dotted moors before zigzagging up to the 443m-high summit. The final stretch is steep and rocky, but the panoramic views from the top provide ample reward.

36 St Kilda: Edge of THE WORLD

ISLAND | BIRDLIFE | DAY TRIP

The tiny archipelago of St Kilda, situated around 100 miles west of the Scottish mainland, is the most remote corner of the British Isles. It is also one of the most beautiful, thanks to its soaring sea stacks, abundant birdlife and fascinating island culture. But splendid isolation doesn't come easy: you'll need money, time and a strong stomach to get here.

VINCENT LOWE/ALAMY STOCK PHOTO ©

How to

Getting here Kilda Cruises and Sea Harris boats depart from Leverburgh on Harris. Alternatively, Go to St Kilda (gotost kilda.co.uk) offers cruises to/from Skye.

When to go Trips run most days between late April and September. Even in summer, inclement weather can force last-minute cancellations; keep an extra day spare as backup.

How much £220 to £260, depending on the operator you go with. Deposits are required for advance bookings.

ANDY SUTTON/ALAMY STOCK PHOTO ©

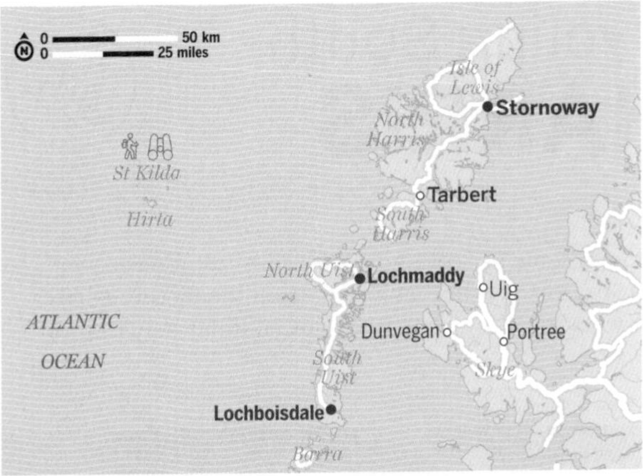

A rocky ride Every St Kilda experience begins with a rough, three-hour boat ride across empty ocean. But stomachs soon settle when **Hirta**, the archipelago's main island, appears over the horizon. It feels like arriving at the edge of the world so it's a surprise when you pull into a quaint little village.

Island life Despite its isolation, St Kilda was home to a tiny community for around 2000 years. Most of those were spent entirely cut off from the rest of civilisation, with islanders sustained by a diet of seabirds. Today you can explore the historic village at the heart of Hirta, as well as the surrounding *cleitean*, stone storage huts built to cure prime cuts of seabird by utilising the reliably strong winds.

Stunning scenery Without doubt, Hirta's biggest draw is its unspoilt nature. Hike along the southern coast to **Ruival** or climb **Conachair** in the north to take in its many varied landscapes, from lush green pastures grazed by rare Soay sheep to sky-scraping cliffs engulfed by screeching clouds of seabirds.

Nesting gannets From glowering grey-brown great skuas to playful orange-beaked puffins, Hirta's birds are a sight to behold. But save some camera memory for the boat journey back, when you will skirt close to St Kilda's colossal sea stacks, swarming with thousands of yellow-headed gannets (and their pungent guano).

Top left Cottages in Hirta
Below Hikers ascending Conachair

Stay on St Kilda

If one day isn't enough, consider camping on Hirta. A small campsite managed by the National Trust for Scotland offers space for six people along with basic toilets, showers and drinking water.
There is no guaranteed electricity supply, wi-fi or mobile-phone signal, and you'll need to bring your own camping stove and food; pack a little extra in case your departure is delayed. It costs £20 per person per night, and you should book as far in advance as possible due to limited space. Email stkildainfo@nts.org.uk or call 01463 732635 to find out current availability.

37 Cycling South HARRIS

BEACHES | BIKING | VIEWS

South Harris is home to some of Scotland's most jaw-dropping coastal scenery. Spend a whole day exploring every inch of it, from the picture-perfect white-sand beaches of the west coast to the heather-dotted lunar landscape of the east.

COLIN PALMER PHOTOGRAPHY/ALAMY STOCK PHOTO ©

Trip Notes

Getting here and around In summer, there are daily ferries to Tarbert from Uig on Skye. Timetables are on the CalMac website. There's no bike hire in Tarbert, but you can rent one at Bike Hebrides in Stornoway on Lewis or bring your own bike on the ferry for free.

When to go Stick to summer for milder weather.

Summary Distance: 52 miles. Difficulty: medium to hard (expect climbs in and out of Tarbert).

Turn One Day into Two

If you prefer a more leisurely pace, you can break up your trip with an overnight stay. Picture-perfect Scarista Beach, which lies just under halfway along this route (3 miles beyond MacLeod's Stone), is lined with charming B&B options. It also makes an ideal base for hiking Chaipaval.

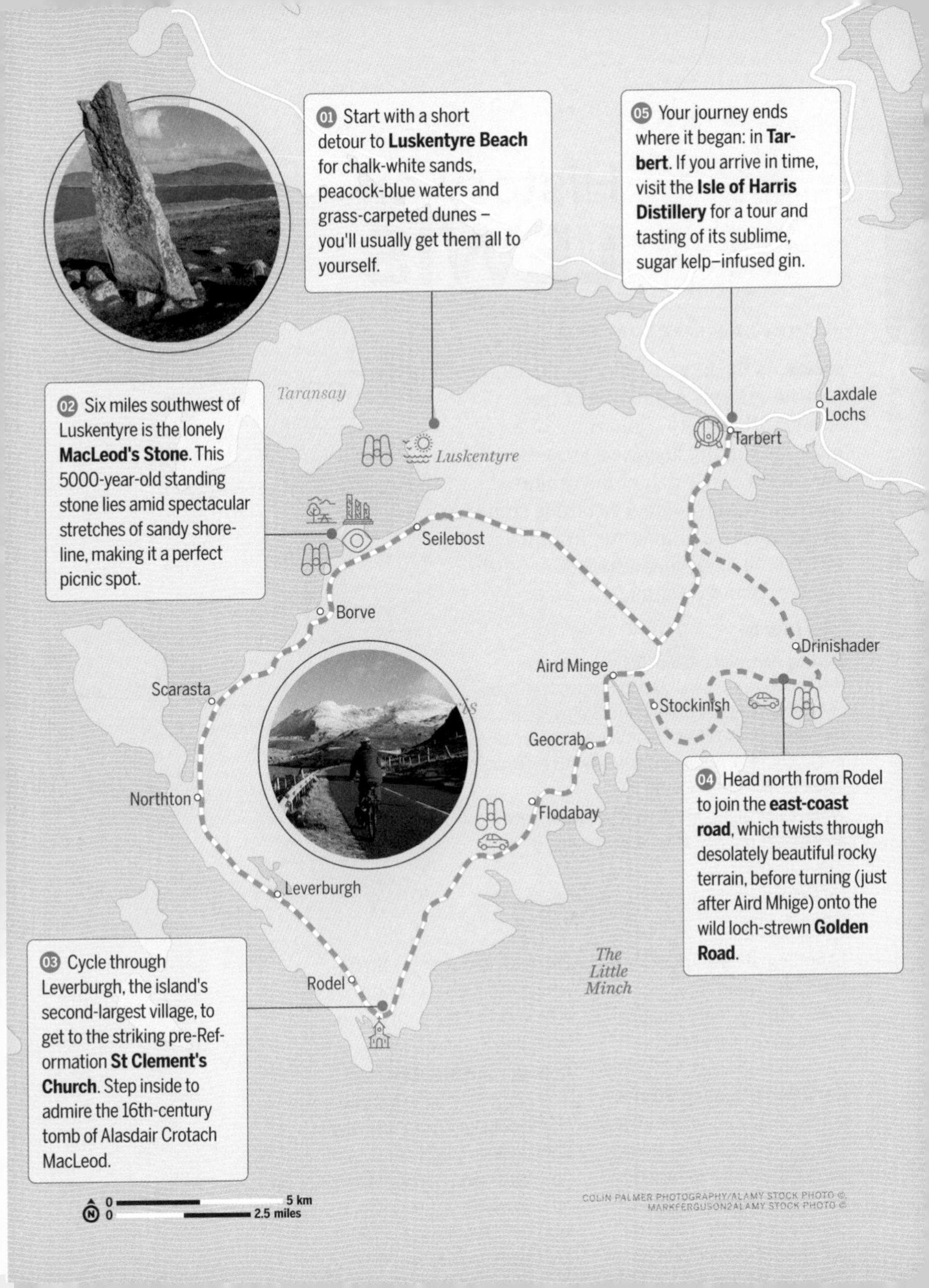

01 Start with a short detour to **Luskentyre Beach** for chalk-white sands, peacock-blue waters and grass-carpeted dunes – you'll usually get them all to yourself.

02 Six miles southwest of Luskentyre is the lonely **MacLeod's Stone**. This 5000-year-old standing stone lies amid spectacular stretches of sandy shoreline, making it a perfect picnic spot.

03 Cycle through Leverburgh, the island's second-largest village, to get to the striking pre-Reformation **St Clement's Church**. Step inside to admire the 16th-century tomb of Alasdair Crotach MacLeod.

04 Head north from Rodel to join the **east-coast road**, which twists through desolately beautiful rocky terrain, before turning (just after Aird Mhige) onto the wild loch-strewn **Golden Road**.

05 Your journey ends where it began: in **Tarbert**. If you arrive in time, visit the **Isle of Harris Distillery** for a tour and tasting of its sublime, sugar kelp–infused gin.

38 History on LEWIS

HISTORY | CULTURE | DAY TRIP

As the largest island of the Outer Hebrides, Lewis is bursting at the seams with history – and three of its most fascinating historical attractions are within easy reach of the capital, Stornoway. Start with a Neolithic stone circle, take in a fascinating Iron Age fortress, then explore a traditional 19th-century island dwelling.

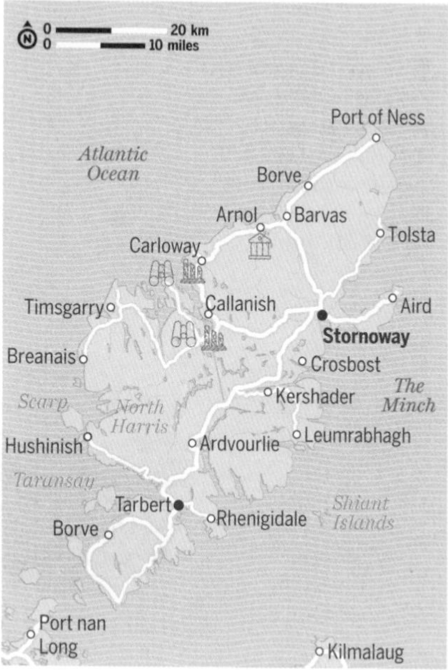

How to

Getting here and around Stornoway can be reached by air (its small airport is served by Loganair) and sea (regular CalMac ferries arrive from Ullapool on the mainland). Getting around is easiest by car, but there is a limited bus service (W2) that stops at Callanish, Carloway and Arnol.

When to go Sights are open year-round; since most are outside, dress weather-appropriately in the wet winter months.

How much Arnol Blackhouse: £6. Callanish and Carloway: free.

Standing stones Travel west from Stornoway for around 17 miles and you'll come to one of Britain's most important prehistoric sights. The **Callanish Standing Stones** comprise 13 large stones laid out in a circle around a central monolith. From here, another 40 smaller stones radiate out in a cruciform. Erected between 3000 and 1500 BCE, Callanish is older than Stonehenge and it offers a better view, overlooking pretty Loch Roag and Bernera island.

Robust roundhouse A little further up the coast lies another ancient site. **Dun Carloway** is an unusually well-preserved Iron Age broch, a type of fortified building unique to Scotland. Built around 200 BCE to protect against seaborne

Top right Callanish Standing Stones
Bottom right Dun Carloway broch

NATALIA YATSKEVICH/SHUTTERSTOCK ©

JOE GOUGH/SHUTTERSTOCK ©

Lewis Chess Pieces

Discovered on the island in 1831, the Lewis Chess Pieces are a set of medieval gaming pieces made from walrus ivory and sperm whale tooth. Their facial expressions are full of character and a testament to the extraordinary skill of their carver(s). See them at the National Museum of Scotland in Edinburgh and the British Museum in London, as well as on long-term loan at the Museum nan Eilean (p200) in Lewis.

Lydia Prosser,
Curator of Medieval Archaeology and History, National Museum of Scotland @NtlMuseumsScot

raiders, parts of its rounded, drystone walls still stand at 9m high, close to its original height. Pop into the nearby visitor centre to learn more about the history and cultural significance of the structure.

Hebridean home Nine miles further north (and 2000 years into the future) is Arnol and its famous **Blackhouse**. This type of dwelling, where a family and its animals lived together under one thatched roof, was commonly used until as recently as the mid-20th century. Step inside to smell the smoke coming off the peat hearth; it's the years of accumulated soot that give the Blackhouse its name. From here, it's just 15 miles back to Stornoway.

Listings

BEST OF THE REST

Outdoor Attractions

Fairy Pools

This collection of enchanting blue-green plunge pools and gentle cascades is one of Skye's most magical sights. Come early or late to avoid the day-tripping crowds.

Armadale Castle Garden

Centred around a semi-ruined 17th-century castle, these vast flower-filled gardens in southern Skye offer spectacular views across to the mainland. A ticket includes access to a fascinating museum on the Clan Donald.

Balranald Nature Reserve

With its mix of rich grassland, sand dunes and wild marshes, this rarely visited reserve on North Uist is a haven for birdlife. Keep an ear out for corncrakes and their distinctive rasping cry.

Our Lady of the Isles

This 9m-high granite sculpture of the Madonna and Child stands on South Uist as a symbol of resistance; it was built on land earmarked for a Ministry of Defence missile facility, scuppering the government's plans.

Sandy Beaches

Traigh Mhòr

Commonly known as Tolsta Beach, this stretch of soft golden shoreline within easy reach of Stornoway is known for its grassy dunes and powerful ocean swells (ideal for surfing).

Traigh Seilebost

Even among the many jaw-dropping beaches of South Harris, Seilebost stands out for its pristine, powdery sands backed by primrose-dotted machair. It also looks across to another stunning beach: Luskentyre.

Traigh Mhòr

Popular with hikers, this inviting white beach at the tip of Barra is also a runway. In fact, it's the only beach runway in the world to handle scheduled airline services.

History Museums

Staffin Dinosaur Museum

One of Skye's most popular family attractions, this museum (founded by local dinosaur hunter Dugald Ross) has an interesting collection of dinosaur footprints and fossils.

Museum nan Eilean

Inside Stornoway's Lews Castle, this new exhibition space showcases various aspects of Hebridean life, from island professions to the Gaelic language. It's also home to six of the famous Lewis Chess Pieces.

Seallam!

Gaelic for 'Let me show you', this visitor centre just north of Leverburgh on Harris has

Armadale Castle Garden

exhibits on Western Isles history and nature. There is also a genealogy centre for those tracing their Hebridean ancestry.

Kildonan Museum

This small museum on South Uist has several interesting artefacts and exhibits on the Uists and the people who live there, as well as a craft shop, cafe and performing arts space.

Island Art Galleries

Dandelion Designs

This charming little gallery in Stein, a crofting township on Skye's Waternish peninsula, showcases a wide range of paintings, photographs and crafts by a mix of local and invited artists.

Raasay Gallery

Works by local artists are featured at this purpose-built gallery space on Skye's neighbouring isle. But the best landscape of all is outside, with spectacular views across the sea to the Cuillin Hills.

Island Darkroom

Overlooking loch-covered moorland, this photography gallery in Lewis displays beautiful prints created in the on-site darkroom. Hands-on workshops let you try analogue film processing and printing for yourself.

Skoon Art Gallery

South Harris' east coast has many fine art galleries, including Mission House, Finsbay and Holmasaig. But if you have limited time, head straight for Skoon, set within a renovated crofthouse.

Hebridean Handicrafts

Isle of Skye Candle Company

This artisan producer sells wax candles as well as reed diffusers, soaps and bubble baths. Fragrances are inspired by Scotland,

GREG BALFOUR EVANS/ALAMY STOCK PHOTO ©

Harris Tweed jackets

allowing you to take home the aromas of whisky, seaweed and heather.

Borgh Pottery

A working studio near the northern tip of Lewis selling hand-thrown ceramics inspired by the local landscape. Watch artist Sue Blair at work on her potter's wheel and take home a souvenir.

Tarbert Tweed Shop

No trip to the Outer Hebrides is complete without picking up some Harris Tweed. This Tarbert store has an array of tweed items, from suit jackets to soft furnishings, hats to handbags.

Hebridean Jewellery

Overlooking pretty Iochdar Beach on the northwest coast of South Uist, this out-of-the-way jeweller specialises in handcrafted silver and gold creations incorporating traditional Pictish and Celtic designs.

Scan to find more things to do in Skye & the Outer Hebrides online

ORKNEY
CULTURE | LANDSCAPES | HISTORY
Experience Orkney online

▸ **Hop to Papa Westray** (p206)

▸ **Neolithic Orkney** (p208)

▸ **Creative Orkney Trail** (p210)

▸ **5000 Years od Orkney Creativity** (p212)

▸ **St Magnus Way Walk** (p214)

▸ **Listings** (p216)

ORKNEY

Trip Builder

Explore bookable experiences in Orkney online

Visitors to this archipelago, at times more akin to Scandinavia than Scotland, are lured by islands brimful with ancient monuments and landscapes steeped in Viking sagas. Bygone eras are chronicled in stone, but it's the people who are the real preservers of the past.

Pay respects to Orkney's patron saint at **St Magnus Cathedral** (p214)
1–2 hours

Climb 176 steps for breathtaking views at **North Ronaldsay Lighthouse** (p217)
1 hour

Take the world's shortest scheduled flight between **Westray** and **Papa Westray** (p206)
1 day

Explore a village older than the Egyptian pyramids at **Skara Brae** (p209)
½ day

Watch a traditional Orkney chair maker at work in **Kirkwall** (p211)
1 hour

Inhale the sea air on a hike along the **Yesnaby cliffs** (p216)
½ day

PQL89/SHUTTERSTOCK ©

Practicalities

ARRIVING

Kirkwall Airport Serves direct flights from major Scottish cities. On arrival take the bus 3 miles to Kirkwall.

Ferries To Orkeny, sail from Thurso to Stomness, and from Gill's Bay to St Margaret's Hope.

CONNECT

Connect to free public wi-fi at the Kirkwall iCentre and some Mainland businesses. Access in the outer isles is very limited.

MONEY

Carry a few pounds of loose change for local honesty boxes selling eggs, vegetables, cakes, preserves and baked goods.

WHERE TO STAY

Town/Village	Pro/Con
Kirkwall	The bustling central hub of the islands; it can get busy.
Stromness	Quaint and historic maritime character, but with few evening options.
St Margaret's Hope	Close to the best spots for marine wildlife, though far from town.

GETTING AROUND

Car Necessary to explore beyond the main towns and attractions.

Bus Run regularly between Kirkwall and Stromness; rural buses can be infrequent.

Ferry & plane Both depart from Mainland to the outer isles, but be aware, there is no public transport on these islands.

EATING & DRINKING

Pattie Supper A local speciality of mince, potatoes and onion deep-fried and served with chips.

Fattie Cutties Fruity biscuits originating from Westray; buy them in independent food stores.

Bere Bannocks These flat breads are made from an ancient local barley. Top them with butter or cheese.

Must-try sweet treat

Orkney Fudge (p217)

Best local seafood

Murray Arms Hotel (p217)

JAN–MAR
Cold with short daylight hours; good chance of seeing the Northern Lights.

APR–JUN
Temperatures fluctuate between low and mild; the best time for festivals.

JUL–SEP
Warm temperatures and longest daylight hours; ideal for outdoor exploring.

OCT–DEC
Low temperatures and shorter days; few tourists, so attractions are quiet.

39 Hop to Papa WESTRAY

NATURE | BEACHES | HERITAGE

With a good wind, the flight between the Orkney islands of Westray and Papa Westray takes close to one minute; on a bad day, it's nearer to two. Either way, it still qualifies as the world's shortest scheduled flight, confirmed by the *Guinness Book of Records*. But it's not all about the journey; Papa Westray is a destination worth delving deeper into.

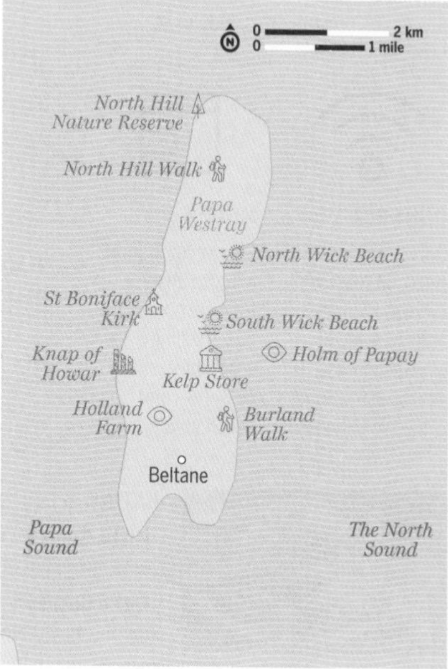

How to

Getting there Book a return flight from Kirkwall to Papa Westray with Loganair. Most outbound flights stop at Westray before continuing to Papa Westray, but check with the airline before booking. The island itself is walkable.

When to visit Year-round, although weather is best in spring and summer.

Top tip On return to Kirkwall Airport, collect your personalised souvenir flight certificate.

Local tip Orcadians shorten Papa Westray to 'Papay'.

Uncover the past Dating back to around 3800 BCE, **Knap of Howar**, a Neolithic farmstead, has the oldest standing stone buildings in northwest Europe. Just along the coast, take sanctuary in **St Boniface Kirk**; Pictish stones found in the kirkyard indicate a religious site much older than the current 12th-century building. The **Kelp Store** has exhibits detailing Papay's rich history and heritage, while the agricultural museum at **Holland Farm** is a time capsule of a lost way of life.

Nature walks In spring and summer, the rare maritime heathland of **North Hill Nature Reserve** is blanketed in a vivid tapestry of wildflowers,

Top right Knap of Howar
Right South Wick Beach

An Uninhabited Island

A community-owned boat ferries visitors across to the uninhabited island of Holm of Papay, just off the east coast of Papa Westray. The best preserved and most remarkable of the three Neolithic chambered cairns found here is also the largest. Modern skylights illuminate the interior, allowing you to pass through confidently. Book in advance via the Papay Ranger on Facebook.

including the rare Scottish primrose. The **North Hill Trail** skirts the coast for 4 miles and takes in the seabird nesting colonies at Fowl Craig. The cliffs bustle with guillemots, razorbills, fulmars and even a few puffins between April and July. Alternatively, head 2.5 miles along the **Burland Walk** to the wetlands around St Tredwell's Loch where wildfowl glide the calm waters and waders feed along its fringes.

Empty beaches Amble across the fine white sands of neighbouring North Wick and South Wick beaches on the east coast where local seals are likely to be your only companions. At the south end of the island, aquamarine shallows are bordered by a serene horseshoe bay at Bothican.

40 Neolithic ORKNEY

ARCHAEOLOGY | MONUMENTS | STONE CIRCLES

Roam across Orkney and you are transported to an age when people forged communities of stone. Their legacy has left an imprint on the landscape for millennia, no more so than at the Heart of Neolithic Orkney, an epicentre of significant monuments designated a Unesco World Heritage Site. Towering stone circles, somber burial cairns and ancient dwellings remain shrouded in mystery.

DANITA DELIMONT/ALAMY STOCK PHOTO ©

How to

Getting around A car offers more freedom (hire one in Kirkwall) or take a local Stagecoach bus from Kirkwall to the main sites mentioned.

When to visit Attractions are open year-round but can be very busy in summer, especially on cruise ship days.

Tour tips Book in advance for entry to Maeshowe. Free tours of Ring of Brodgar and Stones of Stenness take place during summer. For tour info visit historic environment.scot.

JAROSLAV SEKERES/SHUTTERSTOCK ©

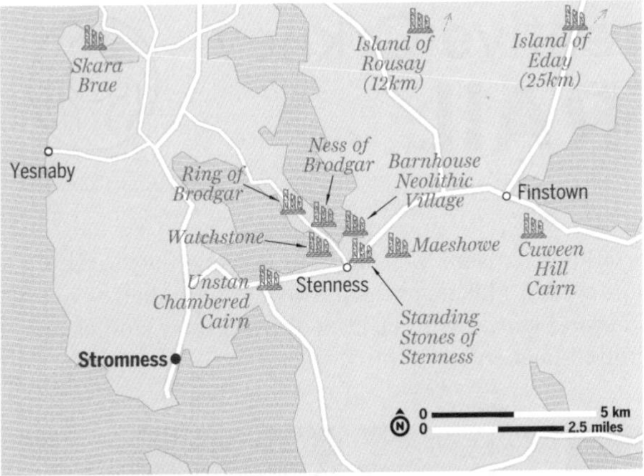

An ancient tomb The passageway of **Maeshowe** leads to a surprisingly spacious chamber where giant sandstone slabs defy gravity and Viking graffiti is scrawled across the walls. Entry to this 5000-year-old tomb includes an informative guided tour.

Towering standing stones Nearby, the **Stones of Stenness** dwarf everything around them. Linger by the hearth among the towering sentinels where locals likely gathered around 3000 BCE. Make the short walk to **Barnhouse**, a Neolithic settlement discovered in 1984. Although not as impressive as Skara Brae, they share many features and dates to a similar period.

Neolithic excavations On the footpath or drive to Ring of Brodgar, you will first be greeted by the **Watchstone**, one of several solitary standing stones, before reaching **Ness of Brodgar** where yearly excavations reveal new clues about the Neolithic people of Orkney and beyond. In summer, visitors can watch archaeologists as they continue to unearth the extensive complex of buildings. At just over 4000 years old, the neighbouring **Ring of Brodgar** is a relative youngster in this ancient landscape. Set in a natural amphitheatre, the purpose of Britain's third-largest stone circle remains an enigma.

A 5000-year-old village Thanks to **Skara Brae** being cocooned under a layer of earth, the prehistoric village has been magnificently preserved. Stone beds and dressers are equivalents of what we use today. A visitor centre houses finds from the settlement.

Top left The entrance to Maeshowe
Bottom left Ring of Brodgar

Less Crowded Neolithic Sites

Unstan Chambered Cairn Distinctive pottery named Unstan Ware and human bones were found during excavations of this 5000-year-old burial monument on the Mainland.

Cuween Hill Chambered Cairn Human and dog skulls discovered here, also on the Mainland, reveal ancient burial rituals. Beware, you will need to crawl into this shadowy tomb.

Island of Rousay Make the short ferry crossing to the 'Egypt of the North', home to over 150 ancient attractions. Midhowe Chambered Cairn is one of the finest.

Island of Eday Attracting few tourists, you will likely have Vinquoy Chambered Cairn and one of Orkney's tallest standing stones to yourself.

41 Creative Orkney TRAIL

ART | CRAFTS | SHOPPING

In workshops across Orkney, artisans welcome you in while they carve, spin, engrave, turn, paint and weave. Makers enthusiastically share their techniques, inspiration and island stories with visitors. Browse their studios and leave with a unique handcrafted memento.

MARKFERGUSON2/ALAMY STOCK PHOTO ©

Trip Notes

Getting around For flexibility, a car is recommended; hire one in Kirkwall. Reach outer islands by Orkney Ferries or Loganair. Buses run frequently between Kirkwall and Stromness but are infrequent in rural areas. Download the Traveline app to plan public transport.

When to go Several workshops only open in spring and summer.

Top tip Pick up a trail booklet from the VisitScotland Information Centre in Kirkwall.

Orkney Chairs

For centuries, Orcadians have huddled by their firesides in a high-back or hooded Orkney chair. Constructed from a wooden frame with a backing handwoven from local oat straw, the style is unique to the islands. Once considered simple furniture, it is now exhibited as a Scottish design icon in V&A Dundee.

01 Visit Alison Moore's workshop in **Dounby** for gemstone jewellery that reflects her geology background. Next door, Castaway Crafts sells handmade Tweed products and items from over 100 local artists.

02 Travel 3 miles south to **Harray** where Andrew Appleby's ceramics at Fursbreck Pottery and the wood-turned designs in Michael Sinclair's studio are heavily influenced by Orkney's Neolithic past.

03 Ten miles further on in **Kirkwall**, the tradition of making Orkney chairs continues at Orkney Handcrafted Furniture and Scapa Crafts. Robin Palmer creates tactile ceramics, and Ortak runs tours of their jewellery workshop.

04 Continue on 6 miles for a lunch break at The Kirk Gallery & Café in **Tankerness**. The renovated church showcases the jewellery collections of Sheila Fleet, while the cafe serves up Orkney cuisine.

05 Finish 17 miles further south at **Hoxa Tapestry Gallery**. It's a proper family affair – mother, daughter and son combine their artistic talents to produce tapestries, rugs, paintings and yarns.

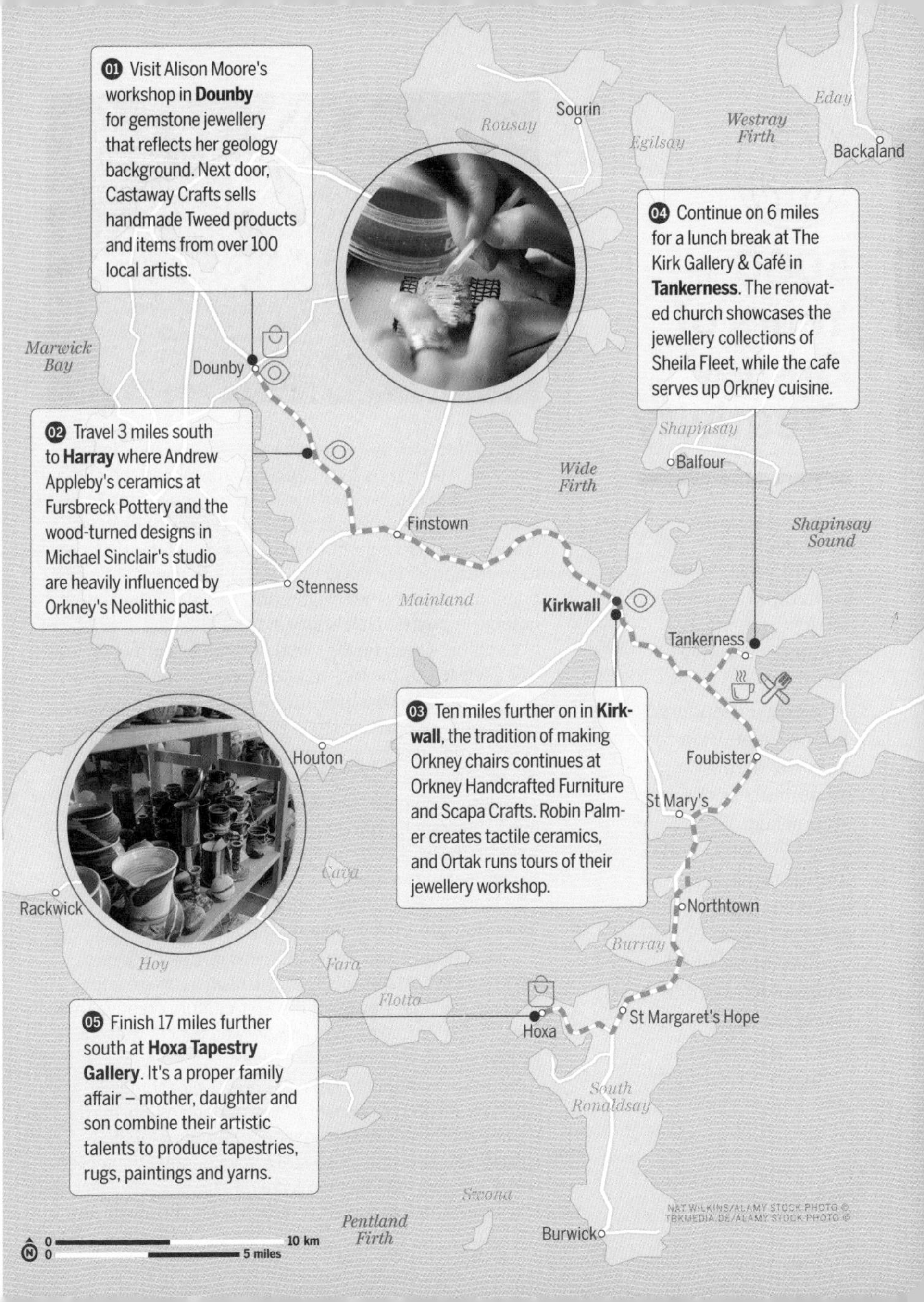

5000 Years of Orkney Creativity

ISLAND DESIGNS FASHIONED BY ANCIENT ARTISANS

Contemporary crafters are just the latest chapter in Orkney's 5000-year-old story of talented islanders. Taking inspiration from the earliest inhabitants of the archipelago, they keep alive skills and traditions passed down from previous generations. A number of astonishing archaeological finds reveal the origins and progression of Orkney's creative past.

Left Orkney jewellery
Middle Spinning wheel
Left Artisan crafting an Orkney chair

TBKMEDIA.DE/ALAMY STOCK PHOTO ©

When a Neolithic potter sat down to work on their latest creation, it is unlikely they could have predicted the stir their humble vessel would make five millennia later. At first glance, the pottery sherd uncovered at Ness of Brodgar is fairly unremarkable, but expert analysis of the surface has revealed a hauntingly personal link to one of Orkney's original artisans – their fingerprint. This is not the only notable impression left in clay at the site; a rare imprint of Neolithic woven textile found on another pottery sherd was likely left by the maker's clothing.

This era was a time of transformation with the introduction of pottery, polished stone and large-scale monuments. Despite rudimentary apparatus, there is evidence of exquisite workmanship among the New Stone Age communities, who designed objects with both function and fashion in mind. Inspiration from Orkney's prehistoric past can be found in the work of today's makers, who depict standing stones and tombs in jewellery and artwork; while others take literal inspiration from ancient discoveries by styling bowls and pots on millennia-old designs.

As the Bronze and Iron Ages rolled in, metalworkers joined the list of Orkney's skilled artisans. If there had been an Iron Age version of the 21st-century creative trail, potters, textile makers and jewellery designers would all be plying their trade much like today.

What we know about Orkney's creative past mainly comes from archaeologists sifting through murky earth, waiting for the soil to surrender another piece of the jigsaw. Now and again they strike gold, or something even better – wood. Wooden items are rare finds as organic material can deteriorate quickly, which is why the discovery

WERNER FORMAN/UNIVERSAL IMAGES GROUP/GETTY IMAGES ©

HEMIS/ALAMY STOCK PHOTO ©

of a perfectly preserved 2000-year-old carved wooden bowl at The Cairns dig site is all the more extraordinary. What makes it even more unusual are the intricate bronze repairs, showcasing a harmony of old and new craftsmanship. The recovery of an intact piece of clothing conserved in a peat bog was another scarce gift from the Iron Age. An expert study of the 2000-year-old 'Orkney Hood' has revealed masterful spinning and weaving skills.

Further innovation came when the Vikings arrived, importing a new wave of ideas, techniques and handcrafted global goods and, more significantly, a new language and culture. Treasure troves from boat burials and concealed hoards have brought to light their appreciation of highly decorative jewellery and ornate personal possessions. One of the most curious finds from Orkney is the Scar Dragon Plaque, featuring two intricately carved dragon heads. It is perhaps the Norse era more than any other that can claim the biggest influence on today's designers. Gallery windows across the islands are filled with beautifully crafted keepsakes engraved with Norse runes and mythical creatures. Just as the Viking artisans traded their goods around the world by boat, Orkney's current creatives sell their wares to international visitors travelling on ferries and cruise liners, and in some ways very little has changed, other than the boats being bigger.

> Inspiration from Orkney's prehistoric past can be found in the work of today's makers...

Learn a Local Craft

Orkney Creative Hub was set up to support and nurture a new wave of local artists and designers. Although visitors are very welcome at their weekly workshops, they are not packaged as tourist experiences. Most participants are local residents looking to learn new skills, including weaving, spinning, painting and felting. Sessions offer an authentic opportunity to join Orkney's creative movement and craft your own unique souvenir under the tutorship of a professional artisan. Introductory sessions covering a variety of artistic disciplines generally last several hours and take place at venues across Kirkwall. Workshops must be booked online in advance at orkneycommunities.co.uk/orkneycreativehub.

42 St Magnus WAY WALK

HIKING | SCENERY | PILGRIMAGE

Set foot in the story of Orkney's patron saint as you hike 58 miles from the location of his martyrdom in Egilsay to his final resting place in St Magnus Cathedral (pictured below). The waymarked pilgrim trail weaves along attractive coastline, past significant historical sites, and unveils wide open vistas before arriving at the heart of the islands in Kirkwall.

Trip Notes

Getting here & around Orkney Ferries runs a regular service between Tingwall and the start of the route in Egilsay. Stagecoach buses run close to the beginning and end of each section, although they can be infrequent.

When to visit The weather is best in spring and summer.

Short on time Walk 11.5 miles from Orphir to Kirkwall taking in history and scenery.

Top tip Download the St Magnus Way app.

The Story of St Magnus

The legacy of St Magnus continues to shape Orkney's culture despite more than 900 years passing since his martyrdom. Born Magnus Erlendsson, he co-ruled Orkney with his cousin Haakon in what started as a harmonious relationship but later severely deteriorated. During peace talks on the island of Egilsay, Haakon betrayed Magnus and ordered his murder. Initially buried where he lay, his body was subsequently transferred to Birsay where miracles were attributed to his gravesite. These wonders saw him canonised, and when his nephew founded St Magnus Cathedral in honour of his uncle, Magnus' relics were interred in one of the pillars.

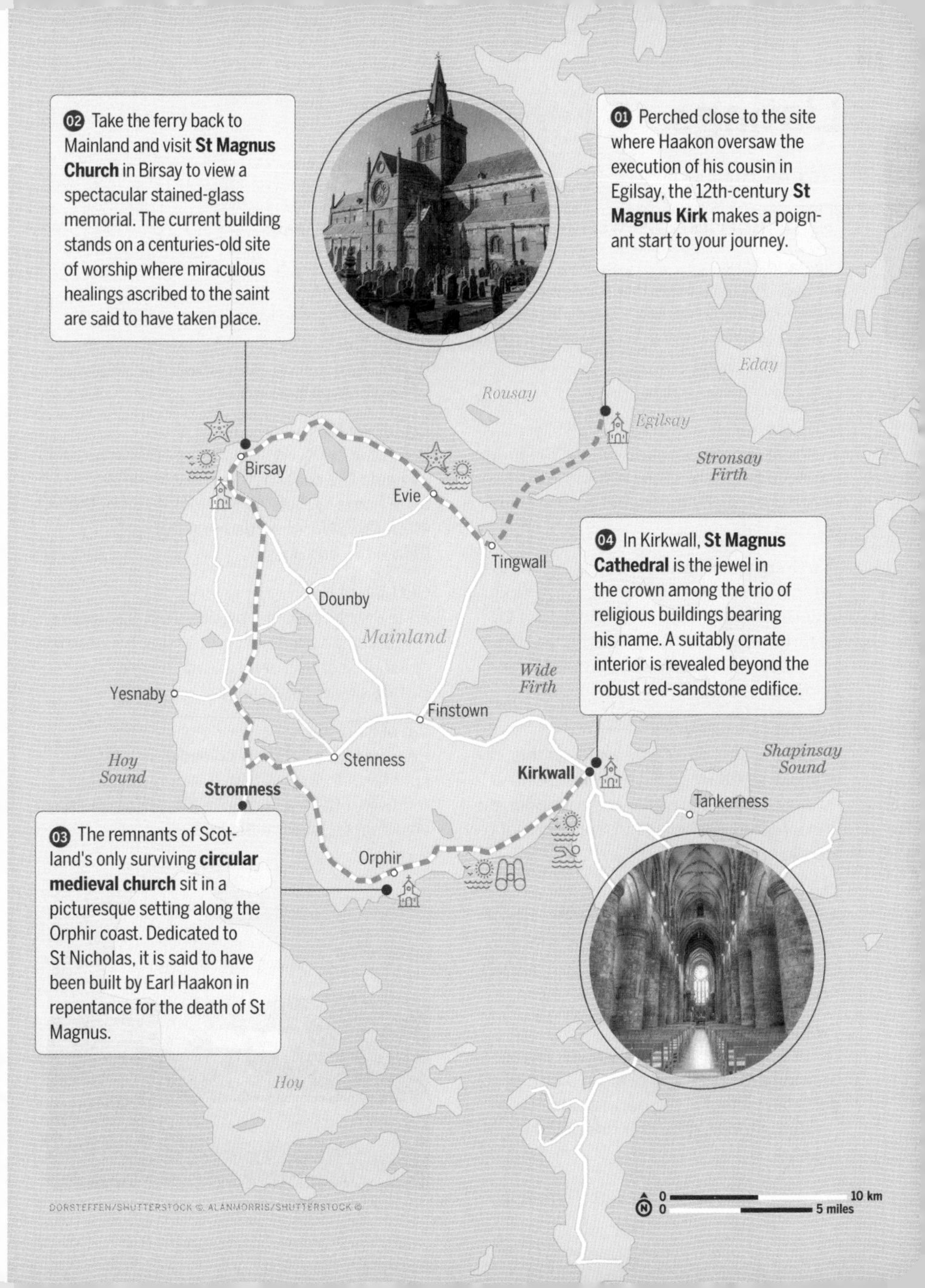

01 Perched close to the site where Haakon oversaw the execution of his cousin in Egilsay, the 12th-century **St Magnus Kirk** makes a poignant start to your journey.

02 Take the ferry back to Mainland and visit **St Magnus Church** in Birsay to view a spectacular stained-glass memorial. The current building stands on a centuries-old site of worship where miraculous healings ascribed to the saint are said to have taken place.

03 The remnants of Scotland's only surviving **circular medieval church** sit in a picturesque setting along the Orphir coast. Dedicated to St Nicholas, it is said to have been built by Earl Haakon in repentance for the death of St Magnus.

04 In Kirkwall, **St Magnus Cathedral** is the jewel in the crown among the trio of religious buildings bearing his name. A suitably ornate interior is revealed beyond the robust red-sandstone edifice.

Listings

BEST OF THE REST

Distilleries & Breweries

Highland Park
For over 200 years this distillery on the outskirts of Kirkwall has been producing single malts revered around the world. Join a tour to discover its Viking origins.

Scapa
Orkney's lesser-known whisky distillery has an enviable coastal outlook. Avoid the front entrance and walk up the cliff trail from Scapa Beach, arriving by the 'secret' scenic back door instead.

The Orkney Distillery
Sample the range of award-winning Kirkjuvagr Gin, distilled in a sleek black cafe-bar on Kirkwall's waterfront. Tour behind the scenes or craft your own gin under expert guidance.

Deerness Distillery
A friendly-family welcome awaits at this bespoke self-built distillery in the country. Award-winning gin, vodka and coffee liqueur are bottled and labelled by hand in an entirely artisan process.

The Orkney Brewery
A Victorian schoolhouse provides a unique setting for a brewhouse and cafe. Education in craft beer takes place in the old classroom, kept authentic with original features.

Swannay Brewery
Served up in bars around Orkney, the beer brewing process takes place in a former dairy farmstead in the north of Mainland where visitors can buy bottles direct from the source.

Coastal Trails

Yesnaby
Follow the trail along the striking sandstone cliffs at Yesnaby in Mainland. Weathered arches and craggy sea stacks, continually beaten by a boiling sea, provide dramatic vistas at every turn.

Brough of Birsay
Cross the causeway at low tide and circumnavigate the coast of this small landmass once home to Picts and Vikings. Explore the impressive Norse settlement, but return before the tide does.

Old Man of Hoy
A steady climb up the hillside from Rackwick reveals a panorama encompassing the north coast of Scotland before reaching one of Britain's tallest sea stacks.

Vat of Kirbister
Relax on a thoughtfully placed bench by a spectacular rock arch in Stronsay. Despite relatively little effort required to get there, the view makes this a gratifying rest stop.

Scapa's beach and distillery

History & Heritage Tours

St Magnus Cathedral
Climb to the upper levels of Orkney's 12th-century masterpiece for a bird's-eye view over Kirkwall. The history revealed en route makes this an illuminating excursion.

Barony Mill
Listen to the wooshing waterwheel and clickety-clack machinery at work as an ancient form of barley called bere is transformed into flour. Little has changed at this mill in Birsay since the 19th century.

North Ronaldsay Lighthouse
The views of Orkney and Shetland from the top of Britain's highest land-based lighthouse, and the 176 steps to get there, will take your breath away.

Local Foodie Favourites

Beiting & Brew £
This street-food van in Kirkwall has gained a cult local following, serving up traditional Orkney ingredients with a unique twist. The menu changes regularly but the surprising combinations are constant.

Argo's Bakery £
Freshly made pastries attract a lunchtime queue in Stromness. Pick up a Bere Bannock, a savoury Orcadian bread, and don't miss the Orkney Fudge if you have a sweet tooth.

Murray Arms Hotel, St Margaret's Hope ££
Regulars flock here for their seafood, landed daily from the family boat and served up in generous platters. The hand-dived scallops melt in the mouth.

Birsay Bay Tearoom £
Between April and September, this popular cafe in Birsay serves up 'Taste of Orkney' daily specials, best enjoyed with a cup of tea while gazing out at sea views.

Brough of Birsay

Festivals & Events

Orkney Folk Festival
During May, traditional tunes, singing, conversation and laughter drift from pub doors and venues around Stromness and beyond. Festival tickets and local accommodation get booked up well in advance.

St Magnus International Festival
For a week around midsummer, the sun barely sets and the islands come alive with music, dance and theatre. Reserve some stamina for the late-night Festival Club.

North Ronaldsay Sheep Festival
Join volunteers to repair the drystone wall protecting the island's native seaweed-eating sheep. Taking place over a fortnight each summer, additional local cultural events enhance the experience.

The Kirkwall Ba'
On Christmas Day and New Year's Day, rival factions play a traditional game of mass street football across the town. The dramatic spectacle has no rules and no time limit.

Scan to find more things to do in Orkney online

SHETLAND
RAW | INSPIRING | WILD
Experience Shetland online

▸ **Exploring Fair Isle** (p222)

▸ **Land of the Vikings** (p224)

▸ **Unforgettable Unst** (p226)

▸ **Flora & Fauna** (p228)

▸ **Mousa Broch's Petrels** (p230)

▸ **Exploring Geology** (p232)

▸ **Listings** (p234)

SHETLAND
Trip Builder

Flanked by the North Atlantic and the North Sea, Shetland's 100-island cluster is where Scotland meets Scandinavia. Closer to the Arctic Circle than London, the dramatic landscape, shaped by fire and ice, has an ingrained Norse feel unlike anywhere else.

Hike to the most northerly part of the UK at **Hermaness** (p226)
½ day

Go beyond Ronas Hill and discover the **Lang Ayre's secluded beach** (p233)
1 day

Stand on the flank of a volcano at **Eshaness** (p233)
½ day

Hop on a boat trip to the seabird colonies of **Noss** (p233)
½ day

Take a jewellery-making workshop at **Red Houss** in Burra (p234)
1 day

Walk through 5000 years of human history at **Jarlshof** (p234)
½ day

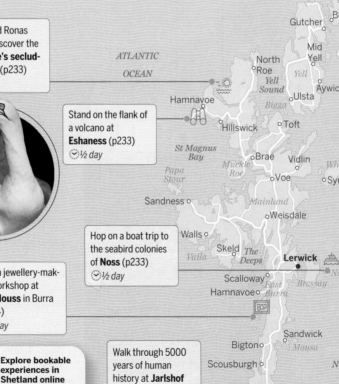

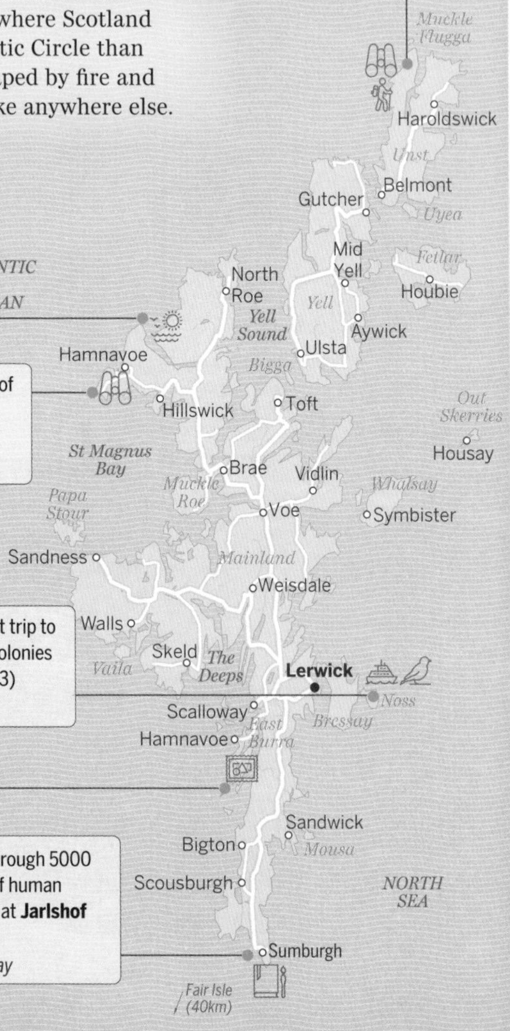

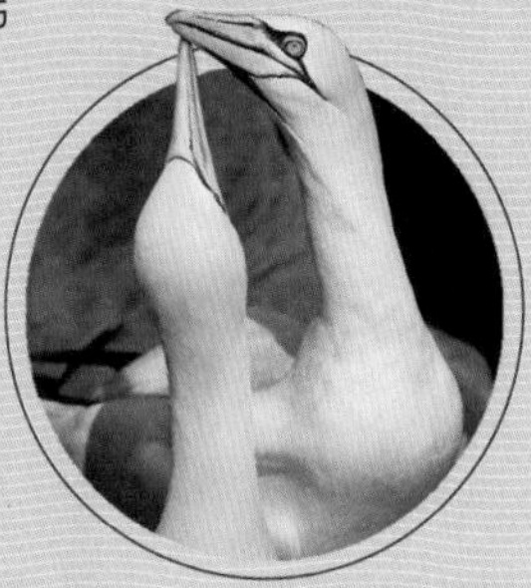

Explore bookable experiences in Shetland online

Practicalities

ARRIVING

Sumburgh Airport Located 24 miles south of Lerwick, handles regular flights from Aberdeen, Edinburgh, Glasgow, Inverness and Kirkwall.

NorthLink Ferry Terminal Just 2 miles from Lerwick town centre, sails daily to and from Aberdeen.

FIND YOUR WAY

Lerwick's Tourist Centre is excellent for advice and maps. Roads are well signposted and locals are happy to give tips and directions.

MONEY

Carry cash – many shops, attractions, honesty boxes and ferries don't accept card payments and ATMs are restricted to Lerwick.

WHERE TO STAY

Town/Village	Pro/Con
Lerwick	Guesthouses and B&Bs are best for a friendly, warm welcome.
Scalloway	Picturesque, close to town and a welcoming village feel.
North Isles	Get away from it all and enjoy a self-catering island retreat in Unst, Yell or Fetlar.

GETTING AROUND

Car The best way to reach Shetland's beauty spots. Buses are frequent, but routes are limited.

Inter-island ferries Provide sea links to nine of Shetland's inhabited islands by car or as a foot passenger.

Hiking The best way to enjoy the stunning coastal scenery.

EATING & DRINKING

Shetland seafood & meat Look out for local rope-grown mussels, fresh Burra lobster at the Dowry (p235), and the Cullen skink soup at Peerie Shop Cafe (p235).

Sunday Teas These pop-up tearooms are great places to experience local hospitality, with everything from cupcakes and bannocks to eggs and jams.

Best for Scandi-style
The Dowry (p235)

Must-try drink
Shetland Reel Gin

JAN–MAR	APR–JUN	JUL–SEP	OCT–DEC
These are often the coldest months but spring emerges slowly. Up Helly Aa is the highlight.	Temperatures can remain cool. June sees 19 hours of daylight.	Average August temperatures are 15°C. This is the busiest season.	Stormy weather is common. Look out for the Northern Lights (aurora borealis).

43 Exploring FAIR ISLE

KNITTING | BIRDWATCHING | ISOLATION

Isolated and rural, the tiny island of Fair Isle is a vibrant, forward-thinking community and, most famously, home to Shetland's distinctive and colourful Fair Isle knitting. Fair Isle is also a walkers and birders paradise, so if you want to remove yourself from the hustle and bustle of everyday life, and you crave open spaces and big horizons, then Fair Isle is for you.

CINDY HOPKINS/ALAMY STOCK PHOTO ©

How to

Getting here There are two options: ferry or plane. The 12-passenger ferry departs from Grutness, close to Sumburgh Airport, and takes 2½ hours. Flights depart from Tingwall Airport, carry a maximum of six passengers and take 25 minutes. Booking in advance is essential with only several sailings and flights a week.

When to go May to September for fair weather and seabirds.

Top tip Fair Isle involves careful planning and the necessity to be adaptable and flexible. Boat crossings can be rough.

MARIANNE TAYLOR/SHUTTERSTOCK ©

Far left Fair Isle knitwear
Bottom left Great skua in flight
Left Sheep Craig

A Paradise for Knitters & Birders

Halfway between Shetland and Orkney, Fair Isle is home to about 40 permanent residents. Clearances and emigration led to a drastic decline in population in the 19th century. The island was bought by the National Trust in 1954 and has since bucked the trend of island depopulation.

Birding An important ornithological centre, Fair Isle's world-famous **Bird Observatory** was lost to fire in 2019. With support from locals and famous faces such as actor Douglas Henshall, fundraising has allowed plans to begin a replacement.

Knitwear Famed for its distinctive Fair Isle knitwear featuring bright colours and bold designs, the island is the home of genuine Fair Isle, a style that has swept through the knitting world and is celebrated during the annual **Shetland Wool Week**. For an even more immersive experience, book a knitting holiday with **Fair Isle with Marie** and discover the intricacies of Fair Isle patterns, techniques, yarns and colours to create a unique piece of knitwear to take home. You'll also experience life on a real working croft.

Culture & walking Fair Isle has some of the most beautiful walks in Shetland with highlights including the impressive **Sheep Craig** and **Malcolm's Head**. It has a rich cultural tradition of music, fishing and the famous straw-backed Fair Isle chairs, stylistically different to those from Orkney (p210). Fair Isle's cultural heritage is thoughtfully depicted in the small **George Waterston Museum**.

Shetland TV Series

Shetland has become increasingly popular as a destination in recent years. The islands' starring role in the *Shetland* series, a fictional TV crime drama based on the popular novels by author Ann Cleeves, has helped to raise its profile, planting it on the worldwide stage. The main character, Detective Inspector Jimmy Perez, comes from Fair Isle, and several episodes were filmed in the isle, showcasing its allure and natural beauty. Douglas Henshall, who plays DI Perez, has become a real advocate for the island in recent years, championing fundraising efforts to rebuild the island's world-famous Bird Observatory.

Land of the Vikings

ON THE TRAIL OF THE VIKINGS

Visitors are instantly struck by the 'otherness' of Shetland. The Vikings left an indelible mark on the people, place and landscape, and the lack of Scottishness is marked by the absence of the ubiquitous haggis, kilts and bagpipes. Shetland is culturally Scandinavian, with Norse place names and dialects, flaming fire festivals and a history that sits apart from Scotland.

Left A replica Viking longhouse, Unst
Middle Scalloway Castle
Right Participants in Up Helly Aa festival

CLEMENT PHILIPPE/ARTERRA PICTURE LIBRARY/ALAMY STOCK PHOTO ©

Viking Shetland

Evidence of Vikings in Shetland is found from the settlement sites at Jarlshof in the south to Unst in the north. No part of the islands escaped this assimilation into Scandinavia from around 850 CE, giving rise to 600 years of Norse rule. Viking rule more or less obliterated pre-Norse culture in Shetland. There is little indication of what place names and language looked like before the Vikings arrived from western Norway and, until a few hundred years ago, the main language spoken in Shetland was a form of Old Norse, known as Norn. Shetland's unique position in the centre of the North Atlantic made it the perfect stepping-stone for Norse colonisation westward. Shetland lies equidistant to Norway and Scotland, and the cultures of both have fed the unique character and cultural heritage of the islands.

Scottish Assimilation: 1469

The 600-year period of Scandinavian rule ended in 1469 when Shetland and Orkney were pawned to Scotland as a wedding dowry. Princess Margaret of Denmark was to marry King James III of Scotland, but King Christian of Denmark couldn't afford the dowry. To secure the marriage and retain peace between nations, he pawned Orkney and Shetland, intending to repurchase them later. This never happened, and Shetland has remained part of Scotland ever since. Where Shetland had once sat proudly in the Viking world's centre, it now sits on the UK's periphery.

Shetland's transition into Scotland wasn't an easy one as land-hungry Scottish landowners moved on the isles in the hope of extending power and influence in the courts of Edinburgh with their newly gained northern estates. Scalloway Castle, built by the notorious Earl Patrick Stewart, stands as a ruin and testament to this oppressive time.

YURIY CHERTOK/SHUTTERSTOCK ©

ANDREW J SHEARER/SHUTTERSTOCK ©

Up Helly Aa

Shetland's Scandinavian heritage is today celebrated in the annual Up Helly Aa fire festivals held throughout the isles between January and March. The largest of the 10 Viking-inspired fire festivals is held in Lerwick on the last Tuesday of January.

Attracting thousands of visitors every year, the torchlit procession, led by the Guizer Jarl (chief Viking), weaves its way around the streets of Lerwick with over 1000 men carrying burning torches. After the procession, the *guizers* (participants) throw the burning torches into a replica Viking longship. The atmosphere is electric as street lights are extinguished: visitors throng the streets, jostling for the best view, and the smell of paraffin and smoke permeates everything. After the ceremonial burning, a night of celebration commences as a dozen halls welcome the squads of *guizers* to perform a sketch or dance and festivities continue until the following morning.

> Shetland's transition into Scotland wasn't an easy one...

Despite what is often believed, Up Helly Aa is not an ancient festival passed down from Norse times but a festival with its roots in Shetland's Victorian era.

A Musical Tradition

Shetland's musical culture is unlike any other, and the tradition of fiddle playing is strong. Rooted in the islands' Scandinavian past, Shetlanders are renowned for their musical abilities. This is celebrated in the annual **Shetland Folk Festival**, attracting thousands of musicians every year.

Viking Place Names

Around 870 CE, Viking explorer Flóki Vilgerðarson, known as Hrafna Flóki (Raven Flóki), visited Shetland with his family before sailing northwest to discover Iceland. Preparing to leave, Flóki went into the hills to gather young ravens. Used as navigational aids, ravens help find land. While absent, his daughter, Geirhildr, fell through the ice on Girlsta Loch and drowned. Local legend tells that her body was buried on the loch's island. Girlsta is a derivation of her name, Geirhildr, coming from Geirhildarvatn (Geirhildr's lake/water). About 95% of place names in Shetland derive from Old Norse.

44 Unforgettable UNST

WILDLIFE | HIKING | ARCHAEOLOGY

Combining outstanding wildlife experiences and a sunset hike to the UK's most northerly point, this one-day trip is an unforgettable adventure. Scout for otters in the morning with a local guide before striding out across some of Shetland's most dramatic landscapes to chase the sunset and spot puffin and gannet colonies.

How to

Getting here Unst is a two-ferry hop from Shetland's Mainland; to get there, hire a car or go with a guide as transport links within Unst are limited. Follow the A970 from Lerwick to Toft before catching the 15-minute ferry to Yell. Drive through Yell (18 miles) to the ferry at Gutcher, which takes you on the five-minute crossing to Belmont, Unst. Booking is recommended.

Tours Otter-sighting tours can be booked with Shetland Nature.

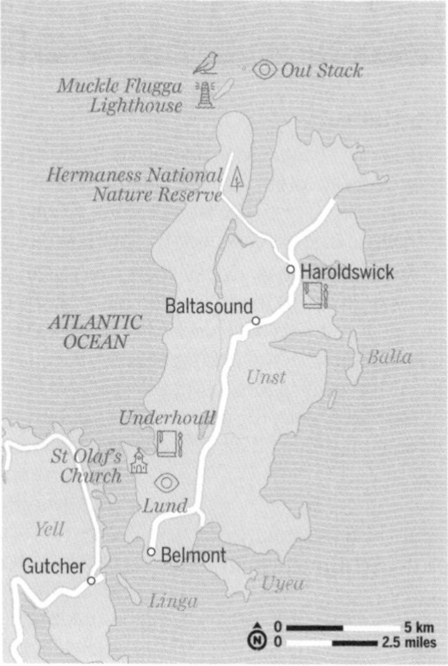

Wildlife spotting Start by tracking the charismatic otter with local guides **Shetland Nature**. Unst is one of the best places to see otters in their natural environment. Known locally as the *draatsi*, Shetland's otters live on the saltwater shores. Elusive and hard to spot, an expert guide is the best way to spot them.

Hiking Hike to the UK's most northerly point, **Hermaness National Nature Reserve**, for an 'edge of the world' feeling, and enjoy views of **Muckle Flugga Lighthouse** and **Out Stack**. Hermaness boasts large colonies of puffins and gannets, and sometimes a passing whale. Time your visit with the setting summer sun.

Top right Eurasian otter
Right Birdwatching at Hermaness National Nature Reserve

HUGH HARROP/ALAMY STOCK PHOTO ©

ARTERRA PICTURE LIBRARY/ALAMY STOCK PHOTO ©

Eurasian Otters in Shetland

A carnivorous four-legged and semi-aquatic mammal that feeds primarily on fish, and with a face as cute as any teddy bear, it is little wonder Eurasian otters are as popular as they are charismatic. Living their lives along our remote coast to the rhythm of Shetland's tides and feeding from our rich inshore seas, they are found here in higher density than anywhere else in the world.

Brydon Thomason, *native Shetland naturalist, otter specialist and tour operator at Shetland Nature*

Archaeology Unst is thought to be the Vikings' first landfall, and with 60 known longhouse sites, it's clear that it was an important place. Visit the reconstructed longhouse and longship at **Haroldswick**. Step back into Neolithic Shetland at the **Lund** standing stone, an impressive 3.5m monolith. Visit the ruined **St Olaf's church** featuring Viking graves (9th to 11th century) and Hanseatic merchant Segebad Detken (1573). Keep your eyes peeled for seals hauled up on the nearby beach. And, following the Vikings, visit the excavated longhouse and Iron Age broch at **Underhoull**.

FLORA & FAUNA

01 Killer Whales
Killer whales can often be seen hunting seals inshore. The same animals move between Iceland, Shetland and mainland Scotland.

02 Otters (Draatsi)
Shetland has the highest density of otters in Europe. See them feeding just offshore at mid to low tide.

03 Seals – Common and Grey (Selkies)
Shetland has two species present in nationally important numbers. Common seals pup in June and grey seals in October.

04 Puffins (Tammie Nories)
Shetland's auks – puffins, razorbills and black guillemots – mate for life and return to the same nest site every spring.

05 Gannets (solans)
With huge wingspans enabling long-distance feeding trips, and a liberal diet, populations of this large seabird have increased.

06 Red-necked Phalaropes (Peerie Deuks)
In an unusual role reversal, males raise chicks while females seek another partner. Incredibly, they winter near the Galapagos Islands!

07 Arctic Terns (Tirricks)
With the world's largest migration, terns see more daylight than any other species, but are threatened by changing sea temperatures.

07

08

09

10

11

12

13

08 Great Skuas (Bonxies)
Shetland hosts 40% of the world's population. Recent sandeel shortages mean they now feed on other seabirds.

09 Fulmars (Maalies)
Shetland's most abundant seabirds have a distinctive stiff-winged flight and have only been resident since the late 19th century.

10 Rare Plants
Edmondston's chickweed is found only on the Unst serpentine. On the Keen of Hamar it grows alongside other rare Arctic alpines.

11 Orchids (Curl-dodie)
Shetland remains flower-rich – visitors are able to enjoy a proliferation of wildflowers, including several species of orchid

12 Curlews (Whaaps)
Less intensive farming in Shetland, compared to mainland UK, means Shetland's populations of curlew, lapwing and redshank are stable.

13 Blanket Bog
Shetland's blanket bog is globally important, capturing and storing carbon, regulating water and supporting a range of plants and birds.

45 Mousa Broch's PETRELS

BIRDS | ARCHAEOLOGY | SIMMER DIM

The incredible culmination of one of the wonders of the natural world takes place within the walls of a 2000-year-old broch, the best preserved in the world, under the magical half-light of midsummer. The sight of the storm petrel, one of Britain's smallest seabirds, returning to its nesting grounds will leave a lasting impression.

DAVID TIPLING PHOTO LIBRARY/ALAMY STOCK PHOTO ©

How to

Getting here The 15-minute crossing departs from Sandsayre pier in Sandwick (unless otherwise advised); all sailings are weather dependent.

When to go The Mousa Boat operates evening tours (Monday, Wednesday and Saturday) from late May to mid-July and daily trips from April to September. Tours allow two to three hours on the island.

Cost £30/10 per adult/child for the evening. Day tours, without the storm petrel experience, cost £16/7 per adult/child (mousa.co.uk).

CLEMENT PHILIPPE/ARTERRA PICTURE LIBRARY/ALAMY STOCK PHOTO ©

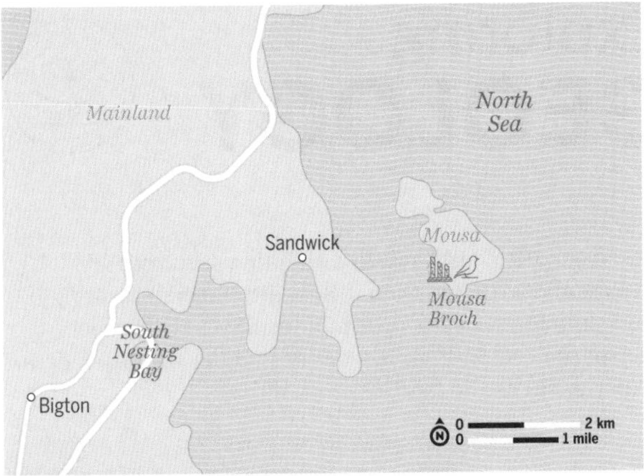

Top left An inquisitive storm petrel
Bottom left Mousa Broch

Mousa: Wildlife & Archaeology Collide

Unforgettable wildlife Nesting within the walls of a 2000-year-old broch, the tiny and enigmatic storm petrels are the star of this evening tour. The drystone walls of the magnificent Iron Age structure are brought to life as the seabirds return to their nests from the sea. With an unmistakable call, described by ornithologist Bobby Tulloch as similar to a 'fairy being sick', these night-time marvels make for a stirring sight.

60° north Mousa is metaphorically sliced in half by the 60° north latitude line that passes through the island. Visitors can take a moment to rest on a driftwood bench that marks this milestone positioning that gives 19 hours of daylight in summer and only six hours in the winter.

RSPB Nature Reserve Mousa is rich in wildlife, with a colony of noisy Arctic terns, and the ever-present great skua breeds on open moorland. Other birds to expect are shags, black guillemots, fulmars, red-throated divers and the Shetland wren, a unique subspecies, slightly larger and darker with a flatter song than its UK counterpart. Both common and grey seals are to be seen, and, if you're lucky, an otter or passing whale.

Abandoned Remnants of a thriving 19th-century community can be viewed in the stone remains of homes on the island, which once supported 11 families.

A Note on Brochs

Unique to the north and west of Scotland and built throughout the mid-Iron Age (2000 years ago), brochs are archaeological enigmas. Shetland boasts around 120 brochs, most standing in ruin. Brochs are round, stone structures constructed using two drystone walls – an inner and outer – with a staircase between to reach the top. Archaeologists debate their purpose – were they defensive or offensive? Were they storehouses or high status 'manor houses' for local chieftains? Nobody knows. Shrouded in mystery, they carry much intrigue about how past societies lived and worked.

46 Exploring GEOLOGY

DAY TRIPS | TOURING | ADVENTURE

Enjoy stunning hikes, dramatic coastlines, breathtaking scenery and uninterrupted horizons at Shetland's Unesco Global Geopark, formed by fire, ice, colliding continents and vanishing oceans over billions of years. The rich and varied geology can be experienced on foot, by boat or paddle, with each area offering a distinct set of experiences as the landscape unfolds.

ALANMORRIS/SHUTTERSTOCK ©

How to

Getting around You'll need a car and a good Ordnance Survey map to cover the whole island.

Slow down Journey to all four corners of Shetland's Mainland and the island of Unst, taking in the greatest geological treasures. Travel at your own pace and work these suggestions into your itinerary, ensuring that you don't miss any highlights.

Planning tip Treat this as a week-long itinerary, with each area taking at least a day.

LIZ MILLER/SHUTTERSTOCK ©

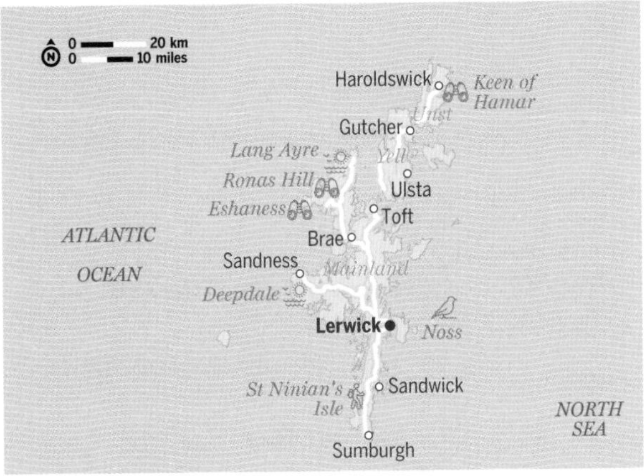

Northmavine Explore the rugged north, home to gneisses almost three billion years old – over half the Earth's age. At **Eshaness**, discover Shetland's volcanic past and stand on the UK's best cross-section through a volcano. Explore the tundra-like landscape of **Ronas Hill**, searching for rare Arctic alpines, and hike on to the **Lang Ayre**, one of Shetland's longest and most isolated beaches.

Unst Search the rocky hillside of **Keen of Hamar**, which remains unchanged since the ice age, and seek out Edmondston's chickweed. The geological diversity of Shetland has allowed for many species of rare plants to thrive. Those like Edmondston's chickweed can't be found anywhere else in the world.

East coast Experience the impressive 180m-high sandstone cliffs of **Noss**, where a boat trip or island hike will take you into the heart of one of the UK's most important seabird colonies, home to thousands of nesting gannets, guillemots, puffins and more.

West Mainland Hike to the impressive shingle beach at the foot of **Deepdale** valley, formed by glacial meltwater, and enjoy the breathtaking coastal scenery, punctuated by headlands and offshore stacks. This walk, from the Dale of Walls beach, is best done to coincide with the sunset across the bay of Deepdale.

South Mainland Stroll across the sandy tombolo at **St Ninian's Isle** and walk the island circular towards the impressive 9th-century treasure hoard discovered within the remains of a 12th-century chapel in 1958.

Left Rock formation at Eshaness
Bottom left Edmondston's chickweed

Shetland's Unesco Global Geopark

Shetland's unique landscapes, seascapes, natural history, human history and culture all grew from the underlying geology. Geologically speaking, Shetland is mainland Scotland in miniature. Within an hour's drive, you can stand on the bed of an ancient desert lake, look over the wall of an eroded volcano, or walk on the roots of a vast mountain range or across the Earth's mantle rocks beneath a vanished ocean. Shetland's landscape has been described as a 'Wow! around every corner', and an 'Open-air museum of rocks'.

By Allen Fraser, *Shetland geologist whose vision began Shetland's journey to becoming a Unesco Global Geopark.*

Listings

BEST OF THE REST

Prehistoric Treasures

Jarlshof Prehistoric & Norse Settlement

One of Shetland's archaeological highlights lies on its southernmost point. Visitors are transported through the ages from the Neolithic to the medieval.

Culswick Broch

Hike some of Shetland's best coastline to this dramatic red granite broch; enjoying commanding views, this untouched corner of Shetland is well worth exploring.

Stanydale Temple

Tucked within the heart of Neolithic Shetland, this archaeological ruin is a quiet retreat.

Viking Unst

With a replica Viking longship and longhouse at Haroldswick, and excavated longhouses at Underhoull, Hamar and Belmont, Unst represents the first landfall of the Vikings in the UK.

Heritage Highlights

Shetland Museum & Archives

This museum nestled on Lerwick's historic waterfront is the best starting point for understanding Shetland's history.

Old Haa Museum

Housed within a 17th-century laird's house on the island of Yell, this museum has local history displays, a gift shop, a tearoom, an exhibition space and an impressive walled garden.

Hoswick Village

The tightly knit village is both unusual and unexpected in Shetland. At its heart, the visitor centre houses displays, local arts and crafts, and a bright tearoom. There are numerous trails, a beach, two knitwear shops, a jewellery studio, play park and cake fridge to discover.

Journey through the Arts

The Craft Trail

Visit open studios throughout the islands (shetlandartsandcrafts.co.uk).

The Shetland Gallery

The UK's most northerly gallery features contemporary island artists in its spacious and modern gallery in Yell.

Bonhoga Gallery

With arts, crafts and a fantastic cafe, set within a historic mill, Bonhoga has one foot in the past, and the other firmly bedded in the present with a contemporary gallery feel.

Red Houss Shetland

Red Houss studio is a treasure trove of creativity, selling watercolours of iconic Shetland crofthouses and handcrafted silver jewellery. Hosts silversmithing and painting workshops too.

ALANMORRIS/SHUTTERSTOCK ©

Replica Viking longship, Haroldswick

Lerwick's Food Highlights

The Dowry £

For Scandi-style and delicious local produce, including local lobster, The Dowry adds a real cosmopolitan feel to Lerwick's Commercial St.

Peerie Shop Cafe £

Tucked down one of Lerwick's historic lanes, the daily soups at this cafe are unmissable. Get in quick on a Friday, as the Cullen Skink sells quickly.

Fjara £

Sitting on the water's edge at Breiwick, this is an ideal spot to watch for passing otters and seals.

Trips & Tours

Sea Kayak Shetland

Explore Shetland's geology from the water – with caves, geos, voes and stacks, every inch of the coastline is waiting for you.

Knitting & Hiking with Shetland Wool Adventures

If knitting needles and hiking boots get your creativity flowing, this is the perfect combination of textile exploration and off-the-beaten-track hikes.

Seabirds & Seals

Visit the heart of one of Shetland's main gannet colonies, overlooked by the dominating Noss cliffs. Just a short boat trip from Lerwick.

Garths Croft

Take a tour around a traditional working croft on the island of Bressay where you have the opportunity to hand feed native Shetland sheep and see other heritage breeds.

Knit & Purl

Jamieson & Smith

Located 1 mile from Lerwick's town centre, you'll find a range of yarns, kits, books and homeware made from 100% Shetland wool.

The Dowry, Lerwick

Jamieson's of Shetland

Specialising in native Shetland wool, visit the shop in Lerwick (home to the world-famous yarn wall!) or the mill in Sandness.

Anderson & Co

Anderson & Co in Lerwick is perfect for traditional hats, gloves, mittens, jumpers and cardigans with the signature Fair Isle yolks.

Shetland Textile Museum

Two miles from the town centre, knitters and spinners demonstrate local skills in a restored 18th-century fishing böd featuring Fair Isle, lace and tweed exhibitions.

A Musical Journey

Mareel

Music, cinema and creative arts centre in Lerwick hosting regular live gigs from local and visiting musicians.

The Lounge Bar

Tucked up one of Lerwick's picturesque historic lanes, The Lounge Bar has weekly live music and impromptu live sessions.

Scan to find more things to do in Shetland online

Practicalities

ARRIVING 238

GETTING AROUND 240

SAFE TRAVEL 242

MONEY 243

RESPONSIBLE TRAVEL 244

ACCOMMODATION 246

ESSENTIALS 248

Right Hiker above the Assynt landscape

EASY STEPS FROM THE AIRPORT TO THE CITY CENTRE

Edinburgh is the primary point of entry for most visitors to Scotland, with the country's biggest international airport here. Located 8 miles west of the city centre, the airport has one terminal and it is easily navigable. The terminal has the usual selection of pubs, restaurants, shops, ATMs and car-hire desks. You can also fly into Glasgow, Aberdeen and Inverness.

AT THE AIRPORT

SIM cards
Prepaid SIM cards for unlocked phones can be purchased at the airport's WHSmith branch. There are four branches of the retailer inside the terminal. Shops are open based on daily flight departure times.

Currency Exchange
International Currency Exchange (ICE) outlets are located in the middle of the departure lounge after security and at International Arrivals. Opening hours are timed to flight departures and arrivals. Rates are better at banks in the city.

NATALIA SVISTUNOVA/SHUTTERSTOCK ©

WI-FI
Free wi-fi (two hours only) is available for all passengers and customers at Edinburgh International Airport.

ATMS
There are a number of bank machines in the airport – bear in mind they issue the Scottish Pound (£).

CHARGING STATIONS
Plug-sockets-a-plenty are dotted around the terminal.

ENTRY & EXIT FORMALITIES

Entry Make sure you've got your passport and supporting documents (visas and landing cards; double-check on the UK government website at gov.uk/government/organisations/uk-visas-and-immigration). If arriving on a domestic flight from elsewhere in the UK, head straight to baggage claim.

Exit Prepare for your departure by knowing what you can and cannot take through security; see edinburghairport.com/prepare. If taking whisky home, check your home country's customs rules.

GETTING TO THE CITY CENTRE

Edinburgh Trams offers a super-smooth 35 minute ride direct from the arrivals plaza, with 15 stops between the terminal and St Andrew Sq in the city centre. Key stops en route include Haymarket, the West End and Princes St. Purchase tickets from staff or at the ticket machine.

Airlink 100 departs every 30 minutes (4.30am to 12.30am) Monday to Sunday from directly outside the Arrivals hall to St Andrew Sq, taking 25 minutes. Other services include Skylink 200 to Ocean Terminal, Skylink 300 to Surgeons' Hall and Skylink 400 to Fort Kinnaird. Pay with cash or use a contactless bank card.

By bike Edinburgh's terminal is linked to the local cycle path network by Eastfield Rd. From here, cycle paths and quiet routes can be followed almost all the way into the city centre.

HOW MUCH FOR A

Taxi
£20
20mins

Bus
£4.50
25mins

Tram
£6.50
35mins

Taxi
Edinburgh's black cabs are the fastest way into the city. Trips take around 20 to 30 minutes. The Uber drop-off/pick-up zone is in the car park outside the Arrivals hall.

Plan Your Journey
Download the Traveline Scotland app to figure out the most convenient way to get wherever you want to go in the city or further afield.

Travel card
Purchase a Ridacard for unlimited travel across all Edinburgh Trams (all zones), Lothian city buses, NightBus services and airport buses. A one-week pass costs £20/17/10 for an adult/student/child (aged five to 15). Day tickets, excluding Airlink, cost £4.50/2.20 for an adult/child.

OTHER POINTS OF ENTRY

Glasgow Airport is 9 miles west of the city. Taxis pick up outside the arrivals gate. Expect to pay around £20; it takes about 20 to 30 minutes. Glasgow Airport Express service 500 runs 24/7 to and from Buchanan Bus Station. Tickets cost £9/5 for an adult/child.

Aberdeen Airport is 6 miles northwest of Aberdeen's city centre. The journey to Union Sq Bus Station takes 20 minutes. There are a number of airline services, including First Bus X27, Jet Service 72 and Service 747.

Inverness Airport is 9 miles northeast of Inverness city centre. The journey takes around 15 minutes. Service 11 is your direct connection between the airport and city centre. Buy tickets from the driver or online in advance.

Ferries There are a number of car and passenger ferries to Scotland. Popular routes include those from Belfast (Northern Ireland) to Cairnryan in Dumfries and Galloway with Stena Line and Larne (Northern Ireland) to the Cairnryan with P&O.

TRANSPORT TIPS TO HELP YOU GET AROUND

Scotland's cities, glens and far-flung islands are most memorably explored with your own wheels. Vehicle hire is straightforward, and exploring the network of single-track roads north of the Central Belt is all part of the adventure. Public transport can lower your carbon footprint between the main cities, but beyond urban centres services can at times be rudimentary.

CAR OR CAMPER VAN HIRE

Car hire is available countrywide, with rates slightly more expensive the further north you travel. Camper vans are ideal for exploring the Highlands and islands, though it's worth noting that road trips are now more popular than ever and locals have a love-hate relationship with RVs and motorhomes.

AUTOMOBILE ASSOCIATIONS

The AA, RAC and Green Flag offer breakdown cover and roadside assistance throughout Scotland. They are also handy resources, providing online travel tools, including route planners, traffic alerts and maps. Check for reciprocal agreements with organisations in your own country before travel.

CAR RENTAL PER DAY

from £18

Petrol approx £1.23p/litre

Car ferry ticket from £16

GO GREEN

Increasingly, Scotland is embracing greener forms of transport. Electric chargers and vehicle plug-in points are growing exponentially, and Orkney offers the UK's gold standard, with more charging stations per kilometre than anywhere else, plus Britain's first fleet of e-campervans. The country's cycle network is also expanding, with The Great North Trail offering a route from the Borders all the way to John O'Groats and Cape Wrath.

BOAT

Boats serve Ireland's offshore islands. Ferries also operate across rivers, inlets and loughs, providing useful shortcuts, particularly for cyclists. Scenic cruises operate on many of Ireland's loughs and waterways.

TRAIN

Ireland's rail network is limited but trains are a quick and comfortable option for certain intercity routes, including Belfast to Dublin and Dublin to Cork. Services are operated by Iarnród Éireann (Irish Rail) in the Republic and NI Railways in Northern Ireland. For the best fares, book in advance.

DRIVING ESSENTIALS

Drive on the left; the steering wheel is on the right.

Single track road

On single-track roads, use passing places to let oncoming drivers pass.

60

Speed limit 60miles/h; 30miles/h in urban areas unless otherwise posted.

A zero tolerance policy to drink driving is in effect. Blood alcohol limit 0.05% (0% for drivers under 20).

Be wary of deer warning signs, particularly at nighttime.

PLANE
A secret pleasure is flying to Scotland's islands. Swoop low over silver sands to Islay or Shetland, or land on the world's only tidal beach runway on Barra. In Orkney, you can take the world's shortest commercial flight between Westray and Papa Westray at just 90 seconds. Loganair is the main carrier.

TRAIN Reliable, if expensive, national rail provider ScotRail connects everywhere from Burns Country to Thurso and Wick in the far north. For particularly scenic routes, consider the West Highland Line from Glasgow to Mallaig or the Kyle Line from Inverness to Kyle of Lochalsh. Find timetables and tickets at scotrail.co.uk.

FERRY Caledonian MacBrayne (shortened to CalMac) offers the lion's share of routes to the Inner and Outer Hebrides, while NorthLink Ferries and Pentland Ferries are the best bets to get to Orkney and Shetland.

KNOW YOUR CARBON FOOTPRINT
A road trip from Edinburgh to Inverness would emit 43.6kg in a car and 21.8kg on a motorbike, per passenger. The same journey by train emits 13.8kg and 7.7kg by bus.
There are a number of carbon calculators online that allow you to estimate the carbon emissions generated by your journey.

ROAD DISTANCE CHART (MILES)

	Edinburgh	Glasgow	Aberdeen	Dundee	Perth	St Andrews	Inverness	Dumfries	Portree	Fort William
Edinburgh	–									
Glasgow	42	–								
Aberdeen	127	146	–							
Dundee	57	81	55	–						
Perth	44	63	87	22	–					
St Andrews	52	73	80	14	34	–				
Inverness	157	169	104	137	112	147	–			
Dumfries	73	76	210	145	123	137	232	–		
Portree	236	216	215	216	192	226	114	288	–	
Fort William	146	110	154	126	102	140	67	180	108	–

SAFE TRAVEL

The biggest threat to travellers in Scotland is heading into the great outdoors unprepared. Crime rates in the cities are on a par with others across the UK, but it's still advisable to show common sense and treat people and places with the same respect you would back home.

MOUNTAINS

Scotland's mountain environments can change rapidly, bringing everything from snow to hurricane-force winds to the odd dose of sunburn. Leave details of your route with someone, take the right kit and don't go beyond your own limits. If you have an accident, call 999 or 112 and ask for the Police and Mountain Rescue (scottishmountainrescue.org).

SEAS & RIVERS

Those beautiful bays, rivers and crystal-clear water look appealing, but unexpected North Atlantic swells and strong currents are all too common. Keep an eye on tide times and the weather, and check with locals before taking the plunge.

ROADS

Scotland has plenty of roadside hazards, ranging from fence-hopping deer to wayward sheep and cattle. The best advice is to drive slowly and avoid dusk and dawn, when animals like red deer are at their most active.

Theft and street attacks do sometimes occur in Scotland's largest cities. Glasgow, Edinburgh and Aberdeen city centres see the majority of problems, especially late on a Friday or Saturday night and commonly involving alcohol or drugs. Dial 999 in an emergency.

EDINBURGHCITYMOM/SHUTTERSTOCK ©

ARTVELL/SHUTTERSTOCK ©

MONEY Scotland is moving towards a cashless society and contactless bank cards are the norm in cities and towns. Remote island communities and villages lag behind – carry cash and a card so you don't get caught out.

BITES & STINGS

To avoid being bitten by midges, horseflies, and ants, cover your li and stick to places where there is a breeze. Ticks, found in wet woodland, moorland and long grass, can carry Lyme disease, so they should be removed quickly.

COVID-19

In light of the coronavirus pandemic, there are various requirements in place for travellers to Scotland. If you feel ill or need more advice, visit gov.scot/publications/coronavirus-covid-19-getting-tested.

QUICK TIPS TO HELP YOU MANAGE YOUR MONEY

CREDIT CARDS (Visa, MasterCard) are accepted everywhere and are a prerequisite for car hire. Credit cards can also be used for cash advances at banks and from ATMs, but such transactions can incur hefty charges. Increasingly, because of the coronavirus pandemic, many shops, cafes and restaurants accept card only.

ATMS

ATMs can be found across the country, though, increasingly, high street banks are closing, with services going online. Contactless payment is available practically everywhere.

BANKNOTES

The variety of different British banknotes can be baffling. All Pound Sterling (£) notes printed in Scotland are valid across the breadth of the United Kingdom.

CURRENCY

Pound Sterling £

HOW MUCH FOR A

Coffee £2.50

Dram of whisky £4

Dinner for two £40

TIPPIING

Although there are no fixed rules, a 10% to 15% gratuity is now expected by most waiters, particularly in cities and large towns. Often, this will be included in your bill, however, you are not obliged to pay it. For taxis, most people round the fare up to the nearest pound.

COSTS

Factor in a £80-a-night hotel, a £20 train ticket, £30 on food and a few £10 pub rounds and you won't get much change from a daily budget of £150. If hostelling or camping, £70 to £100 is more realistic.

DRINKING WATER

Scotland has some of the freshest, cleanest water anywhere on the planet. Bring a reusable bottle and help save on plastic and your budget.

TAXES & REFUNDS

Following Brexit, Britain is no longer an EU member state and the practice of refunding VAT paid by travellers has ended.

DISCOUNTS & TIPS

Many attractions, activities and transport options offer discounts for seniors, students and families travelling with children.

Sights Historic Scotland offers the money-saving Explorer Pass, which includes free entry to more than 70 attractions.

Train Fares are cheaper when you travel at less busy, off-peak times.

Ferries Ferry operator CalMac offers 30 different island-hopping tickets that are valid for one month to help save time with bookings.

RESPONSIBLE TRAVEL

Tips to leave a lighter footprint, support local and have a positive impact on local communities.

ON THE ROAD

Look for the Thistle logo (visitscotland.org) on your accommodation. It's Visit Scotland's grading system for driving quality and shouting about success.

Observe the Scottish Outdoor Access Code (outdooraccess-scotland.scot). The act provides a guide for everyone to explore the great outdoors in a safe and responsible manner.

Go electric. It's easy to hire an electric vehicle and take advantage of charge points: Scotland is home to more than 1500 chargers country-wide (chargeplacescotland.org/live-map).

Avoid crowded places and come back when it's less busy. Stick to marked roads, tracks and paths, leaving only footprints.

Be beach safe. Scotland's seas are unpredictable, with cold temperatures and rip currents, even during the height of summer. Visit RNLI (rnli.org) for guidance.

Take part in habitat restoration, or volunteer to help save Scotland's red squirrels. For listings of volunteer programs, see Visit Scotland (visitscotland.com).

CHRISTIAN MUELLER/SHUTTERSTOCK ©

GIVE BACK

Shop local at farmers markets and farm shops to sample fresh products and support Scottish businesses throughout all four seasons.

Choose visitor attractions, sights and distilleries that are committed to sustainable practices and responsible tourism ahead of ones that aren't. A good resource is Visit Scotland (visitscotland.org).

Enjoy Scotland's two stunning national parks – the Cairngorms and Loch Lomond & the Trossachs – responsibly. You'll need a permit if you wish to wild camp, and fires are not permitted in some areas.

Plant a tree. Join charity Trees for Life in planting native woodland to restore Caledonian Forest in the Highlands (treesforlife.org.uk).

DOS & DON'TS

Do 'Fàilte' (embrace) and respect the Gaelic language.

Don't forget remember that tap water is safe to drink, and pure unfiltered waters run from rivers and streams.

Do eat out for a good cause at Social Bite (social-bite.co.uk). Its Edinburgh, Glasgow and Aberdeen restaurants and cafes support Scotland's homeless community.

LEAVE A SMALL FOOTPRINT

Spend more time in one area. Travel slowly to reduce the pressure on the country's most famous destinations and don't cram too much in. Save the stress, and become more richly acquainted with this beautiful country.

Use designated toilets and dispose of motorhome and camper van chemical waste and grey water responsibly. The Northwest Highlands, in particular, has only a limited number of accessible facilities.

#TakItHame. Carry a spare bag and if you see rubbish when out hiking, walking or climbing, pick it up and take it with you.

LEONARD ZHUKOVSKY/SHUTTERSTOCK ©

SUPPORT LOCAL

Eat locally. From bread to beer to fish to fresh fruit, buy from local producers around the country (foodanddrink.scot/support-local).

Source unique souvenirs like Harris Tweed and Orkney handicrafts directly from the makers. Social enterprise platforms **Buy Social Scotland** (buysocialscotland.com) and **Love Local Scotland** (lovelocal.scot) list recommended artisans.

CLIMATE CHANGE & TRAVEL

It's impossible to ignore the impact we have when travelling, and the importance of making changes where we can. Lonely Planet urges all travellers to engage with their travel carbon footprint. There are many carbon calculators online that allow travellers to estimate the carbon emissions generated by their journey; try resurgence.org/resources/carbon-calculator.html. Many airlines and booking sites offer travellers the option of offsetting the impact of greenhouse gas emissions by contributing to climate-friendly initiatives around the world. We continue to offset the carbon footprint of all Lonely Planet staff travel, while recognising this is a mitigation more than a solution.

RESOURCES

visitscotland.com
outdooraccess-scotland.scot
johnmuirtrust.org
keepscotlandbeautiful.org

UNIQUE AND LOCAL WAYS TO STAY

Sleep in a medieval town house surrounded by history or camp under the stars for free on a beach – Scotland offers something for every taste and budget. Often hotels and guesthouses are located inside historic buildings gone glam – from castles to coaching houses – and nothing beats them for atmosphere. For an only-in-Scotland experience, rough it at a remote bothy.

HOW MUCH FOR A

Bothy Free

Campsite from **£12 per pitch**

City-centre hotel £80

MARK CANNING/SHUTTERSTOCK ©

WILD CAMPING

Wild camping is permitted throughout Scotland, offering unrivalled access to the country's dramatically different landscapes and seasons. There are exceptions to this rule: in popular spots throughout the Cairngorms (pictured above) and Loch Lomond & the Trossachs, wild camping is restricted to certain permit-only pitches and by-laws prohibiting camping and firelighting are in effect.

HOSTELS

Not-for-profit charity Hostelling Scotland (hostellingscotland.org.uk) has more than 60 properties scattered across the country. From the lochside to the trail path, highlights include those on the West Highland Way and the North Coast 500. A standout is the Loch Ossian Youth Hostel at Corrour, with no vehicle access and located on a wildly remote swathe of Rannoch Moor.

BLACKHOUSES

Once used to house both farmers and livestock, a blackhouse is a frozen-in-time, thatched dwelling synonymous with the Outer Hebrides. Inside, they exude a country-chic vibe, with history hewn into the walls. Lewis, in particular, has a number to stay in or rent, including Gearrannan (pictured; gearrannan.com), a self-catering option on the windswept Atlantic coast.

NINA ALIZADA/SHUTTERSTOCK ©

BOTHIES

Bothies are a uniquely Scottish form of rustic, shelter-style accommodation, and to stay in one is to see the country's landscape at its rawest and most unadorned. Many are off-grid, almost closely guarded secrets, requiring long walks or bike rides to reach their random locations. Others offer different sorts of challenges, sitting on unsignposted, lonely passes, with only the most basic of facilities.

Commonly, all are free to stay in as long as you embrace the bothy philosophy. You'll have to embrace the slow pace, carry in all your supplies (food, sleeping bag and candles), fetch water from a nearby stream and share the cottage with whoever else turns up for the night. Due to their popularity, some have stoves and sleeping platforms, but most are no-frill, two-roomed shepherd's cottages with a dusty fireplace. It's also worth noting that there is no booking system and reserving a bed at one isn't possible. And yet, what an adventure. A night overlooking an empty beach or picturesque glen? It's what backpacking dreams are made of.

The Mountain Bothies Association (mountainbothies.org.uk) is an excellent resource.

Price: Free

BOOKING

VisitScotland's cross-country network of 26 iCentres can help with accommodation reservations, as well as tour bookings and buying tickets for public transport. Book well in advance in peak tourist season, from June to August. Edinburgh is at its busiest throughout the Fringe Festival in August and during Hogmanay in December.

Lonely Planet (lonelyplanet.com/hotels) Find independent reviews, as well as recommendations on the best places to stay, and then book them online.

The Camping and Caravanning Club (campingandcaravanningclub.co.uk) Membership association with a great selection of top-rated sites.

Hidden Scotland (hiddenscotland.co/accommodation) Holiday bookings with everything from lodges and log cabins, to dog-friendly options and hot tub havens.

Scotland's Best B&Bs (scotlandsbestbandbs.co.uk) The only 4- and 5-star B&B association in the country, offering a great selection of reliable guesthouses.

Scottish Cottages (scottish-cottages.co.uk) Rental listings with more than 1500 cottages to suit all family sizes and budgets, including many eco-friendly options.

VisitScotland (visitscotland.com/accommodation) Online accommodation bookings, especially good for quirky options, glamping and guesthouses.

★★★★

VisitScotland operates a Quality Assurance scheme whereby all businesses that have a Star award have been inspected by assessors to ensure visitors enjoy a high-quality experience from start to finish.

ESSENTIAL NUTS-AND-BOLTS

ALCOHOL

It's the lifeblood of Scotland and 'taking a drink' is deeply rooted in the country's national psyche, whether for better or worse. And it's spelt whisky, without the 'e'.

TIPPING

There isn't a big tipping culture in Scotland, though it is common in restaurants and for taxi journeys.

SMOKING

It's illegal to smoke in any pub, restaurant, nightclub and hotel, except within designated outdoor areas.

FAST FACTS

Time Zone
GMT+1

Country Code
+353

Electricity
230V/50Hz

GOOD TO KNOW

Citizens from 139 countries are automatically issued a temporary visa on arrival, typically valid for 90 days.

Scottish banknotes are different to those in England.

Driving etiquette: move into lay-bys to let oncoming traffic pass.

The legal drinking age in Scotland is 18.

Mobile phone signal can be hit or miss across the country – even close to a major city.

ACCESSIBLE TRAVEL

Larger hotels have wheelchair-friendly rooms (book in advance). Euan's Guide reviews hotels with all write-ups done by disabled travellers (euansguide.com).

Accessible dining varies dramatically. It's always best to call the restaurant, cafe or pub in advance to make sure of access.

City transport stations have elevators or ramp access at street level. Station staff will help you on and off the train with a temporary slope. Ask at the ticket counter.

Museums and attractions often have different entrances, but varying is considered 'accessibility'. Accessible Travel Hub (accessibletravel.scot) is a great resource for planning journeys.

Wheelchairs and other equipment can be booked for short-term use from the British Red Cross (redcross.org.uk).

Download Lonely Planet's free Accessible Travel guide from lptravel.to/Accessible-Travel.

WINTER
Many attractions, museums, guesthouses and hotels close in winter (usually from November to March).

BREXIT
From 1 October 2021, you need a valid passport to enter the UK from the EU; EU identity cards can no longer be used.

FOOTBALL
The national sport can be a divisive subject and unsavoury. Especially in Glasgow, which splits into either Rangers or Celtic.

Pubs are hubs of community life and not just for drinking world-class beers, ales and whiskies in. They act as social centres for live music, quizzes, events and getting the lowdown on what's going on. You'll also pay a fraction of the price for meals compared to a restaurant, and breakfast, lunch and dinner are often on the menu.

FAMILY TRAVEL

Licensing laws mean children under 14 often can't be in pubs that sell meals after a certain time.

Admission to castles, museums, art galleries and more is often wonderfully free for all ages.

Restaurants commonly have high chairs and children's menus.

Train travel is £1 return each for up to four kids for every paying adult at the weekend. See scotrail.co.uk.

Breastfeeding in public is widely accepted and actively encouraged by government campaigns.

Child seats are not available in taxis.

KILTS

Non-Scots are actively encouraged to wear and buy kilts – this is taken as a heartfelt tribute, not an act of cultural appropriation.

There are few do's or don'ts: go casual or formal, with a jacket or without. It's all about the freedom.

Underwear is optional, but the proper way to wear a kilt is without.

THIRDFLOORDRAFT/SHUTTERSTOCK ©

LGBTIQ+ TRAVELLERS

Outright discrimination is unusual and the Scottish government actively campaigns for inclusivity regardless of sex or gender; however, travellers have reported isolated incidents of being turned away when checking into hotels in rural areas.

The Rainbow Index ranks Scotland as one of the top four countries in all of Europe for LGBTQI+ equality and human rights.

Glasgow and Edinburgh have large, vibrant gay and lesbian communities, with annual Pride events and parades celebrating Scotland's LGBTQI+ heritage and future.

Follow Pink Saltire (@PinkSaltire) to keep up with issues and learn about events and meet-ups.

Index

A

Aberdeenshire Coastal Trail 114-17
accessible travel 248
accommodation 246-7
activities 16-23
animals 99, 228-9, *see also* wildlife watching, *individual animals*
Anstruther 95
archaeological sites 140-1, 208-9
  Callanish Standing Stones 198
  Dun Carloway 198-9
  Dunadd Fort 141
  Glebe Cairn 141
  Jarlshof Prehistoric & Norse Settlement 234
  Kilmartin Glen 142-3
  Knap of Howar 206
  Nether Largie 141
  Temple Wood Stone Circle 141
  Unst 227-8
  Viking Unst 234
arts 14, 64-5, *see also* crafts, design, films, literature, murals, music
Arthur's Seat 54
ATMs 238

B

Beltane Fire Festival 22
Ben More 131
Ben Nevis 156-7
birdwatching
  Cape Wrath 171
  Fair Isle 223
  Hirta 195
  Mousa Broch 230-1
  Mull 144
  Mull of Galloway 86
  Noss 233, 235
  Staffa 131
Blackford Hill 51
blackhouses 199, 246
boat tours
  Central Highlands 161
  Loch Ness 153
  Northern Highlands 179
boat travel 240
bothies 247
Braemar Gathering 18
breweries 216
Brexit 249
Burns, Robert 87

C

Caithness 174-5
Caledonian Canal 153
Calum's Road 192-3
camping 246
canoeing & kayaking 107, 131, 133, 161, 235
Cape Wrath 170-1
car travel 12-13, 240-2, *see also* driving tours
castles 8, 100-3, 104-5
  Armadale Castle Garden 200
  Balmoral Castle 159
  Blackness Castle 45, 55
  Blair Atholl Castle 159
  Bothwell Castle 72
  Caerlaverock Castle 83
  Carnasserie Castle 141
  Castle of Old Wick 168
  Castle Stalker 144
  Craigmillar Castle 45
  Culzean Castle 81
  Drumlanrig Castle 81
  Dumbarton Castle 70-1
  Dunnottar 116
  Dunrobin 169
  Dunure Castle 83
  Dunvegan Castle 191
  Edinburgh Castle 45
  Fatlips Castle 86
  Floors Castle 81
  Glamis Castle 123
  Inveraray Castle 144
  Kinloch Castle 161
  Lauriston Castle 45
  Loch Leven Castle 102
  New Slains Castle 117
  Rothesay Castle 145
  St Andrews Castle 106
  Stirling Castle 102-3
Central Highlands 146-61, **148-9**
  accommodation 151
  drinking 151, 161
  festivals & events 151
  food 151
  money 151
  navigation 151
  planning 148-9
  travel seasons 150
  travel to/from 150
  travel within 150
  wi-fi 151
Central Scotland & the East itineraries 30-1, **30-1**
children, travel with 249
churches & cathedrals
  Elgin Cathedral 123
  Glasgow Cathedral 67
  Rosslyn Chapel 45
  St Clement's Church 197
  St Magnus Cathedral 215, 217
  St Magnus Church 215
  St Magnus Kirk 215
climate 16-23, 32
climate change 245
convents & monasteries
  Arbroath Abbey 122
  Dundrennan Abbey 86

000 Map pages

Inchcolm Abbey 55
Melrose Abbey 83
Paisley Abbey 72
Pluscarden Abbey 122-3
Covid-19 33, 242
crafts 122, 145
Fair Isle 223
Northern Highlands 179
Orkney 210-11, 212-13
Outer Hebrides 201
Shetland 234-5, 235
Skye 201
Crail 95
Crannog Centre 106
currency 243
customs regulations 238
cycling 10-11
Caithness 174-5
Cape Wrath 171
Crinan Canal 140
Dundee 120
Great Cumbrae 86
Harris 196-7
Loch Ness 152-3
Southern Scotland 84-5

D

Dalnawillan Lodge 175
Dean Village 47
design 120-1
disabilities, travellers with 248
distilleries 113
Ardnahoe 133, 135
Balblair Distillery 178
Bowmore Distillery 134
Bunnahabhain 133
City of Aberdeen Distillery 123
Clydeside Distillery 73
Dalwhinnie Distillery 160
Deerness Distillery 216
Dewar's Aberfeldy Distillery 160
Edinburgh Gin Distillery 55
Glenlivet 160
Glenrinnes Distillery 123
Highland Park 216
Isle of Harris Distillery 197
Isle of Raasay Distillery 192
Kilchoman 133
Kingsbarns Distillery 95, 107
Lagavulin Distillery 133
Laphroaig 133
Orkney Distillery 216
Royal Lochnagar Distillery 159
Scapa 216
Talisker Distillery 191
driving tours, *see also* car travel
Central Highlands 158-9
North Coast 500 179
Secret Coast 138-9
Skye 190-1
Snow Roads Scenic Route 160
Dundee 120-1
Dunfermline 101

E

Edinburgh 36-55, **38-9**
accommodation 41
drinking 41, 54-5
festivals 41, 42-3
food 41, 54, 55
hills 50-1
history 44-5
money 41
navigation 41
planning 38-9
travel seasons 40
travel to Edinburgh 40
travel within 40
wi-fi 41
Edinburgh Festival Fringe 17, 42-3
Eigg 161
Eildon Hills 79
etiquette 245, 249
Eurasian otters 226, 227, 228
events, see festivals & events

F

Fair Isle 222-3
Fairy Glen 188
Fairy Pools 200
family travel 249
ferries 240, 241
festivals & events 14, 16-23, *see also individual events*
Braemar Gathering 158
Common Ridings, the 87
Edinburgh Festival Fringe 17, 42-3
Edinburgh International Book Festival 43
Edinburgh International Film Festival 43
Edinburgh's Hogmanay 21, 43
Highland Games 119
North Ronaldsay Sheep Festival 217
Orkney Folk Festival 217
Royal National Mòd 19
Scottish Traditional Boat Festival 115
Shetland Folk Festival 225
Spirit of Speyside Festival 119
St Magnus International Festival 217
Up Helly Aa 21, 225
World Pipe Band Championships 16
Fife 88-107, **90-1**
accommodation 93
drinking 93
food 93, 94, 106, 107
money 93
planning 90-1
travels seasons 92
travel to/from 92
travel within 92
wi-fi 93
Fife Coastal Path 94-5
films 35, 154-5
food 9, *see also individual locations*
football 249

G

Gardenstown 116
geography 32
geology 232-3
Glasgow 56-73, **58-9**
accommodation 61

Glasgow *continued*
drinking 61, 62-3, 73
entertainment 69, 72-3
food 61, 62-3, 73
history 66-7, 68-9
money 61
navigation 61
planning 58-9
shopping 61
tours 72
travel seasons 60
travel to/from 60
travel within 60
wi-fi 61
Glen Clova 160
Glenan Wood 139
golf 51

H

Harris 6
Highland Clearances 172-3
Highland Games 176-7
Highlands & Islands
itineraries 26-7, **26-7**
hiking 8, 10-11
Aonach Eagach 157
Ben Nevis 156-7
Braeriach 157
Buachaille Etive Mòr 157
Crinan Canal 140
Culswick Broch 234
Deepdale 233
Dùn Caan 193
Fair Isle 223
Great Cumbrae 86
Hermaness National Nature Reserve 226-7
Loch Leven Heritage Trail 102
Loch Ness 152
North Hill Nature Reserve 206-7
Old Man of Hoy 216
Schiehallion 97, 157
St Abbs Head Nature Reserve 79
Trotternish 186-9
Yesnaby 216
history & historic sites 8, 93
Battle of Bannockburn Visitor Centre 107
Blackhouse 199
Culloden 160
Grave of Flora MacDonald 188
Moot Hill 101
Stirling Bridge 103
history 8, *see also individual locations*
Hoswick Village 234

I

Inner Hebrides 130-1
insects 33, 242
Iona 131
islands 6-7, *see also individual locations*
Islay 5, 132-3
Isle of Raasay 192-3
itineraries 24-31, *see also individual regions*

K

killer whales 228
Kilmartin Glen 142-3
kilts 249
Kirkwall 211

L

language 33, 116
Largs Viking Festival 19
Leith 52-3
Lewis 198-9
LGBTIQ+ travellers 249
lighthouses 160, 217
Lismore 144
literature 34, 48-9
Lochinver 178
Loch Lomond 139
historyLoch Morlich 161
Loch Ness 152-3
Lochdhu 175
Lochinver 178
Lunga 131

M

Mackintosh, Charles Rennie 65, 67
MacLeod's Stone 197
Malt Whisky Trail 5, 119
midges 33, 242
mobile phones 32, 77, 238, 248
monasteries, *see* convents & monasteries
money 238, 243
monuments & memorials
Emigrants Statue 173
Our Lady of the Isles 200
Scott Monument 49
Wallace Monument 103
William Wallace Statue 86
Mousa Broch 230-1
Mull 6
murals 64-5, 167
Murrayfield Stadium 47
museums & galleries 55
Bonhoga Gallery 234
Burrell Collection 72
Dandelion Designs 201
Devil's Porridge Museum 87
Dundee Contemporary Arts 121
Gallery of Modern Art 72
George Waterston Museum 223
Holland Farm 206
House for an Art Lover 72
Hoxa Tapestry Gallery 211
Island Darkroom 201
Jim Clark Motorsport Museum 87
Kelvingrove Art Gallery & Museum 67
Kildonan Museum 201
McManus Art Gallery & Museum 121
Museum nan Eilean 200
Museum of Lead Mining 87
National Museum of Scotland 55
Old Haa Museum 234
People's Palace 67
Perth Museum & Art Gallery 106
Raasay Gallery 201

000 Map pages

Riverside 67
RRS Discovery 121
Scottish Fisheries Museum 106
Scottish National Gallery of Modern Art 47
Seallam 200-1
Shetland Gallery 234
Shetland Museum & Archives 234
Skoon Art Gallery 201
Skye Museum of Island Life 188
Staffin Dinosaur Museum 200
V&A Dundee 14, 121
Writers' Museum 49
music 13, 34, 63, 72-3
Belladrum Tartan Heart Festival 17
Ceilidh Place 178
Celtic Connections 21
Edinburgh Music Tours 55
Glasgow 63, 72-3
Shetland 235

N

national parks & reserves
Balranald Nature Reserve 200
Black Wood of Rannoch 97
Falls of Clyde 79
Forsinard Flows Nature Reserve 168
Fowlsheugh Nature Reserve 116
Galloway Forest Park 78, 79
Hermaness National Nature Reserve 226-7
North Hill Nature Reserve 206-7
RSPB Nature Reserve 231
St Abbs Head Nature Reserve 79
Unesco Global Geopark (Shetland) 232-3
neolithic sites 208-9
Barnhouse 209
Callanish Standing Stones 198
Cuween Hill Chambered Cairn 209
Island of Eday 209
Island of Rousay 209
Jarlshof Prehistoric & Norse Settlement 234
Maeshowe 209
Ness of Brodgar 209
Ring of Brodgar 209
Skara Brae 209
Stanydale Temple 234
Stones of Stenness 209
Unstan Chambered Cairn 209
Watchstone 209
Northeast Scotland 108-23, **110-11**
accommodation 113
drinking 113
food 113, 122
money 113
navigation 113
planning 110-11
travel seasons 112
travel to/from 112
travel within 112
wi-fi 113
Northern Highlands 162-79, **164**
accommodation 165
drinking 165
food 165
money 165
planning 164
travel seasons 165
travel to/from 165
travel within 165
wi-fi 165
Northern Scotland itineraries 28-9, **28-9**

O

Oban 136
Old Man of Storr 189
Orkney 7, 202-17, **204**
accommodation 205
drinking 205
food 205, 217
history 212-13
money 205
planning 204
travel seasons 205
travel to/from 205
travel within 205
wi-fi 205
Outer Hebrides 180-201, **182-3**
accommodation 185
drinking 185
food 185
money 185
planning 182-3
travel seasons 184
travel to/from 184
travel within 184
wi-fi 185

P

palaces & stately homes 45, 80-1, 86, 102, 106, 159
Papa Westray 206-7
parks & gardens
Armadale Castle Garden 200
Castle Kennedy Gardens 85
Glamis Castle 123
Gordon Castle Walled Garden 123
Inverewe Gardens 179
Johnston Gardens 123
Jupiter Artland 55
Langley Park Gardens 123
Logan Botanic Gardens 86
Mellerstain House 86
Pitmedden Garden 123
Royal Botanic Gardens 47
Perthshire 88-107, **90-1**
accommodation 93
drinking 93
food 93, 106, 107
money 93
planning 90-1
travels seasons 92
travel to/from 92
travel within 92
wi-fi 93
Peterhead Prison 117
Portpatrick 84, 85

Puck's Glen 138
puffins 131, 228

Q

Quiraing 187

R

Rannoch 96-7
responsible travel 244-5
River Tay 98-9
River Tummel 97
Royal Highland Show 17
Royal Mile 45
Royal Observatory 54
RRS Discovery 121
ruins 85, 117, 139, 141, 153, 168, 227

S

safe travel 242
seafood 94-5, 106, 136-7
seals 19, 115, 228
Shetland 218-35, **220**
  accommodation 221
  drinking 221
  food 221, 235
  history 224-5
  money 221
  navigation 221
  planning 220
  travel seasons 221
  travel to/from 221
  travel within 221
skiing 20, 161
Skye 6, 180-201, **182-3**
  accommodation 185
  drinking 185
  food 185
  money 185
  planning 182-3
  travel seasons 184
  travel to/from 184
  travel within 184
  wi-fi 185
Southern Highlands & Islands 124-45, **126-7**
  accommodation 129
  drinking 129
  food 129
  money 129
  navigation 129
  planning 126-7
  travel seasons 128
  travel to/from 128
  travel within 128
  wi-fi 129
Southern Scotland 74-87, **76**
  accommodation 77
  drinking 77, 87
  food 77, 87
  history 82-3
  money 77
  planning 76
  travel seasons 77
  travel to/from 77
  travel within 77
  wi-fi 77
Speyside 118-19
sporting events
  Braemar Gathering 18
  Halkirk Highland Games 178
  Highland Games 119, 176-7
  Kirkwall Ba' 217
  Mountain Bike World Cup 23, 161
  Six Nations 22
St Andrews 95
St Kilda 194-5
St Magnus Way 214-15, **214**
Staffa 131
stargazing 54, 78, 131, 160
Stirling 88-107, **90-1**
  accommodation 93
  drinking 93
  food 93, 106, 107
  money 93
  planning 90-1
  travels seasons 92
  travel to/from 92
  travel within 92
  wi-fi 93
Stone of Destiny 101
storm petrels 230-1
Strathnaver 173
street art 64-5
surfing 115, 179
swimming 117

T

taxis 239
tipping 243, 248
Tiree 131
tours 72, 144, 235
train travel 166-9, 240, 241
travel seasons 16-23, 249
travel to/from Scotland 238-9
travel within Scotland 240-1
Trotternish 186-9

U

Unst 7, 226-7
Up Helly Aa 21

V

Vikings 224-5, 234, 227

W

Wallace, William 86, 103
walking, *see* hiking
waterfalls 79, 138, 167, 187
Water of Leith 46-7
weather 16-23, 32
websites 35, 245
West Highland Way 161
West Island Way 144
Westray 206-7
whale watching 17
whisky 4-5, 54-5, 113, 118-19, 132-3, 134-5
  Glasgow 73
  Northern Highlands 178
  Spirit of Speyside Whisky Festival 22
  World Whisky Day 23
white-water rafting 97, 107
wi-fi 32, 238, *see also individual locations*
wildlife watching 19, 46, 97, 99, 107, 133, 144, 171, 191, 226-7

000 Map pages

MIKE MACEACHERAN

Mike MacEacheran is an award-winning, Edinburgh-based travel journalist and guidebook author who has contributed to several Lonely Planet titles. He writes for *National Geographic*, the *Times* and the *Telegraph*, filing stories from 115 countries. His favourite? Silly question.

@MikeMacEacheran

My favourite experience is skiing in Glencoe. On a golden winter's day, with the right snow conditions, nowhere in the world beats it.

JOSEPH REANEY

Joseph Reaney is a travel journalist and editor who divides his time between Edinburgh and Prague. As well as contributing to Rough Guides, *National Geographic* and Forbes Travel Guide, he runs travel content writing agency World Words (world-words.com).

josephreaney.com

My favourite experience is St Kilda. When it comes to off-the-beaten-track adventures in Scotland, it's hard to beat this beautiful, isolated archipelago.

NEIL ROBERTSON

Neil has been exploring his home country extensively since 2012 as a travel writer and blogger as *Travels with a Kilt*. A Glasgow boy at heart, he has recently become a Highlander, living on the Lochaber coast.

@travelswithakilt

My favourite experience is a relaxed wander along the River Kelvin, between Kelvingrove Park and the Botanics, through the heart of the city's West End. .

NEIL WILSON

Based in Perthshire, Neil has been a full-time writer since 1988, working on more than 80 guidebooks for various publishers, including the Lonely Planet guide to Scotland. He is also an active hill-walker, mountain-biker, sailor, snowboarder and rock-climber.

@neil3965

My favourite experience is climbing Schiehallion. The view from the summit never gets old, with the peaks of Glen Coe shimmering beyond Rannoch Moor.

THIS BOOK

Design development
Lauren Egan, Tina Garcia, Fergal Condon,

Content development
Anne Mason

Cartography development
Wayne Murphy, Katerina Pavkova

Production development
Mario D'Arco, Dan Moore, Sandie Kestell, Virginia Moreno, Juan Winata

Series development leadership
Liz Heynes, Darren O'Connell, Piers Pickard, Chris Zeiher

Commissioning Editor
Daniel Bolger

Product Editor
Joel Cotterell

Book Designer
Fergal Condon, Clara Monitto

Cartographers
Mark Griffiths, Rachel Imeson

Assisting Editors
Gabrielle Innes, Anne Mulvaney, Monique Perrin

Cover Researcher
Lauren Egan

Thanks Kristopher Clifford, Gwen Cotter, John Taufa

Our Writers

SUSANNE ARBUCKLE

Born in Glasgow, Susanne is the founder of *Adventures Around Scotland* travel blog and a travel writer based in Orkney. Her articles specialising in Scotland's lesser-visited destinations have featured in a variety of online and traditional publications.

@ScotAdventures

My favourite experience the Aberdeenshire Coastal Trail as the route encompasses an enthralling diversity over a relatively short distance.

COLIN BAIRD

Colin lives in Edinburgh, blogging about cycling and travelling in Scotland. His ambition is to see the whole country by bike. He's covered a lot of miles and filled his notebooks with wonderful experiences to share with his followers.

@cyclingscot

My favourite experience is the Far North Line. I love the changing landscape and hopping off at rural stations to explore on my bike.

KAY GILLESPIE

Edinburgh-local Kay Gillespie travels Scotland for a living and shares her experiences online as The Chaotic Scot, focusing on quirky stays, local cuisine, and public transport. An island-hopper for life, Kay has visited over 60 Scottish Islands to date.

@thechaoticscot

My favourite experience is taking a boat trip with Staffa Tours to the turquoise-fringed shores of Lunga to see thousands of puffins up close: a sight you never forget.

LAURIE GOODLAD

Writer and tour guide Laurie is a Shetlander with a passion for her island home and culture. Curator by trade and a keen writer, she writes a travel blog and is working on a book detailing the history of Shetland.

@shetlandwithlaurie

My favourite experience is witnessing the return of the storm petrels to the 2000-year-old Mousa Broch at midsummer. The culmination of nature and archaeology is breathtaking.